You Can Knit That

YOU CAN

FOOLPROOF INSTRUCTIONS *for* FABULOUS SWEATERS

KNIT THAT

AMY HERZOG

PHOTOGRAPHY BY KAREN PEARSON

ABRAMS | NEW YORK

CONTENTS

Introduction

Of all of the things a hand-knitter can make, sweaters seem to be the most intimidating. In the years since my first book, *Knit to Flatter*, was published, I've met countless knitters who can create heirloom lace shawls with 7 charts and complicated constructions without thought…but then look decidedly nervous when I suggest they try to make a simple Stockinette vest.

Why is this so? Clearly, it's not knitting skill—in fact, sweaters are some of the most simple projects around, skill-wise. All you really need to successfully knit a sweater is to keep a consistent gauge and know some basic increases and decreases. (Translation: If you've made a scarf that looks rectangular and has some stitch patterning, then you're ready for sweaters.)

What, then, is so frightening? I think most of the nervousness centers around two core issues:

- Sweaters need to *fit*, and we have plenty of store-bought garments that we're stacking the fit of our hand-knits up against. So it's easier to tell when we've failed!

- Sweaters are a big investment in both time and materials, and it's often difficult to tell whether things are working until the very end of the process. This makes for stressful and worry-filled knitting—the opposite of why most of us have taken up this hobby!

The resources out there for prospective sweater knitters don't really help combat this intimidation. There's perilously little simple guidance aimed at demystifying the sweater, and lots of anecdotal evidence that sweaters are difficult (such as pictures of disappointing garments online). So much information is out there, in fact, that it's tough for a novice sweater knitter to distinguish what's really important (like considering the fabric you're creating) from the details that honestly don't make or break a sweater (like knowing exactly what kind of shaping to use where).

I'm here to help.

My previous books have demystified fit in the most precise of all hand-knit sweaters: the set-in-sleeve sweater with waist shaping. My clear-cut, you-can-do-it approach has helped thousands of knitters to make tailored, fitted garments they love to wear. If you're reading these words, and have worked with me to get a sweater you love, thank you. Now, *You Can Knit That* stretches beyond the tailored, fitted sweater and helps you create hand-knitted sweaters of *other*, more fit-forgiving types, that you will adore just as much.

For those of you who looked at my first two books and felt intimidated: *don't despair!* The book you have in your hands will get you started on successful sweater knitting in the easiest, most gentle way possible—with sweaters that are more forgiving in terms of fit, and honest, up-front advice about what needs to be considered (and what doesn't).

My goal in this book remains the same as in everything that I do: I want to help you create garments with your hands that you reach for day in and day out, because they're comfortable and look great.

But *unlike* some of the sweaters you've seen from me before, the sweaters in this book represent the whole universe of hand-knit sweaters—from boxier, looser, swathe-you-in-luscious-fabric open cardigans (see page 93), to casual, comfortable beach wear (see page 97), to that colorwork sweater that made you want to be a knitter in the first place (see page 142). And of course, we'll cover the fitted, cabled pullover I've been helping people create and love for years (page 160).

Most of the sweaters in this book are lower-stakes, fit-wise, than the classic tailored pullover—they're a little looser, a little less glued to your shoulders, a little more relaxed. This means you can approach them with lower stakes and worry less while you're knitting them than some other sweaters you've seen.

I've organized the book so that you can either work through it cover-to-cover, or skip around as garments call to you.

In chapters 1–3 (pages 8–45), I give you practical advice on the most important concepts in sweater knitting (and let you know what's safe to ignore in most patterns), from the swatching stage to the finishing stage. Short exercises let you nail the core techniques in a low-stress, low-stakes way by encouraging you to "minify" and practice on swatches.

In chapters 4-9, I give you advice and sweater patterns grouped by the way their pieces come together, a.k.a. their construction styles. Are they worked all in one? With raglan shaping? A gorgeous yoke? Each chapter presents you with a set of garments that reflects the most wearable, fantastic aspects of that construction.

Further, each chapter includes a small "mini" project that lets you produce a successful sweater with all the relevant techniques from that section, but on a smaller scale. Sweaters for kids aren't nearly as intimidating as sweaters for adults, so each chapter starts with a more approachable pattern sized from 1 to 10 years. These will help you to learn on more manageable garments, and build up your confidence in how a particular sweater comes together before starting one for yourself or a full-sized loved one.

It's my hope that you'll look through these pages and find a sweater (or five) that resonates with you, one that you've seen in the store and know you could improve upon if you made it yourself. Further, I hope that my guidance gives you the skills and confidence you need to actually cast on. Because truly, there's no feeling like wearing a stunning sweater you've made with your own two hands.

It's easier than you think—I can't *wait* to see yours.

BEFORE *the* KNITTING

Got a sweater you're dying to make? Awesome!
You can knit that. But before you pick up the
needles and go, there are some simple things you
can do to set yourself up for success.

The Swatch

Bring up swatching in any group of knitters and
you'll probably get a variety of opinions, including several groans. But swatching doesn't have to
be an unpleasant chore!

For many knitters, the cycle of swatch unhap-
piness goes like this: First, we start by thinking
of swatching as a checkbox to mark off before we
get to the *real* knitting. Then, when we finish the
swatch and realize we haven't matched the pattern's gauge on the first try, we get frustrated and
give up on the swatch altogether. This makes
our swatch knitting less predictive of what our
gauge will be, so when we finally knit the sweater,
it's a different size than the swatch indicated it
would be.

This cycle of frustration leads to the angry
knitter's battle cry: *Lying swatches and the lies
they tell!*

But in reality, swatching isn't just a checkbox
to mark off before we get to the "real knitting."
Instead, swatching is our chance to work out any
kinks with the project before we start knitting
the final piece. It's like a sewist's muslin or an
artist's draft sketch.

One more mind-set shift before we get into
the nitty-gritty of swatching well: Your swatch will
never be wrong. Swatching is your practice time—
you can test-drive the fabric of your piece with
it, you can predict how large your stitches will be
with it, and you can use it to decide whether or
not you like either of those outcomes. But in the
end, your swatch isn't wrong, even if you hate
it. Instead, you're learning what you dislike on a
small piece of fabric instead of waiting until you
finish the entire piece!

SWATCHING PREDICTIVELY

One of the most important things your swatch
can tell you is how large your stitches will be
when you actually knit the project itself. The
size of your stitches, in terms of their width and
height, is called your *gauge*: The width of your
stitches is your *stitch gauge*, and the height of
your stitches is your *row gauge*. Gauge is often
given as a (fractional) number of stitches and
rows over 4" (10 cm).

You can't make a successful sweater without
knowing how big your stitches will be. A good,
predictive gauge swatch will tell you.

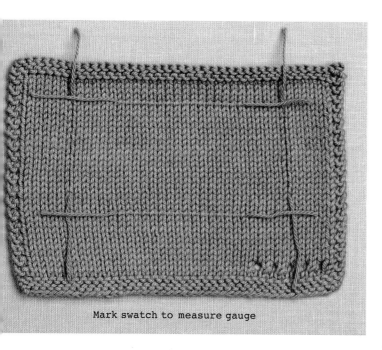

Mark swatch to measure gauge

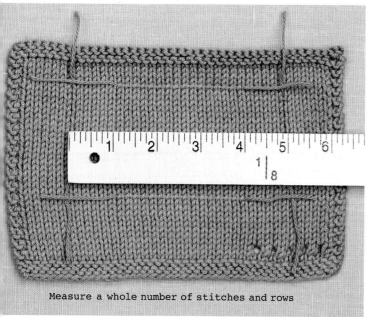

Measure a whole number of stitches and rows

I'm here to buck tradition and say that your goal isn't to *match* the pattern's gauge, necessarily, but instead to *predict* the gauge you'll get when you sit down and knit your garment. (There are strategies for adapting to a different gauge than the pattern specifies, ranging from knitting the instructions for a larger or smaller size to drafting a whole new pattern. But no strategies in the world can help you if you can't predict your gauge ahead of time!)

So how can you ensure your swatch is a faithful predictor? Really, it's about keeping you from lying to yourself, intentionally or unintentionally.

Here's my process for making a reliably predictive swatch:

1 CAST ON AT LEAST 35, BUT FEWER THAN 50, STITCHES. You want to have enough stitches on the needle that your hands settle into their routine, but not so many that each row fills you with dread.

2 WORK FOR AT LEAST 5" (12.5 CM). Your swatch needs to be long enough that your hands have the feeling and impression of a good amount of fabric hanging off the needles. Many knitters find their gauge is slightly different in that first inch or two than it is once they've gotten into a rhythm.

3 QUICK-MEASURE YOUR PRE-WASHED GAUGE (OPTIONAL). While your gauge shouldn't change much simply because your swatch got wet (it's the same amount of yarn, after all), some knitters like the security of measuring their fabric's gauge at this point. It's okay if you want to measure now, but just make sure to use your washed gauge for any actual calculations!

4 WASH YOUR SWATCH, AND LET IT DRY NATURALLY. No pinning here! Get your swatch nice and wet, squeeze the water out without handling the swatch too much, and let it dry without stretching or shaping it. This serves two purposes.

First, you'll get to see the nature of the final fabric: Did the wool bloom? How does the fabric feel? (More on that in the next section.) But second, and more important for this discussion, you'll get to see what your gauge will be after you've washed the garment when you're actually moving in it, rather than what you can force the gauge to be when it's lying flat and pinned to a blocking board.

5 PLAY WITH YOUR SWATCH FOR A WHILE BEFORE MEASURING IT. Again, you're trying to see what this garment's fabric will be like as you use it in real life! So live with your swatch for a day or two. Put it in your pocket, carry it to your desk, and fiddle with it throughout the day. Reserve all judgment and rulers until you've lived with the fabric for a bit.

Once you have a swatch that's been through a bit of real life, you've eliminated a number of the "lying to yourself" pitfalls.

Do you like the way your swatch fabric feels? Is it something you want to make into a sweater? If so, now you're ready to measure your gauge. To measure accurately and reduce the chance of "hopeful" gauge numbers, I recommend the following:

1 MARK THE MAXIMUM NUMBER OF STITCHES YOU THINK ARE "GOOD DATA" FOR PREDICTING YOUR GAUGE. This probably means you're not marking off the few edge stitches on each side.

I like to block this section off with a contrasting color of yarn for easier measuring. Mark nearer the top of the piece, since it's more likely that you've settled into your knitting groove by the time you're near the end. See the top photo on the opposite page for an example.

2 MEASURE THE PRECISE WIDTH OF THOSE STITCHES WITH A RULER. This way, instead of estimating a fraction of a stitch (e.g., 22.25 stitches in 4" [10 cm]), which is difficult and prone to result in errors even for very experienced knitters, you're letting the ruler tell you exactly how many fractions of an inch your stitches measure. You'll wind up with a number that's something like 32 stitches in 7.5 inches.

3 DO THE SAME FOR ROWS. In this case, you might not want to count the rows closest to your cast-on edge. A more typical set of measurements for rows might be 18 rows in 2.875 inches.

4 NOW, DIVIDE TO GET YOUR PER-INCH STITCH AND ROW GAUGES. Continuing with these examples, our stitch gauge is 32 stitches/7.5 inches = 4.27 stitches per inch, and our row gauge is 18 rows/2.875 inches = 6.55 rows per inch.

Now, these numbers aren't likely to match what's written in your pattern exactly! That's okay—*it's much more important to know what your gauge will be than to match the pattern entirely.*

First, see exactly how far off you are: Divide the stitch counts in the size you'd typically choose by your true per-inch stitch gauge. This will tell you how far off the pattern's measurements will be if you take no further steps. If the measurements are too far off, you can do the same calculation for the next size up (if your stitches are smaller than the pattern's gauge) or the next size down (if your stitches are larger). It's pretty likely that simply knitting the instructions for a different size will give you a garment that works!

Hand-Knitted Fabric

If you follow my swatch checklist, it will not only give you the best prediction possible of the size of your stitches, but it will give you a gauge swatch that is large enough for you to get a great sense of the fabric you're creating. This is really important, since it will help you decide whether the fabric you're getting is a good one for your project!

SWEATERS AND FABRIC

Different hand-knitted items make different demands of their fabric as being on a continuum from easy (i.e., no demands) to difficult (i.e., that fabric has a tough life ahead of it!).

At the easy end of the scale, we have scarves and shawls. They make literally no demands on their fabric at all—they just have to rest around your neck and shoulders, supported by your body. There's no abrasion, no gravity, no structural requirements. In fact, scarves and shawls tend to be most pleasing when their fabric is very *unstructured*, because loose fabric is easily squished fabric!

At the difficult end of the scale, we have socks. Socks have a tough life. They take a long time to knit, so you want them to last. But they're constantly being rubbed and moved around inside shoes and under our feet, leading to *tons* of abrasion. They require a fabric that's iron-tight to last well.

Sweaters are somewhere in the middle. They need to deal well with both abrasion (especially under the armpits) and some gravity (assuming the garment is the proper size for you, your body won't be filling it out completely everywhere). So your sweater fabric needs to be much stronger and harder-wearing than your average shawl.

On the other hand, your sweater fabric can't be so tight that it won't stretch easily as you move. So some flexibility is required, and the typical sock fabric is tighter than what will work well in a sweater.

How do you tell whether your sweater fabric will wear well? I have three tests for you: one that will test your gauge given the yarn you've chosen, one that will test your fabric's spring and elasticity, and one that will test your fabric's structure.

1 THE POKE TEST. To see whether you're knitting at a tight enough gauge for the yarn you've selected, try to poke a bit of your pinky finger or nail all the way through the spaces between the stitches. Unless you're working with yarn that's at Aran weight or larger, you shouldn't be able to do so—you should see a nice tight mesh instead. If you can poke your finger (or part of it) through, go down a needle size and swatch again.

2 THE SPRING TEST. To see whether your fabric will be able to keep its shape as you wear it, test how well your fabric springs back when stretched. (Note: You should get a nicely springy fabric even out of completely inelastic yarn!) Place your swatch, WS up, on a flat smooth surface like a table. The fabric should be able to move around freely. Making a triangle with your fingers and thumb, press down and stretch your fingers and thumb apart. First, note whether your fabric stretches easily. If it doesn't, go up a needle size and try again. Now, let go. Your stitches should spring back together instantly. Your swatch may even move! If the stitches are sluggish about returning to form, your fabric is too loose and you need to go down a needle size.

3 THE STRUCTURE TEST. Now you need to tell how well each stitch keeps its neighbors in line. Unlike the previous two tests, a fail on this test isn't necessarily a deal breaker! Instead, this test teaches you about the way your fabric will act

Wool/silk
and wool/alpaca
held together

60% wool/
30% alpaca/
10% angora

70% alpaca/
30% wool

Acrylic/
wool/nylon

100% wool

50% wool/
50% alpaca

50% wool/
50% alpaca

when you've got a lot of it. The goal of the test is to see how movement in one part of the fabric affects the rest.

Again placing your swatch on a very smooth surface with the WS up, take both index fingers and press down firmly toward one corner of the swatch. Making little half-circles or figure-eights with your fingers while pressing down firmly, see how much of the swatch you can move by shifting your one corner.

If you can move most (or all!) of the fabric of the swatch as you move your fingers, your fabric is structural and can handle a tougher job (for example, an open cardigan with cables). If moving one portion of the swatch doesn't cause the rest to move (hint: this will be true of the drapiest fibers), that's a sign that you'll need to strongly support your fabric with a sturdy silhouette—one with seams around the shoulders and arms.

If you're having trouble getting a fabric that will wear well even after trying a different needle size, consider whether your yarn choice is the issue. Some yarns are harder to work into a sweater fabric than others! The most knitter-friendly sweater yarns:

FEEL SLIGHTLY ELASTIC IN THE HANDS AND ARE EASY TO TENSION. The single most challenging thing about knitting a sweater, for many knitters, is keeping a consistent tension through the entire garment. This is much easier if your chosen yarn has good elasticity, and feels pleasant and smooth running through your fingers.

ARE DURABLE AND ABRASION RESISTANT. Some yarns are so delicate that they pill, snag, or otherwise get damaged just during the swatching process! Be on the lookout for these warning signs—they may mean that your yarn isn't really a great match for sweaters.

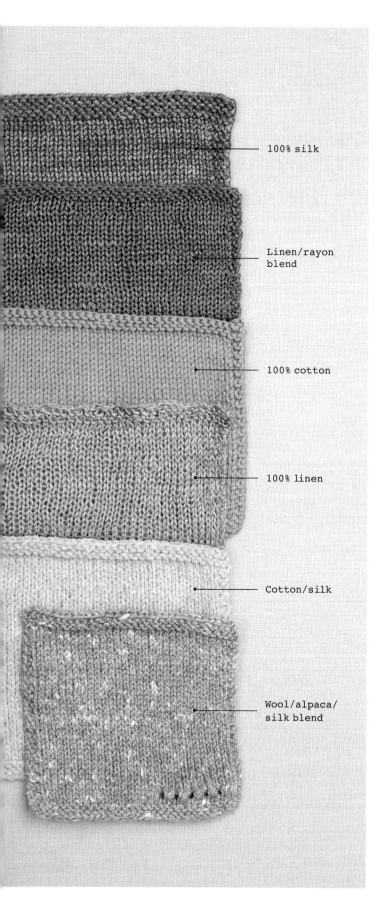

100% silk

Linen/rayon blend

100% cotton

100% linen

Cotton/silk

Wool/alpaca/silk blend

REQUIRE LITTLE IN THE WAY OF SPECIAL HANDLING WHEN WET. Some yarns, 100% superwash wools in particular, can get unwieldy and require careful handling when wet to keep from distorting or growing. This isn't necessarily a deal breaker, but if your fabric seems fine before you get it wet and things go wrong when you're washing your swatch, consider using a different yarn for your first few sweaters.

ARE SOMETHING YOU LIKE! Finally, the best sweater yarn in the world is the wrong choice for you if you find it unpleasant to use, or dislike the fabric it makes. Life is too short to work with yarn we don't like, so be honest with yourself!

LOOK & FEEL

Have a fabric that will stand up well to the rigors of sweater wearing? Great! Now there's just one more set of things to consider before beginning your garment: how the fabric looks and feels, and whether the fabric matches your design.

Most of the words we use to describe our fabric's look and feel—words like *drape, stitch definition, heft, fluidity*—come from the yarn's fiber content instead of its gauge. Different fibers bring different properties to the fabric party, regardless of the gauge at which they're knit. The cheat sheet below, and photographic examples on page 13 and opposite, will help you figure out the right fibers for your project.

WOOL is a gloriously forgiving fiber for the knitter, as it is smooth, relatively light, and has great elasticity and memory. This means that your sweater will keep its shape well when worn, because after your movements have stretched the fabric, the stitches will go back to the place they started. This is great news if you'd like your sweater to keep its shape when worn. Wool also traps body heat well, and is very warm to wear.

ALPACA is a dense, warm, drapey fiber that tends to be a bit more slippery than wool. Its combination of weight and drape produces a beautiful Stockinette fabric, but pure alpaca is a tough choice for a design with cabling or that's loosely knit, as the fabric may droop and stretch out of place. This droop and stretch won't correct itself, as alpaca is not an elastic fiber.

SILK is one of the most gloriously drapey, fluid fibers around. It's also incredibly strong and has a nice luster. It isn't very elastic compared with wool, though it does keep its shape a bit better than rayon or linen if worked snugly.

COTTON is on the heavy side. It is the absolute opposite of elastic, but it is incredibly durable and soft. Cotton wicks moisture away from the body and releases it quickly by evaporation, so it makes a great choice for warmer-weather garments.

LINEN is another inelastic, moisture-wicking, incredibly durable fiber. When compared with cotton, linen offers more drape and a more fluid feel to the fabric. Linen fabric feels better the more it's worn.

RAYON, or viscose, came to be when manufacturers were looking for a way to re-create silk with synthetic materials. It offers a beautiful color, a smooth feel, and absolutely no elasticity. It's also quite slippery, so a 100% rayon yarn would have to be knit very tightly to stay in shape on your body—it works much better as a blend.

NYLON is primarily a "helper" fiber in hand-knitting, used to add strength and durability to other yarns, and as structural components in some more unusual yarn constructions. (For example, it could form a binding core for hairy brushed yarns, or a casing for yarns where loose bits of fiber are blown into a tube.) You'll typically find nylon as part of a blend with another material.

ACRYLIC is often either blended with a natural fiber or used on its own, when ease-of-care is the foremost concern. It's relatively grippy, offers good stitch definition, and has a fairly smooth look. Acrylic, like nylon, also adds strength and memory to your fabric—in fact, acrylic has so much memory that blocking won't change this fiber at all! Your fabric after washing will look and feel exactly like your fabric before washing.

If this all sounds like a lot to keep track of, don't worry! Just remember that most yarns want to be knit at a fairly firm gauge for sweater knitting, and if there's one fabric quality or another at the top of your wish list for a certain design, you can achieve that quality by selecting yarns of the right fiber.

If *several* of the qualities listed above are what you're after, the yarn world has you covered! Many yarns on the market as of this writing are blends of more than one fiber. So if you want the luster and drape of silk, and the elasticity and warmth of wool, choose one of the many wool-silk blends out there. If you're hankering for the smooth, soft feel of cotton but want some elasticity, too, a cotton-wool blend might be what you're after. For a summer-weight sweater with more drape and sheen, a linen-rayon blend might be just the ticket.

For more information on yarns and fibers, I cannot recommend Clara Parkes's *Knitter's Guide to Yarn* and *Knitter's Guide to Wool* highly enough. They're excellent resources, fun to read, and belong on every knitter's shelf.

STITCH PATTERNING

If you're feeling overwhelmed, you can stop here! Once you have a structured fabric that makes you happy, knit a great (plain) sweater and come back to this section later.

But, as you move beyond basic sweaters, you'll probably want to add, change up, or otherwise play around with stitch patterning in your sweaters. And when you do, you'll need to think about how your chosen stitch pattern and chosen fabric get along.

Generally, sweaters work best when there's only one "star," so if the yarn is busy, the stitch pattern should take a seat, and vice versa. It's a good idea to make a small swatch of your stitch pattern before beginning to make sure the pattern and your yarn get along. (But you knew that, right?)

In addition to "Do I like it?" there are three important things to consider:

1 **STITCH DEFINITION** refers to how crisply and quickly you can identify the outline of a particular stitch. A smooth 100% silk would offer high stitch definition; a fuzzy woolen-spun tweed yarn offers almost none. Generally speaking, the stronger the stitch definition, the more polished and refined the fabric will look. The fuzzier the stitch definition, the more rustic your garment will feel.

2 **PATTERNING VISIBILITY** is related to stitch definition, but isn't quite the same. If you're adding a stitch pattern to part (or all) of a sweater, how clearly can that patterning be seen? Several things can affect this visibility, including stitch definition and the inherent busyness of the yarn itself. Things like blooms, halo, tweedy textures, and color changes can all obscure stitch patterning.

3 **COLOR** is the last thing to consider when matching a fabric to a design. Is the color solid, semisolid, or variegated? If it's semisolid or variegated, you're likely to be happier pairing the yarn with simpler designs and simple or small-scale texture stitch patterns. Consider how the yarn looks knit up into fabric, rather than just in the hank, before making a firm decision on a yarn/design pairing. Finally, if the yarn is hand-painted, be sure to alternate hanks every two rows as you knit to keep the pooling and color differences between skeins to a minimum!

DEFINITION, COLOR, AND VISIBILITY (clockwise from top left): The nubby cotton/silk tweed "fuzzes up" the Shoreside Vest; variegation obscures the Speedster Raglan stitch pattern; super-crisp stitches let the cables of the Horseshoe Pullover shine.

Anatomy of a Knitting Pattern

If you have a fabric you like, a design you love, and confidence in your gauge, you're ready to roll. Before you cast on, here's a brief primer on the knitting pattern itself—what information it contains, how that information can help you, and what parts of the pattern you should feel free to improvise.

KNITTING PATTERN SECTIONS

Each knitting pattern contains three separate kinds of information for you: what I like to think of as a summary, the instructions themselves, and then visuals to help you keep the 10,000-foot view of what you're doing in your head.

1 PATTERN SUMMARY. This is everything you need to know at a glance—what sizes the pattern comes in (hopefully listed by finished bust or chest circumference), the exact yarn that was used in the sample, the materials you'll need to have on hand to make the project, and the gauge the numbers are based on.

- *Use it for:* Selecting a size, preparing your notions, getting a starting point for your needle size, understanding how the combination of fibers, yarn, and gauge produced the sweater you see in the picture.

- *Feel free to change:* Needles! You should definitely use whatever needles you need to come close to the listed gauge. Also feel free to substitute yarn, keeping in mind that you'll need to stay as close to the listed yarn as possible (in terms of weight, yarn construction, and fiber composition) to get a similar result.

2 ACTUAL INSTRUCTIONS. These instructions form the core of the pattern. They tell you exactly what to do with your needles step by step. It's always a good idea to start by scanning the pattern closely—it will help you build a picture in your mind of the process of knitting the sweater. It will also help you identify those necessary-but-irritating *at-the-same-time* instructions before you reach them!

- *Use it for:* Knitting! These instructions specify the bulk of your actual knitting.

- *Feel free to change:* The numbers, to match your body's specific needs. All hand-knitting patterns are crafted to a standardized set of measurements—in my first two books, I affectionately call the woman represented by these measurements "Ms. Average." Since your measurements are likely to differ from Ms. Average's in some respect, you should feel encouraged to alter the instructions so that your sweater will be perfect for you! We'll cover more on how to do this in chapter 2 (page 23).

3 VISUALS. These portions of the pattern—the pattern's schematic and charted stitch pattern instructions—give you important visual cues about your knitting. The pattern's schematic (see opposite) is a gold mine of helpful stuff. It tells you what the pieces of knitting should look like as they come off your needles, and provides you with detailed information about exactly how big they should be in every dimension.

- *Use them for:* Getting a great visual sense of how your stitch pattern looks, in overview form, and of how your knitted pieces should look when you're finished blocking.

- *Feel free to change:* The schematic in particular will give you the information you need to change the pattern's numbers to suit your own body.

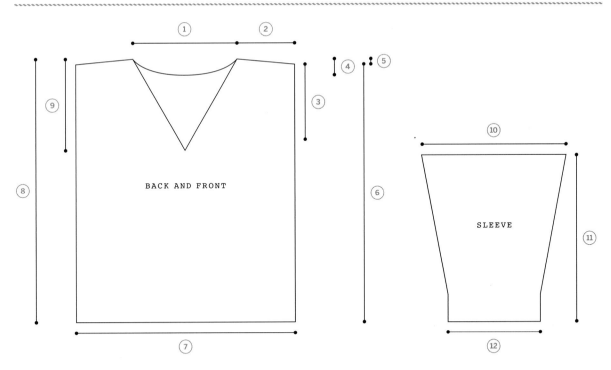

PATTERN SCHEMATIC

All the measurements given with the schematic represent the actual dimensions of the knitted pieces after blocking but before any seaming.

The flat top to the sleeve at the top right, along with notched arms on the body pieces, mean this schematic is for a drop-shoulder sweater, like the ones in chapter 6.

You can check the shoulder fit of the size you've selected by adding the neck and shoulder widths together (1)+(2)+(2), and comparing that with your, or your recipient's, shoulders.

BACK AND FRONT

1 9¾ (9¾, 10, 10¾, 11, 11¾, 12, 12, 12¾, 12¾, 13, 13)"
25 (25, 25.5, 27.5, 28, 30, 30.5, 30.5, 32.5, 32.5, 33, 33) cm

2 4¾ (5¼, 5½, 5¾, 6, 6¼, 6½, 7, 7¼, 7¾, 8½, 9½)"
12 (13.5, 14, 14.5, 15, 16, 16.5, 18, 18.5, 19.5, 21.5, 24) cm

3 6 (6½, 7, 7½, 8, 8½, 9, 9½, 10, 10½, 11, 11)"
15 (16.5, 18, 19, 20.5, 21.5, 23, 24, 25.5, 26.5, 28, 28) cm

4 1½"/4 cm

5 ½"/1.5 cm

6 23½ (23¾, 24, 24½, 25, 25½, 26, 26½, 27, 27½, 28, 28)"
59.5 (60.5, 61, 62, 63.5, 65, 66, 67.5, 68.5, 70, 71, 71) cm

7 19 (20, 21, 22, 23, 24, 25, 26, 27, 28, 30, 32)"
48.5 (51, 53.5, 56, 58.5, 61, 63.5, 66, 68.5, 71, 76, 81.5) cm

8 24 (24¼, 24½, 25, 25½, 26, 26½, 27, 27½, 28, 28½, 28½)"
61 (61.5, 62, 63.5, 65, 66, 67.5, 68.5, 70, 71, 72.5, 72.5) cm

9 7¾ (8, 8½, 9, 9½, 10, 10½, 11, 11½, 11½, 11½, 11½)"
19.5 (20.5, 21.5, 23, 24, 25.5, 26.5, 28, 29, 29, 29, 29) cm

SLEEVE

10 12 (13, 14, 15, 16, 17, 18, 19, 20, 21, 22, 22)"
30.5 (33, 35.5, 38, 40.5, 43, 45.5, 48.5, 51, 53.5, 56, 56) cm

11 15½ (15½, 15½, 16, 16, 16, 16½, 16½, 16½, 16½, 17, 17)"
39.5 (39.5, 39.5, 40.5, 40.5, 40.5, 42, 42, 42, 42, 43, 43) cm

12 8¼ (8¼, 9, 9, 9, 9¼, 9¼, 9¾, 10¼, 10¾, 11, 12)"
21 (21, 23, 23, 23, 23.5, 23.5, 25, 26, 27.5, 28, 30.5) cm

Charts (see below) tell you, in visual form, exactly how to work the stitch pattern in your garment. They're more helpful (in my opinion) than line-by-line written instructions, because they give you a sense of how the whole stitch pattern comes together. And with the advent of smart phones and tablets, apps that keep track of your place in the chart help make them easy to use, too!

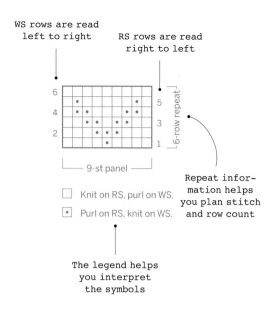

WS rows are read left to right

RS rows are read right to left

6-row repeat

9-st panel

☐ Knit on RS, purl on WS.

⊡ Purl on RS, knit on WS.

Repeat information helps you plan stitch and row count

The legend helps you interpret the symbols

Difficulty Levels

To give you a sense of what you're getting into with each project, I've created a set of sweater-specific difficulty levels and ranked each pattern in this book according to them. There are a few different sources of challenge when knitting a sweater: the number of stitches, the amount of stitch patterning, how many different pieces you have to create, and how intense the finishing is (trims, edgings, and button bands). Each project in the book is given a ranking from 1–5 ball(s) of yarn:

- *Difficulty 1:* These projects rank "easy" in each of the challenge areas. They feature minimal finishing, are small-size or large-gauge, and use minimal stitch patterning.

- *Difficulty 2:* These projects are still pretty simple overall, but may have one slightly more intense challenge area.

- *Difficulty 3:* These projects have one challenge area that is as complicated as it gets, or multiple challenge areas might be of medium intensity.

- *Difficulty 4:* Nothing could be called "easy" about these projects, though the dial isn't turned to 11 on all of them.

- *Difficulty 5:* These projects are the pinnacle of sweater knitting. They'll have complicated stitch patterning, "at-the-same-time" instructions and shaping, and intricate or interesting finishing.

Mini Exercises

Your success as a sweater knitter increases like crazy the more intuition you build into your hands . . . but nobody wants to knit dozens of sweaters to get that intuition!

The answer? Use swatches and mini projects to help your intuition grow with the fewest number of stitches possible. Each chapter in this book will include mini exercises to help you get used to sweater knitting.

In these first three chapters, the minis will be shown as exercises that focus on swatching for a specific purpose. Once we get into the patterns, each type of garment will be offered as a children's-sized smaller package, so that you can get all the techniques and idiosyncrasies worked out before you tackle a garment at full adult size.

This chapter's mini exercises (see opposite) are all about fabric.

MINI EXERCISES

MINI #1 Choose three yarns out of your stash (or from your local yarn store) at random. Pick a pattern from this book, and knit swatches of each yarn on three different needle sizes: the recommended size listed in the pattern, one needle size up, and one needle size down.

Wash and dry the swatches as described on page 10, and then play with them for a little while. What words would you use to describe the fabrics you made?

How do those words relate to the fiber qualities listed?

Which versions do you think would make the best sweater? Socks?

MINI #2 Grab your favorite store-bought sweater or knit top out of your closet. Look closely at its materials and how it's constructed. Sketch out a schematic-style drawing of the pieces you'd need to knit to reproduce the sweater, and make a note of what kinds of yarn you'd need to use to get a similar fabric based on the descriptions I've provided on pages 14–15.

Chapter 1

DURING *the* KNITTING

You have a pattern, a fabric you like, and have predicted your gauge well. Awesome! Now, what should be on your mind while you're actually knitting?

Sizing and Modifications

Sweater patterns are written in sizes based on the full bust/chest circumference. The patterns in this book give a list of *finished measurements*—that is, what the bust/chest of the sweater will measure once it's all put together.

The simplest way to choose a size is to:

- Take the measurement of your own full bust.
- Compare it against the list of finished bust measurements from the pattern you've chosen.
- Choose a size that's within a couple of inches of your own full bust, in either direction, depending on whether you'd like a close-fitting or loose-fitting sweater.

Hand-knitting patterns are like ready-to-wear clothing instructions: They're sized based on an industry-standard chart. So if your measurements are more or less those of the woman whose measurements are described by the chart—whom I refer to as "Ms. Average" on page 18—this approach will work well for you. (Not sure if you're like Ms. Average? Generally speaking, she has a full bust and hips that are roughly the same size, with a smaller waist and shoulders.)

If your measurements *aren't* like Ms. Average's—

say, you have a longer torso or wider shoulders—choosing a size based on your own full bust measurement and knitting the pattern as written will lead you astray, and you'll have to adjust for this otherwise!

A full-on fit discussion is outside the scope of this book (for more detail, please see either my first book, *Knit to Flatter*, which covers this in depth, or my second book, *Knit Wear Love*, which includes a pretty thorough overview). But, to get you started off right, here's a "top 3" list for easy fit adjustments you can make if you're nervous about achieving a proper fit:

1 If your bust and shoulders aren't a Ms. Average B/C cup, choose a size by comparing your *upper torso* to the pattern's full bust measurements:

- Put a measuring tape around your torso as high in your armpits as it can go. If you're smaller busted, let it be a little loose. If you're larger busted, pull it snug.
- Use this number as if it were your full bust when choosing a size to start with. Add ease to it as desired (see page 28 for a discussion on ease), and choose the closest "finished bust circumference" to the resulting number.

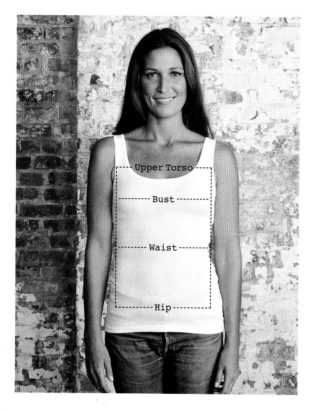

- Now, forget your upper torso—you won't need it beyond this first step.

② Examine the circumference measurements at the waist, bust, and hip for the size you've selected. Are they the right size for your body, once ease is taken into account? *(Remember: Knitwear is forgiving, so as long as the garment is within a couple of inches of your target number, you'll be fine.)*

- If they're not, you'll need to change the stitch count at the point where the garment isn't right for you. Take your desired measurement at that point and multiply it by the stitch gauge from your swatch to get the number of stitches you need.

- You can adjust the back and front of your sweater separately—and that's what you *should* do, especially if you have a larger bust: Make

the front bust width larger than the back bust width to match your body.

③ Examine and compare the pattern's length measurements against your body as well, and adjust if needed.

Modifications might seem daunting, but they're usually pretty simple to work. If you'd like a primer on ease and fit, check out pages 28–29.

Shaping and Other Stuff

I'll be honest—sometimes, knitting patterns are downright vague. There's usually a good reason, though! If a knitting pattern isn't spelling something out exactly, you probably have several options for how to accomplish your task. None of them is more *right* than the other—they just produce different looks, and you might favor some over others. Here's the lowdown on the most common choices you'll have:

CAST-ONS AND BIND-OFFS. In most cases, you can use whichever cast-on or bind-off method you prefer. Personally, I prefer the long-tail cast-on and the regular old in-pattern bind-off, and use them for almost everything I do. If you'd like to learn more about different choices for cast-ons and bind-offs, check out the Recommended Reading List and Resources on page 173.

BUTTONHOLES. As shown opposite, there are a few different ways to work buttonholes, and different people prefer different types. (In almost all cases, I use plain, old two-row buttonholes, but I'm giving you an overview here for completeness.)

- The simplest to work, and the most appropriate if you're using a strong, fairly fine yarn, is the (yo, k2tog) buttonhole. It's neat, easy to work, and is over in a single row. I tend to use it when I'm making a sweater with lots of small buttons.

- The next easiest to work is the two-row or bind-off/cast-on buttonhole. On the first buttonhole row, you bind off 2, 3, or 4 stitches (depending on the size of your button—it should be slightly difficult, but possible, to put the button through the hole). On the following row, cast on the same number of stitches you've bound off.

  There are a few tricks to making this buttonhole sturdy and lovely: First, working the stitches on each side of the buttonhole through their back loops (twisting them) helps to keep the edges strong. Second, working the cast-on stitches through the back loop in the row immediately following the cast-on will help stabilize them. I tend to use this buttonhole as my default.

- The third kind of buttonhole you'll likely find reference to is a one-row buttonhole where you both bind-off and cast on on the same row. You'll need this buttonhole to be one stitch larger, generally speaking, than a two-row buttonhole to achieve the same size opening.

EDGE SHAPING. This is by far the most common offender in the "vague instructions" camp! Patterns will say something like "decrease one stitch at neck edge every RS row 5 times," or "decrease one stitch at each end of every RS row 7 times," etc. Why so vague?

Well, there are a number of different ways to accomplish edge shaping, none of them incorrect. You essentially have two choices to make: where you work the shaping, and how.

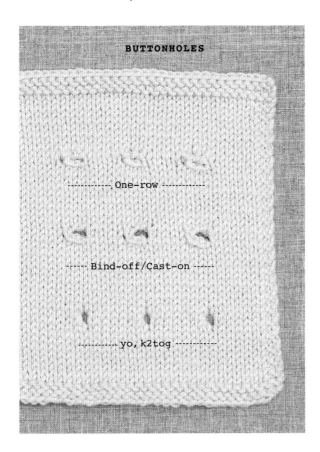

BUTTONHOLES

- - - - - - - One-row - - - - - - -

- - - - - Bind-off/Cast-on - - - - -

- - - - - - - - - yo, k2tog - - - - - - - - -

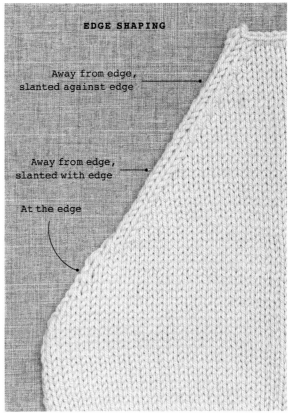

EDGE SHAPING

Away from edge, slanted against edge

Away from edge, slanted with edge

At the edge

- *Where.* Shaping can be worked right on the edge, or one or more stitches in from the edge. When worked on the edge itself, the shaping is hidden within the seam of the finished garment, giving it a very clean look. The downside to this approach is that your seaming gets a bit trickier! Shaping worked one (or two, or three) stitches in from the edge makes for easier seaming, but the shaping then becomes part of the look of the finished piece.

- *How.* If you're shaping one or more stitches in from the edge, the direction your shaping *slants* makes for another choice. Shaping that slants *with* the edge being shaped (i.e., an ssk at the beginning of a RS row, and a k2tog at the end) makes a streamlined, less-noticeable line. Shaping that slants *toward* the edge being shaped (i.e., a k2tog at the beginning of a RS row or an ssk at the end) is more noticeable. This isn't bad—in fact, quite the opposite! It's a technique that was originally found in high-end clothing, and is called "fully fashioned" shaping. The choice of where and how to shape is up to you. Check out the photo on page 25 to see how these options look!

These are the most common culprits for vague pattern instructions, but any time you're unsure about how something should be worked, you can take comfort in the fact that you probably have a few options! In those cases, remember: If you like the way it looks, you're doing it right.

Other Mods

Quite aside from the basic choices of fit and shaping methods, you might want to make some changes to the pattern as written simply for style reasons. The patterns in this book are fundamentally on the simpler side—they're meant to give you wearable, versatile wardrobe staples. This means that sometimes, you might want to use them as a launching point for that more complicated sweater in your head. Usually, "more complicated" will mean adding a stitch pattern or two to the blank slates I've given you in this book. Here's how to do that successfully.

TYPES OF STITCH PATTERNS

A stitch pattern is a particular way of working knits, purls, increases, decreases, cabling, slipped stitches, etc., into a pattern that's pleasing to the eye. I tend to think about them in groups: *texture patterns*, which are usually composed of knits, purls, and the occasional slipped stitch; *lace patterns*, which involve paired increases and decreases (usually yarnovers); and *cables*, which rearrange the order of some of your stitches.

Texture patterns, with their abstract look, are usually the best match for a busily colored or variegated yarn. Their gauge should be close to, or identical to, Stockinette, and they're typically simple to work. The Broken Rib on the sleeves of the Downy Cardigan (page 154) is a great example. Cables tend to look best (and are more functional) when your chosen yarn has some elasticity and memory, because they're heavy! They look lovely in both yarns with crisp stitch definition and fuzzier yarns. I used cables with eyelets added to give some interest to the Maypole pullover (page 135). Lace can look great in almost any yarn, though tweedier yarns and ones that tend to bloom will obscure the patterning

TYPES OF STITCH PATTERNS (clockwise from top left): Eyelets are used to create lace stripes in the Rigging Sweatshirt; the Maypole pullover includes a shrinking cable pattern; the Downy Cardigan uses Broken Rib, a textured stitch pattern.

somewhat. This isn't always a bad thing though! For an example of a clean, unfussy lace, check out the eyelet stripes in the Rigging Sweatshirt (page 68).

Whatever stitch pattern is catching your eye, be sure to swatch it in your intended yarn first before making any final decisions. This needn't be a large gauge swatch like I talked about in chapter 1 (pages 9–11)—just a few inches square to make sure you enjoy how that pattern looks in your chosen yarn!

STITCH PATTERNS AND GAUGE

If you're including just a small panel of stitch patterning, there's no need to do a giant gauge swatch. Chances are that if the pattern is *lace or texture*, any gauge differences won't be large enough to matter in the finished sample. (Keep in mind that while lace *can* be stretched quite wide, when worn in a sweater application, it doesn't stay stretched! So your lace's unblocked, resting gauge is what matters.) *Cables* are really the only kind of stitch pattern that require gauge adjustment, and I have a handy rule of thumb for you:

Since each stitch that gets put on a cable needle is removed from the width of the piece you're knitting, when you're adding a cable to a plain Stockinette garment, add one stitch to your stitch count for each stitch that gets put on a cable needle, over the width of the cable.

Here's an example: If you're working a 4-stitch, 2-over-2 cable cross on the front of a cardigan, you'll need 2 stitches over your Stockinette stitch count to achieve the same width. If you're adding three 3-over-3 cables to the front of a pullover, add 9 stitches to your Stockinette count.

Eases

If ease confuses you, you're not alone! Ease refers to the difference between what your body measures and what the garment measures in some dimension. Your sweaters can and *should* fit you differently at different points on your body.

Generally speaking, the way we look to others is based on how we fill out our clothing. If your sweater is looser at the waist than at the bust and hips, you'll look hourglass in proportion. Busts look larger when the sweater is snug through the bust, and smaller when the sweater is loose.

How you want to look is up to you, but here's a quick rundown on what eases look best from a fit perspective.

FULL BUST -2" to +2" (-5 to +5 cm)

WAIST +2" to +6" (+5 to +15 cm)

HIPS

- *Short and medium sweaters:*
  -2" to +0" (-5 to +0 cm) for anchoring

- *Long sweaters:*
  0" to +2" (0 to +5 cm)

- *Tunic-length sweater*
  (below the curve of the bum):
  +6" (+15 cm) or more, up to +12" (+30.5 cm)
  for an A-line sweater

EASES (clockwise from top left): Positive ease in bust, waist, and hips in the Entangled Raglan; negative ease in bust and hip in the Corner Office Vest; zero ease in bust and hip, positive ease in waist in the Snowdrift Pullover.

Tracking Your Progress

Okay, you're into the actual sweater knitting itself. For some knitters, this blissful time is periodically interrupted by anxiety (Am I doing it right?). So here are a few ways you can double-check your progress and keep on track.

MEASURING

Of course, one way to keep yourself calm while knitting is to spot-check that things are measuring as they should: Does the sweater back actually measure 8½" (21.5 cm) when you reach the waist? Is the back bust actually 20" (51 cm) wide?

To measure, place your knitting on a not-too-grippy, not-too-smooth, flat surface (like a carpet) and uncurl the edges gently. (Smoothing out the fabric on a grippy surface too aggressively will stretch it, and your fabric will curl too much on a smooth surface to effectively measure.) Use a flexible fabric tape measure to check your progress. That's all there is to it!

COUNTING

Of course, if during your swatching your gauge changed from the "as knitting" stage to your "after washing" stage, using a tape measure to measure your work while you go along isn't going to be helpful. In that case, you can count rows to keep on track. If your pattern already has row counts, great! If not, multiply the inches measurement you're aiming for (say, 8½" [21.5 cm]) by your post-washing row gauge (say, 8 rows to the inch). You should have a row count of 68 rows when you move on to the next set of instructions.

In fact, counting rows is less error-prone than measuring, and will lead to easier seaming—it's my approach of choice!

CHECKING A FINISHED PIECE

Once you have an entire piece completed, it can save a lot of anxiety (or ripping, depending on how things turn out) to block the piece and let it dry to sanity-check your progress. (See page 33 for guidelines on how to do this.) If things look good—your piece measures what it should, the fabric is still something you want to wear, etc.—you'll feel confident when knitting the remaining pieces. If not, at least you know before the sweater is finished! Head back to the drawing board, secure in the knowledge that we've all been there with one sweater or another. (I once knit a sweater that could stand up on its own!)

MINI EXERCISES

A great way to figure out your own preferences and needs in terms of stitch patterns, shaping, buttonholes, and more is by making small swatches. So your exercises for this chapter are to re-create my buttonhole and shaping swatches to see which method you prefer, and to explore the way stitch patterns look with different yarns.

Create swatches like the ones shown in this chapter:

BUTTONHOLES

CO 34 sts.

Work 5 rows even in Garter stitch, then switch to Stockinette stitch in the middle with 2 stitches of Garter stitch continuing up each side.

Work around 1½" (4 cm) even, then work three evenly spaced (yo, k2tog) buttonholes with 6 stitches before the first buttonhole and 8 stitches between buttonholes.

Continue in Stockinette stitch for another 1" (2.5 cm), then work three evenly spaced two-row buttonholes.

Repeat for one-row buttonholes.

See pages 24–25 for more information.

EDGE SHAPING

CO 30 sts.

Work around 1" (2.5 cm) in 2 x 2 ribbing, then switch to Stockinette stitch and work an additional 1½" (4 cm).

Work 8 RS-row decreases at the left edge of your swatch in each of three ways: decrease at the edge; decrease 2 stitches away from the edge, slanting to the right; decrease 2 stitches away from the edge, slanting to the left.

BO all stitches.

See pages 25–26 for more information.

STITCH PATTERNS Pull out a stitch dictionary and try a few different stitch patterns in different yarns. What things do you like? What things do you dislike?

....

....

....

....

....

....

....

....

Chapter 2

AFTER *the* KNITTING

You're almost there! You've decided how you want the sweater to look, maybe made some changes to the pattern, and the knitting is complete. You're not totally done though—things still look unfinished. So, how do you get from this mostly done step to wearing your gorgeous sweater?

Blocking

Before you do anything else, you need to block your piece(s). Absolutely everything else you need to do will be made easier by this all-important step. Blocking refers generally to getting your knitted bits ready for the finishing process, and there are a few different ways to do it.

While it's always a good idea to check your yarn label for specific care instructions, pretty much every yarn I've ever personally worked with is best cared for by wet-blocking. Here's how to do this like a champ:

1. First, fill a small bucket, pot, sink, etc., with cold water and a no-rinse wool wash like Eucalan or Soak.

2. Put your pieces in and thoroughly submerge them so they sink. The idea is to get things sopping wet. Let them soak for at least a half hour. (*Confession time: I've forgotten sweater pieces in the water for several hours before. Things turned out just fine.*)

3. Press out most of the water, keeping the pieces wadded together in a tight ball. You can dump your bin out in the bathtub and press down, or if you're nervous about "growth" problems during blocking, you can dump them into a large colander or strainer and press the water out that way. (The only thing you *shouldn't* do at this point is pull on a corner or edge of the fabric—your hand-knit won't be strong enough to carry the weight of the water without stretching.)

4. Get out the rest of the water. I like the *spin-only* cycle of my washing machine, on the low speed—but a less-technological way is to place your pieces on a towel, roll the towel up, and step on it to squeeze the water out.

5. Transport the pieces to your blocking surface. You should still keep your pieces balled up when you're moving them, but nearly all the water should be out at this point, and the pieces should feel fairly light. I use a set of foam exercise mats covered with a dry towel for blocking,

but you can use anything you like—just make sure it's a nice flat surface into which you can put a few pins.

Once your pieces are on the blocking board, it's time to prepare them for drying. I don't like to use a lot of pins in blocking, nor am I a fan of stretching things out. If you've done your gauge calculations correctly, your pieces should basically be the correct size already, and the water will have already worked its magic on your fabric. So this part is mostly about encouraging your edges to lie flat and making your finishing process as easy as possible.

1 Gently but quickly, with a minimum of pulling, get your pieces into approximately the right shape.

2 Measure and pin a few key points only. For example, on the sweater body pieces, I like to place one pin on each of the shoulders, on each side of the fullest part of the chest, and at the hip. If you're working a piece with waist shaping, let the side seams curl under—you want the fabric to retain its curves!

3 Walk away and leave the sweater pieces alone until they're fully, truly bone-dry. *(It's okay to help things along with a fan. It's not okay to lie to yourself about what "dry" is.)*

Unpin, and get ready to finish!

General Finishing Tips

The goal of all finishing is to ensure that there are no unfinished knit edges showing—they're not particularly strong, they're not particularly attractive, and unless there's an edge treatment (ribbing on the hem of a sweater, for example) they have a tendency to curl and cause other problems.

There are three kinds of edges you'll have to finish: a straight vertical edge, such as a cardigan front; a straight horizontal edge, such as the top of a shoulder; or a mixed edge, like a neck opening or a sleeve cap top. In all cases, you'll want to fold/turn exactly one full row and/or column of stitches into the interior of the piece during your finishing.

Whether you're seaming or picking up stitches, you want one even line of stitches and rows against the finished edge. So get familiar with the place you'll be working your finishing! Use a needle or your finger to trace the "ditch" (see illustration opposite) between one row/column of stitches and the next. Notice how there are tiny little boxes of space into which you could insert a needle and yarn. That's where you'll be working.

SEAMING

The first step is to get all your pieces (if necessary) together and make sure the garment looks like, well, a garment. You might be working an entirely all-in-one construction, but even then chances are there's at least a teeny seam somewhere in your sweater. Here's how to do them well.

I prefer mattress stitch for all sweater seaming. The general approach is to attach two pieces of knitting together with smooth yarn (in many cases the yarn you used to knit the sweater), with the RS of the work facing up. Mattress stitching

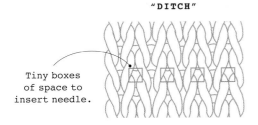

"DITCH"

Tiny boxes
of space to
insert needle.

HORIZONTAL MATTRESS STITCH

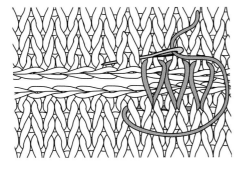

VERTICAL MATTRESS STITCH

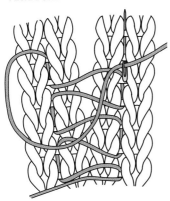

turns the first column of stitches to the inside as you work it. That means you should be looking at the "outsides" of all your pieces when mattress stitching.

There are two fundamental kinds of mattress stitch: for horizontal edges and for vertical edges.

SEAMING A HORIZONTAL EDGE

When you're joining shoulders, underarms, and the like, you're seaming two bound-off edges together—this is horizontal seaming. Lay your knitted pieces out so that the bound-off edges are touching each other. You'll be using your seaming yarn to attach one stitch from the top to one stitch from the bottom, all the way across the edges. Here's how:

1 Thread your yarn through a tapestry needle and begin with the needle on top of your work. Reach down with your needle and "scoop up" both legs of a whole knit stitch on the bottom piece. Pull your yarn through, leaving about a 6" (15 cm) tail.

2 Now, reach with your needle and "scoop up" both legs of a whole knit stitch on the top piece (notice that on this piece, *the stitch is upside down, so it looks like a /\ instead of a \/ !*). Pull the yarn so that there's just a little bit showing.

3 Repeat the last two steps, pulling the yarn tight every inch or so.

When done properly, mattress stitch creates a very strong, neat line and a great anchor point for the sweater to stay in place on your body as you move.

SEAMING A VERTICAL EDGE

When you're joining side and sleeve seams, vertical mattress stitch is the way to go. Lay your knitted pieces out so that the edges you're joining are right next to each other. Remember, you'll be working with the bars between one column of knit stitches and the next. Spend some time finding these bars before you begin. Here's how it goes:

1 Again, thread your yarn through a tapestry needle and begin with the needle on top of your work.

2 Reach down with your needle and "scoop up" the bar between the first two stitches at the bottom of your right-hand knitted piece. Pull your yarn through, leaving a 6" (15 cm) tail.

3 Now, reach with your needle and "scoop up" the bars between the last two stitches on your left-hand knitted piece both in the first row and in the second. Pull the yarn so that there's just a little bit showing in between the two pieces. The yarn will be on top of the edge columns of both pieces.

4 Reach with your needle and "scoop up" the bars between the two edge stitches of the next two rows of the next piece.

5 Continue going back and forth in this way, pulling the yarn nice and snug every inch or so. After you've "zippered" a section together, it should appear like a smooth, unbroken piece of Stockinette fabric.

Side seams, when done properly, are invisible and help keep the sweater from clinging to your stomach. Practice seaming striped swatches together invisibly, as in the Puddle Jumping Cardigan Mini (page 105), to hone your skills!

MIXED EDGES

Once you're a pro at seaming two like edges, you're ready to tackle the big stuff: seaming mixed edges, as in a sleeve cap. There's no real mystery here—it's just a straight-up mix of the two kinds of seaming—but there are things you can do to make the process less intimidating.

- Pin! Pinning your pieces together with removable stitch markers ensures you'll be seaming the correct sections to each other. For sleeve caps, I start by pinning the center top of the sleeve cap to the shoulder seam (A). Then, I add pins at the armhole edges (B). Finally, I place pins every couple of inches along the curved part of the seam (C).

- For other curved edges, follow a similar procedure—that way you'll be sure everything fits together nicely before you start!

For stepped bind-offs like most shoulder seams, mix horizontal and vertical mattress stitch at the point of the "step." Picking up one vertical bar at the edges of the step really smooths out the seam.

Once your sweater pieces are seamed together, it's time to add trim to any "raw" edges left.

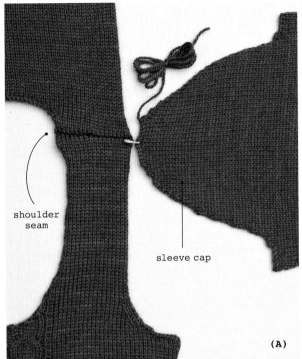

shoulder seam

sleeve cap

(A)

center of sleeve cap to center of shoulder

bind-offs to bind-offs

(B)

attach rest of sleeve

(C)

- You'll be working a mix of vertical and horizontal seaming as you move around the curve.

- Start by pinning together the edges as shown—make sure there are no lumps or gathers before you start!

- Begin and end at the armhole edge your first few times.

- As you seam, make sure you reach your pins at the same time on both the sleeve and armhole edge.

- If it looks wrong, rip it out and redo!

Along Bound-Off Edges

Along a Vertical Edge

Along a Diagonal Edge

PICKING UP STITCHES

Your goal: create a smooth transition between main fabric and trim.

- Along Bound-Off Edges: Pick up one stitch for each stitch.

- Along a Vertical Edge: Pick up one inch (2.5 cm) of stitches for every inch of rows (usually 2 stitches out of 3 rows or 3 stitches out of 4 rows).

- Along a Diagonal Edge: A higher ratio than vertical. Pick up 3 stitches out of 4 rows or 4 stitches out of 5 rows.

Finishing Edges

Okay, that thing looks a lot like a sweater now! But you probably still have a few unruly, unfinished edges to neaten up, particularly if you're knitting a cardigan. Here's the lowdown on finishing edges.

THE BASIC APPROACH

The most common way to trim a raw edge—typically a neckline—is to pick up and knit stitches along that edge, and then work them in a trim stitch pattern (often ribbing) for anywhere from ½" to 2" (1.5 to 5 cm). A few of the patterns in this book also include the *applied I-cord* edge—a method of trimming that's much more discreet. Both require you to pick up stitches.

PICKING UP STITCHES

Much like mattress stitch, picking up stitches should cause one full column or row of stitches to be turned to the inside of your work. Once the edging is worked on your picked-up stitches (or attached to it, as with I-cord), the fabric should flow smoothly from the main part of the knitted piece to the edging—no gathering, no rippling, and no puckering.

The following tips, along with the images at left, will teach you how to pick up stitches properly:

ALONG BOUND-OFF EDGES. With the RS of your work facing you, insert your knitting needle tip, from front to back, under the legs of a bound-off stitch. Wrap your yarn around it and pull a loop of yarn through to the front, leaving it on the needle. You've just picked up one stitch. Repeat, picking up one stitch for each bound-off stitch.

ALONG A VERTICAL EDGE. Here, you'll be pulling loops through the "boxes" next to the edge column of stitches. Once again, with the RS facing you, insert the tip of your needle, from front to back, into the little box made by two bars (the same bars you picked up during mattress stitch on page 36) and the sides of the stitches. Wrap your yarn around it and pull a loop through to the front, leaving it on the needle. You've just picked up one stitch in one row.

Since stitch gauge and row gauge are different, and you'd like your fabric to remain smooth once finished, you don't want to pick up one stitch in every single row. Instead, for each inch of rows, you want to pick up one inch of stitches. Usually this is either two stitches out of every three rows (for example, if your gauge is 4 stitches and 6 rows to the inch) or three stitches out of every four rows (for example, if your gauge is 6 stitches and 8 rows to the inch).

ALONG A DIAGONAL EDGE. Here, you pick up stitches as for a vertical edge, but at an increased rate since diagonal edges are longer, for a given number of rows, than a vertical edge. Typically you'll pick up 3 stitches out of 4 rows, or 4 stitches out of 5 rows, along a diagonal edge.

ALONG MIXED EDGES. Necklines are usually a combination of horizontal, vertical, and diagonal edges. Simply pick up stitches at a rate appropriate for whatever section you're in.

TRADITIONAL EDGINGS

Once you've picked up those stitches, it's time to work your edging. This is as simple as starting a stitch pattern, working until the trim measures what you'd like it to, and then binding off in pattern. But there are a few tips to help your sweater look as professional as it can:

• Your trim will be more stable and attractive if you work the very first row through the back loop, twisting each stitch as you work it.

FINISHING TOUCHES (clockwise from top left): The Collegiate Cardi has pockets and a button band; The Whisper Tee trims cap edges with applies I-Cord; The Corner Office Vest uses decorative shaping and a picked-up neckband.

- When working a deep curved edge, as on a scoop neck, you'll need to decrease some stitches at the curved points to keep the edging from flaring. Try one stitch at each curve, every fourth row.

When working a particularly deep edging on a neckline, like a turtleneck or cowl neck, increase your needle size every 3" (7.5 cm) or so to ensure the fabric of the turtleneck or cowl starts to get squishier as it extends toward the bind-off edge.

APPLIED I-CORD

There are lots of other different options for edgings, of course (Nicky Epstein has a great series of books on the topic), but one edge treatment that I chose for some of the sweaters for this book, and want to talk about specifically, is the applied I-cord.

I-cord is a self-encasing cord of Stockinette stitch. You can make one on any double-pointed needle by casting on 3 or 4 stitches, knitting them, sliding the stitches back to the right-hand side of the needle, bringing the yarn tightly around the back, and knitting them again. Repeat until the cord is as long as you'd like it to be.

I-cord can be *applied*—that is, knit directly onto—any unfinished knit edge. Pick up a line of stitches along that edge and then work the last stitch of the I-cord with a picked-up stitch. This is a neat and unobtrusive trim, particularly for areas like armholes where you may not want a bunch of extra fabric. It's a great technique to have in your finishing arsenal.

Storage and Care

Congratulations! You've made a garment you can't wait to wear. Want to get the longest and most beautiful life possible out of your hand-knits? Here are a few tips:

- Most yarns (yes, even superwash) will last longer and look better if hand-washed. Simply treat the whole sweater like you treated the pieces when you blocked them.

- Be sure to wash your sweater carefully before storing it for the season. Cosmetics, sweat, perfume, etc., will all attract moths (the knitter's bane) to your creation.

- Store sweaters folded, rather than hung— all that gravity is bad for the fabric!

- If your sweater pills, you can shave the fuzzy balls off with any fabric shaver on the market. (Of course, if your sweater is made out of good sweater fabric, you'll see fewer pills than if the yarn was knit loosely—and that's a good thing! As a good friend once said to me, when your sweater pills, it's not magical yarn babies being created—that's your garment disintegrating before your very eyes.)

MINI EXERCISES

Swatches are the perfect place to practice your finishing! Swatch a worsted-weight yarn until you're getting roughly 4 stitches and 6 rows to the inch (2.5 cm). Then, create the following swatches:

SWATCH 1 AND SWATCH 2 Two (roughly) 4" x 4" (10 x 10 cm) square swatches:
Work any kind of ribbing for 1" (2.5 cm), then switch to Stockinette stitch and work for 3" (7.5 cm). Bind off all stitches.

SWATCH 3 AND SWATCH 4 Two mini armhole swatches:

- *Swatch 3 (armhole swatch):*
  Cast on 17 stitches.
  Work 2" (5 cm) even in Stockinette.
  Next row (RS): Bind off 4 sts, work to end. Work 1 row even.
  Next row (RS): Bind off 2 sts. Decrease 1 st at bind-off edge every RS row 3 times.
  Work even until piece measures 8" (20 cm). Bind off remaining sts.

- *Swatch 4:*
  Cast on 20 stitches.
  Work 2" (5 cm) even in Stockinette, ending in a RS row.
  Next row (WS): Bind off 4 sts, work to end. Work 1 row even.
  Next row (WS): Bind off 2 sts, work to end. Decrease 1 st at bind-off edge of your 3rd RS row twice, then every RS row 4 times.
  Next row (WS): Bind off 2 sts. Work one row even.
  Next row (WS): Bind off 2 sts. Work 1 row even. Bind off remaining sts.

SWATCH 5 Finally, a mini neckline swatch:
Cast on 20 stitches.
Work for 2" (5 cm). On your next RS row, bind off 6 stitches. Then, decrease one stitch at the bound-off edge every row 4 times, then every RS row 3 times. Seven stitches remain.
Work for an additional 2" (5 cm), and then bind off all stitches.

Wash and block all your swatches. Then, practice!

VERTICALLY AND HORIZONTALLY MATTRESS STITCH swatches 1 and 2 together to make a pocket. Then pull seams out.

PIN AND SEAM SWATCHES 3 AND 4 TOGETHER like an armhole and sleeve cap, and seam.

PICK UP STITCHES ALONG THE VERTICAL EDGES of swatches 1 and 2, at three different rates, and work for 1½" (4 cm), then bind off.

- First, pick up one stitch in every single row (too many). Notice how the edging starts to curve and ruffle a bit.

- Now, pick up one stitch in every other row (too few). Notice how the edging puckers and gathers.

- Finally, pick up 2 out of every 3 stitches. Notice how the edging lies perfectly flat—this is what you want to see.

PICK UP STITCHES ALONG THE CURVED EDGE of swatch 5, and work an inch of ribbing of any kind. Work the first row through the back loop, and play around with the finished swatch. What parts look good?

....

....

....

....

....

....

What parts do you want to practice more?

....

....

....

....

....

....

VESTS

Vests are just about the easiest sweaters around. They make great layering pieces, and since there are no sleeves to fiddle with, they're fast and simple to knit. They're also a wonderful opportunity to try out new or especially cherished yarns in a lower-stakes way!

In addition to our Buttercup Mini Vest on page 47 (made from simple wool with an easy stitch pattern for building your skill set), I've given you three versatile women's vests in this chapter—a luscious-but-simple V-neck pullover that's great for dressing up or down; an easy, breezy tunic with an A-line shape and lace trim; and a simple cardigan with waist-shaping screw-in closures.

The yarns for these vests encourage you to try some materials that may be new to you, and highlight how the same basic sweater can look vastly different based on the materials used: A soft and cuddly alpaca/wool blend makes for a subtle layering piece; a nubby cotton-silk blend makes you dream of warmer days and ocean breezes; and a sturdy, light woolen-spun yarn creates a piece you'll be able to wear for decades to come.

So what are you waiting for? You can knit that!

Straight shape and small size get you started quickly!

DIFFICULTY LEVEL:

VESTS

BUTTERCUP MINI VEST

Simple stitch patterning

Buttercup Mini Vest

This sweet little vest is both interesting, with the Seed Stitch stripe pattern that adorns the front, and relaxing, with the repetitive Stockinette back. It covers all the techniques you'll need to master for this chapter: using a stitch pattern, shaping, seaming, and finishing neck and armhole edges. It's worked in a workhorse wool that comes in tons of great colors and is economical to boot—what a great gift for a little one!

SIZES
To fit children 1 (2, 3/4, 5/6, 7/8, 9/10) year(s)

FINISHED MEASUREMENTS
22 (24½, 26½, 28, 29½, 31)" [56 (62, 67.5, 71, 75, 78.5) cm]

NOTE: Vest is intended to be worn with 2–4" (5–10 cm) ease in the chest.

YARN
Louet GEMS Worsted [100% merino wool; 175 yards (160 meters)/100 grams]: 2 (2, 3, 3, 3, 4) hanks #80.2654 Golden Rod

NEEDLES
One pair straight needles size US 7 (4.5 mm)

One set of five double-pointed needles (dpns) size US 7 (4.5 mm)

Change needle size if necessary to obtain correct gauge.

NOTIONS
Stitch markers

GAUGE
21 sts and 32 rows = 4" (10 cm) in St st

STITCH PATTERNS

1X1 RIB
(even number of sts; 1-row/rnd repeat)
ALL ROWS/RNDS: *P1, k1; repeat from * to end.

SEED STITCH
(even number of sts; 1-row repeat)
ROW 1 (RS): *K1, p1; repeat from * to end.
ROW 2: Knit the purl sts and purl the knit sts as they face you.
Repeat Row 2 for Seed Stitch.

SEED STITCH STRIPE
(even number of sts; 22-row repeat)
ROWS 1–6: Work in St st.
ROWS 7–8: Work in Seed st.
ROWS 9–16: Work in St st.
ROWS 17–20: Work in Seed st.
ROWS 21–22: Work in St st.
Repeat Rows 1–22 for Seed Stitch Stripe.

NOTE
Armhole and neck decreases should be worked to match the slant of the edge being shaped (when seen from the RS), as follows:

FOR LEFT-SLANTING EDGES:
On RS rows, k1, ssk, work to end; on WS rows, work to last 3 sts, ssp, p1.

FOR RIGHT-SLANTING EDGES:
On RS rows, work to last 3 sts, k2tog, k1; on WS rows, p1, p2tog, work to end.

BACK

CO 58 (64, 70, 74, 78, 82) sts. Begin 1x1 Rib; work even for 1" (2.5 cm), ending with a WS row.
Change to St st; work even until piece measures 8 (8¼, 9, 10, 11½, 13)" [20.5 (21, 23, 25.5, 29, 33) cm] from the beginning, ending with a WS row.

SHAPE ARMHOLES

BO 3 (4, 4, 5, 6, 6) sts at beginning of next 2 rows, then decrease 2 sts every RS row 3 (3, 4, 4, 4, 4) times—46 (50, 54, 56, 58, 62) sts remain. Work even until armhole measures 3¾ (4¼, 4¾, 5, 5½, 6)" [9.5 (11, 12, 12.5, 14, 15) cm], ending with a WS row.

SHAPE NECK

NEXT ROW (RS): Work 10 (11, 12, 12, 12, 13) sts, join a second ball of yarn, BO center 26 (28, 30, 32, 34, 36) sts, knit to end. Working both sides at the same time, decrease 1 st at each neck edge every RS row once—9 (10, 11, 11, 11, 12) sts remain each shoulder. Work even until armhole measures 4¾ (5¼, 5¾, 6, 6½, 7)" [12 (13.5, 14.5, 15, 16.5, 18) cm], ending with a WS row.

SHAPE SHOULDERS

BO 5 (5, 6, 6, 6, 6) sts at each armhole edge once, then 4 (5, 5, 5, 5, 6) sts once.

FRONT

CO 58 (64, 70, 74, 78, 82) sts. Begin 1x1 Rib; work even for 1" (2.5 cm), ending with a WS row.

Change to Seed St Stripe; work even until piece measures 8 (8¼, 9, 10, 11½, 13)" [20.5 (21, 23, 25.5, 29, 33) cm] from the beginning, ending with a WS row.

SHAPE ARMHOLES

Continuing in Seed St Stripe, BO 3 (4, 4, 5, 6, 6) sts at beginning of next 2 rows, then decrease 2 sts every RS row 3 (3, 4, 4, 4, 4) times—46 (50, 54, 56, 58, 62) sts remain. Work even until armhole measures 2¾ (3¼, 3¾, 4, 4½, 5)" [7 (8.5, 9.5, 10, 11.5, 12.5) cm], ending with a WS row.

SHAPE NECK

NEXT ROW (RS): Work 16 (18, 19, 20, 20, 22) sts, join a second ball of yarn, BO center 14 (14, 16, 16, 18, 18) sts, work to end. Working both sides at the same time, decrease 1 st at each neck edge every row 4 (4, 4, 5, 5, 5) times, then every RS row 3 (4, 4, 4, 4, 5) times—9 (10, 11, 11, 11, 12) sts remain each shoulder. Work even until armhole measures 4¾ (5¼, 5¾, 6, 6½, 7)" [12 (13.5, 14.5, 15, 16.5, 18) cm], ending with a WS row.

SHAPE SHOULDERS

BO 5 (5, 6, 6, 6, 6) sts at each armhole edge once, then 4 (5, 5, 5, 5, 6) sts once.

FINISHING

Block pieces as desired. Sew shoulder seams. Sew side seams.

NECKBAND

With RS facing, using dpns and beginning at left Back shoulder, pick up and knit sts around neck shaping, picking up 1 st for every BO st, 3 sts for every 4 rows along vertical edges, and 4 sts for every 5 rows along diagonal edges, making sure to end with an even number of sts. Join for working in the rnd; pm for beginning of rnd. Begin 1x1 Rib; work even for ½" (1.5 cm). BO all sts in pattern.

ARMHOLE EDGING

With RS facing, using dpns and beginning at center underarm, pick up and knit sts around armhole shaping, picking up 1 st for every BO st, 3 sts for every 4 rows along vertical edges, and 4 sts for every 5 rows along diagonal edges, making sure to end with an even number of sts. Join for working in the rnd; pm for beginning of rnd. Begin 1x1 Rib; work even for 2 rnds. BO all sts in pattern.

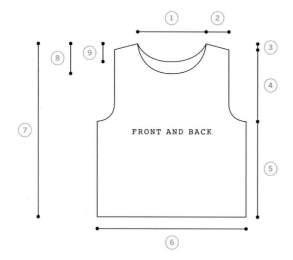

FRONT AND BACK

1 5¼ (5¾, 6, 6½, 6¾, 7¼)"
   13.5 (14.5, 15, 16.5, 17, 18.5) cm

2 1¾ (2, 2, 2, 2, 2¼)"
   4.5 (5, 5, 5, 5, 5.5) cm

3 ½"/1.5 cm

4 4¾ (5¼ 5¾, 6, 6½, 7)"
   12 (13.5, 14.5, 15, 16.5, 18) cm

5 8 (8¼, 9, 10, 11½, 13)"
   20.5 (21, 23, 25.5, 29, 33) cm

6 11 (12¼, 13¼, 14, 14¾, 15½)"
   28 (31, 33.5, 35.5, 37.5, 39.5) cm

7 13¼ (14, 15¼, 16½, 18½, 20½)"
   33.5 (35.5, 38.5, 42, 47, 52) cm

8 2½"/6.5 cm

9 1½"/4 cm

Corner Office Vest

This vest is everything a great layering piece should be—classic, comfortable, and featuring a great deep neckline that shows off your favorite button-down. It is worked in two pieces from the bottom up, and includes waist shaping worked on vertical dart lines, which flatters the body (and sounds way more complicated than it is)! I worked up this vest in an incredibly cozy, quick-to-knit yarn with a nice sheen. If you've never tried knitting with an alpaca-blend yarn before, I encourage you to give it a shot!

FINISHED MEASUREMENTS
30 (31½, 34, 36, 38½, 40, 41½, 44, 46, 47½, 50, 54½)" [76 (80, 86.5, 91.5, 98, 101.5, 105.5, 112, 117, 120.5, 127, 138.5) cm] bust

NOTE: Vest is intended to be worn with 1–2" (2.5–5 cm) ease in the bust.

YARN
Blue Sky Alpacas Extra [55% baby alpaca/45% fine merino wool; 218 yards (199 meters)/150 grams]: 3 (3, 3, 3, 4, 4, 4, 4, 5, 5, 5, 6) hanks #3518 Java

NEEDLES
One pair straight needles size US 8 (5 mm)

One 24" (60 cm) long circular needle size US 8 (5 mm), for Neckband

One 16" (40 cm) long circular needle size US 8 (5 mm), for Armhole Edging

Change needle size if necessary to obtain correct gauge.

NOTIONS
Stitch markers; removable stitch marker

GAUGE
19 sts and 28 rows = 4" (10 cm) in St st

STITCH PATTERN
1X1 RIB
(even number of sts; 1-row/rnd repeat)
ALL ROWS/RNDS: *K1, p1; repeat from * to end.

BACK
CO 72 (76, 82, 86, 92, 96, 100, 106, 110, 114, 120, 130) sts. Begin 1x1 Rib; work even for 2" (5 cm), ending with a WS row decrease 1 st on last row—71 (75, 81, 85, 91, 95, 99, 105, 109, 113, 119, 129) sts remain.

NEXT ROW (RS): Change to St st; work even for 1 row.

NEXT ROW: P24 (25, 27, 28, 30, 32, 33, 35, 36, 38, 40, 43), pm, p23 (25, 27, 29, 31, 31, 33, 35, 37, 37, 39, 43), pm, purl to end.

SHAPE WAIST
DECREASE ROW (RS): Decrease 2 sts this row, then every 14 rows 3 times, as follows: Knit to 2 sts before first marker, ssk, sm, knit to next marker, sm, k2tog, knit to end—63 (67, 73, 77, 83, 87, 91, 97, 101, 105, 111, 121) sts remain. Work even until piece measures 9½" (24 cm) from the beginning, ending with a WS row.

SHAPE BUST
INCREASE ROW (RS): Increase 2 sts this row, then every 10 rows 3 times, as follows: Knit to first marker, M1R, sm, knit to next marker, sm, M1L, knit to end—71 (75, 81, 85, 91, 95, 99, 105, 109, 113, 119, 129) sts. Work even, removing markers on first row, until piece measures 16 (16¼, 16½, 16¾, 17, 17¼, 17½, 17½, 18, 18, 18, 18)" [40.5 (41.5, 42, 42.5, 43, 44, 44.5, 44.5, 45.5, 45.5, 45.5, 45.5) cm] from the beginning, ending with a WS row.

Stitches picked
up around
neck and armhole

DIFFICULTY LEVEL:

VESTS

CORNER OFFICE
VEST

Dart-style
waist shaping

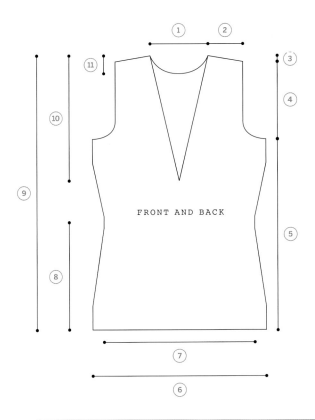

1 5¼ (5¾, 5¾, 6, 6½, 6½, 7, 7, 7, 7, 7¼, 7¾)"
   13.5 (14.5, 14.5, 15, 16.5, 16.5, 18, 18, 18, 18, 18.5, 19.5) cm

2 3¼ (3¼, 3½, 3½, 3¾, 4, 4¼, 4¼, 4½, 4½, 4½, 4¾)"
   8.5 (8.5, 9, 9, 9.5, 10, 11, 11, 11.5, 11.5, 11.5, 12) cm

3 ½"/1.5 cm

4 6½ (7, 7¼, 7½, 8, 8¼, 8½, 9, 9¼, 9¾, 10, 10½)"
   16.5 (18, 18.5, 19, 20.5, 21, 21.5, 23, 23.5, 25, 25.5, 26.5) cm

5 16 (16¼, 16½, 16¾, 17, 17¼, 17½, 17½, 18, 18, 18, 18)"
   40.5 (41.5, 42, 42.5, 43, 44, 44.5, 44.5, 45.5, 45.5, 45.5, 45.5) cm

6 15 (15¾, 17, 18, 19¼, 20, 20¾, 22, 23, 23¾, 25, 27¼)" hip and bust
   38 (40, 43, 45.5, 49, 51, 52.5, 56, 58.5, 60.5, 63.5, 69) cm

7 13¼ (14, 15¼, 16¼, 17½, 18¼, 19¼, 20½, 21¼, 22, 23¼, 25½)" waist
   33.5 (35.5, 38.5, 41.5, 44.5, 46.5, 49, 52, 54, 56, 59, 65) cm

8 9"/23 cm

9 23 (23¾, 24¼, 24¾, 25½, 26, 26½, 27, 27¾, 28¼, 28½, 29)"
   58.5 (60.5, 61.5, 63, 65, 66, 67.5, 68.5, 70.5, 72, 72.5, 73.5) cm

10 10 (10½, 10¾, 11, 11½, 11¾, 12, 12½, 12¾, 13¼, 13½, 14)"
    25.5 (26.5, 27.5, 28, 29, 30, 30.5, 32, 32.5, 33.5, 34.5, 35.5) cm

11 1½"/4 cm

SHAPE ARMHOLES

BO 6 (6, 6, 6, 6, 6, 6, 8, 8, 10, 10) sts at beginning of next 2 rows, 0 (0, 2, 2, 2, 2, 2, 4, 4, 6, 6, 8) sts at beginning of next 2 rows, then decrease 1 st each side every RS row 2 (2, 2, 3, 4, 5, 5, 6, 5, 5, 5, 6) times, as follows: K2, ssk, knit to last 4 sts, k2tog, k2—55 (59, 61, 63, 67, 69, 73, 73, 75, 75, 77, 81) sts remain. Work even until armhole measures 5½ (6, 6¼, 6½, 7, 7¼, 7½, 8, 8¼, 8¾, 9, 9½)" [14 (15, 16, 16.5, 18, 18.5, 19, 20.5, 21, 22, 23, 24) cm], ending with a WS row.

SHAPE NECK

NEXT ROW (RS): K17 (18, 19, 19, 20, 21, 22, 22, 23, 23, 23, 24), join a second ball of yarn, BO center 21 (23, 23, 25, 27, 27, 29, 29, 29, 29, 31, 33) sts, knit to end. Working both sides at the same time, decrease 1 st at each neck edge every RS row twice, as follows: On right neck edge, knit to last 3 sts, k2tog, k1; on left neck edge, k1, ssk, knit to end—15 (16, 17, 17, 18, 19, 20, 20, 21, 21, 21, 22) sts remain each shoulder. Work even until armhole measures 6½ (7, 7¼, 7½, 8, 8¼, 8½, 9, 9¼, 9¾, 10, 10½)" [16.5 (18, 18.5, 19, 20.5, 21, 21.5, 23, 23.5, 25, 25.5, 26.5) cm], ending with a WS row.

SHAPE SHOULDERS

NEXT ROW (RS): BO 8 (8, 9, 9, 9, 10, 10, 10, 11, 11, 11, 11) sts at each armhole edge once, then 7 (8, 8, 8, 9, 9, 10, 10, 10, 10, 10, 11) sts once.

FRONT

CO 72 (76, 82, 86, 92, 96, 100, 106, 110, 114, 120, 130) sts.
Begin 1x1 Rib; work even for 2" (5 cm), ending with a WS row, decrease 1 st on last row—71 (75, 81, 85, 91, 95, 99, 105, 109, 113, 119, 129) sts remain.
Change to St st; work even for 1 row.
NEXT ROW (WS): P18 (19, 20, 21, 23, 24, 25, 26, 27, 28, 30, 32), pm, p35 (37, 41, 43, 45, 47, 49, 53, 55, 57, 59, 65), pm, purl to end.

SHAPE WAIST

DECREASE ROW (RS): Decrease 2 sts this row, then every 14 rows 3 times, as follows: Knit to 2 sts before first marker, ssk, sm, knit to next marker, sm, k2tog, knit to end—63 (67, 73, 77, 83, 87, 91, 97, 101, 105, 111, 121) sts remain. Work even until piece measures 9½" (24 cm) from the beginning, ending with a WS row, and placing marker before center st on last row.

1 st at each neck edge every 4 rows 11 (12, 12, 13, 14, 14, 15, 15, 15, 15, 16, 17) times, as follows: On left neck edge, knit to last 4 sts, k2tog, k2; on right neck edge, k2, ssk, knit to end. AT THE SAME TIME, when piece measures 16 (16¼, 16½, 16¾, 17, 17¼, 17½, 17½, 18, 18, 18, 18)" [40.5 (41.5, 42, 42.5, 43, 44, 44.5, 44.5, 45.5, 45.5, 45.5, 45.5) cm] from the beginning, ending with a WS row, shape armholes as follows:

NEXT ROW (RS): BO 6 (6, 6, 6, 6, 6, 6, 6, 8, 8, 10, 10) sts at each armhole edge once, then 0 (2, 2, 2, 2, 2, 4, 4, 6, 6, 8) sts once, then decrease 1 st at each armhole edge every RS row 2 (2, 2, 3, 4, 5, 5, 6, 5, 5, 5, 6) times, as follows: K2, ssk, knit to last 4 sts, k2tog, k2—15 (16, 17, 17, 18, 19, 20, 20, 21, 21, 21, 22) sts remain. Work even until armhole measures 6½ (7, 7¼, 7½, 8, 8¼, 8½, 9, 9¼, 9¾, 10, 10½)" [16.5 (18, 18.5, 19, 20.5, 21, 21.5, 23, 23.5, 25, 25.5, 26.5) cm], ending with a WS row.

SHAPE SHOULDERS

BO 8 (8, 9, 9, 9, 10, 10, 10, 11, 11, 11, 11) sts at each armhole edge once, then 7 (8, 8, 8, 9, 9, 10, 10, 10, 10, 10, 11) sts once.

FINISHING

Block pieces as desired. Sew shoulder seams. Sew side seams.

NECKBAND

With RS facing, using 24" (60 cm) circular needle and beginning at left Back shoulder, pick up and knit sts around neck shaping, picking up 1 st for each BO st, 3 sts for every 4 rows along vertical edges, and 4 sts for every 5 rows along diagonal edges, making sure to end with an even number of sts. Join for working in the rnd; pm for beginning of rnd. Place removable marker on center Front st. Work 1x1 Rib for 1 rnd, beginning with k1 or p1 as needed to ensure that center Front st is a knit st.

DECREASE RND: Work to 1 st before marked st, s2kp2, work to end—2 sts decreased.

Repeat Decrease Rnd every other rnd until Neckband measures 1¼" (3 cm). BO all sts in pattern.

ARMHOLE EDGING

With RS facing, using 16" (40 cm) circular needle and beginning at center underarm, pick up and knit sts around armhole shaping, picking up 1 st for every BO st, 3 sts for every 4 rows along vertical edges, and 4 sts for every 5 rows along diagonal edges, making sure to end with an even number of sts. Join for working in the rnd; pm for beginning of rnd. Begin 1x1 Rib; work even for 2 rnds. BO all sts in pattern.

SHAPE BUST, NECK, AND ARMHOLES

Note: Bust and neck shaping are worked at the same time for some of the sizes, then neck and armhole shaping are worked at the same time for all sizes; please read entire section through before beginning. Neck shaping will not be completed until after armhole shaping is complete.

INCREASE ROW (RS): Increase 2 sts this row, then every 10 rows 3 times, as follows: Knit to first marker, M1R, sm, knit to last marker, sm, M1L, knit to end. AT THE SAME TIME, when piece measures 13 (13¼, 13½, 13¾, 14, 14¼, 14½, 14½, 15, 15, 15, 15)" [33 (33.5, 34.5, 35, 35.5, 36, 37, 37, 38, 38, 38, 38) cm] from the beginning, ending with a WS row, shape neck as follows:

NEXT ROW (RS): Knit to 4 sts before second marker, k2tog, k2, remove marker, join a second ball of yarn, BO center st, k2, ssk, knit to end. Working both sides at the same time, decrease

WAIST SHAPING

IN MOST CASES, women's hand-knit sweaters look best with at least some waist shaping—that is, making the waist of the sweater smaller than the bust and hips. Used appropriately, this shaping allows your garment to give you a shapely look without being tight or constraining.

There are two fundamental ways to shape the waist of a sweater:

1. EDGE WAIST SHAPING is located within a couple of stitches of the edges of your piece, and is typically slanted with the direction of the edge. The shaping on the front of your sweater matches the shaping on the back, and the shaping is usually fairly gentle.

This is a great choice if you're working an allover stitch pattern in your garment, because this type of shaping disrupts the patterning as little as possible. For an example of this kind of waist shaping, see the Shoreside Tunic on page 54.

2. VERTICAL DART WAIST SHAPING may sound complicated, but it's not! Basically, the shaping is worked identically to edge waist shaping, except it's located within the interior of the sweater's front and back. To work this kind of waist shaping, place markers where the decreases or increases will be worked (a good rule of thumb is to place the markers with roughly one-third of your stitches between the markers on the back, and half of the front stitches between the markers, though they can be moved closer to the sides if that's helpful). Then, work your typical decrease or increase rows at the markers, rather than at the edges. See an example of this kind of waist shaping in the Corner Office Vest on page 49.

The great thing about this kind of waist shaping is that it allows you to work different amounts of shaping on the front and back of the sweater. For example, a small amount of shaping could be worked on the back of the sweater, with the front worked straight to the armholes. This produces a comfortable "sweatshirt"-type look without making your sweater too boxy. (The Revive Cardigan on page 93 includes this shaping on the back only.)

Shoreside Tunic

This vest showcases a completely different look than the others—
it's casual and beachy, thanks to the cotton-silk tweed yarn,
slight shaping, and wide A-line tunic. A simple Roman Stripe lace pattern
decorates the hem to give you some interest without complicating
the simple pattern. The lace is worked on smaller needles than
the rest of the garment, but still ends up wider than the Stockinette;
this creates a casual, slightly rippled effect.

FINISHED MEASUREMENTS
30 (32, 34, 35½, 38, 40, 42, 43½, 46, 48, 50, 54)" [76 (81.5, 86.5, 90, 96.5, 101.5, 106.5, 110.5, 117, 122, 127, 137) cm] bust

NOTE: Tunic is intended to be worn with 1–2" (2.5–5 cm) ease in the bust.

YARN
Classic Elite Yarns Classic Silk [50% cotton/30% silk/20% nylon; 135 yards (123 meters)/50 grams]: 6 (7, 8, 8, 9, 10, 10, 11, 12, 12, 13, 14) balls #6906 Oatmeal

NEEDLES
One pair straight needles size US 5 (3.75 mm)

One pair straight needles size US 4 (3.5 mm)

One 24" (60 cm) long circular needle size US 5 (3.75 mm), for Neckband

One 16" (40 cm) long circular needle size US 5 (3.75 mm), for Armhole Edging

Change needle size if necessary to obtain correct gauge.

NOTIONS
Stitch markers

GAUGE
22 sts and 34 rows = 4" (10 cm) in St st

STITCH PATTERNS

1X1 RIB
(even number of sts; 1-row/rnd repeat)
ALL ROWS/RNDS: *K1, p1; repeat from * to end.

ROMAN STRIPE
NOTE: Since pattern has an odd number of rows, you will alternate working Row 1 on a RS row with working it on a WS row. St count doubles between the edge sts on Row 1; original st count is restored on Row 3.

(even number of sts; 7-row repeat)
ROW 1: K1, *yo, k1; repeat from * to last st, k1.
ROW 2: K1, purl to last st, k1.
ROW 3: K1, *k2tog; repeat from * to last st, k1.
ROWS 4 AND 5: K1, *yo, k2tog; repeat from * to last st, k1.
ROWS 6 AND 7: Knit.
Repeat Rows 1–7 for Roman Stripe.

BACK
Using larger needles, CO 104 (110, 116, 120, 126, 132, 138, 142, 148, 154, 160, 170) sts. Begin 1x1 Rib; work even for ¾" (2 cm), ending with a RS row.
Change to smaller needles; purl 1 row.
Change to St st; work even for 2 rows.
Change to Roman Stripe; work Rows 1–7 five times.
Change to larger needles and St st, beginning with a WS row; work even until piece measures 5¼ (5¼, 5¼, 5¼, 6, 6, 6, 6, 6, 6, 6, 6)" [13.5 (13.5, 13.5, 13.5, 15, 15, 15, 15, 15, 15, 15, 15) cm] from the beginning, ending with a WS row.

SHAPE WAIST
DECREASE ROW (RS): Decrease 2 sts this row, then every 4 rows 15 times, as follows: Knit 1, ssk, knit to last 3 sts, k2tog, k1—72 (78, 84, 88, 94, 100, 106, 110, 116, 122, 128, 138) sts remain. Work even until piece measures 13 (13, 13, 13, 14, 14, 14, 14, 14, 14, 14, 14)" [33 (33, 33, 33, 35.5, 35.5, 35.5, 35.5, 35.5, 35.5, 35.5, 35.5) cm] from the beginning, ending with a WS row.

SHAPE BUST
INCREASE ROW (RS): Increase 2 sts this row, then every 10 rows 4 times, as follows: Knit 1, M1R, knit to last st, M1L, k1—82 (88, 94, 98, 104, 110, 116, 120, 126, 132, 138, 148) sts. Work even, removing markers on first row, until piece measures 19½ (19¾, 20, 20¼, 21½, 21¾, 22, 22, 22½, 22½, 22½, 22½)" [49.5 (50, 51, 51.5, 54.5, 55, 56, 56, 57, 57, 57, 57) cm] from the beginning, ending with a WS row.

Side-seam waist
shaping

Stitch
patterning
at hem

SHAPE ARMHOLES

BO 6 (6, 6, 6, 6, 6, 6, 8, 8, 10, 12) sts at beginning of next 2 rows, then 0 (2, 2, 2, 2, 2, 2, 4, 4, 6, 6, 8) sts at beginning of next 2 rows, then decrease 1 st each side every RS row 3 (3, 4, 5, 5, 7, 8, 8, 8, 8, 8, 7) times, as follows: K2, ssk, knit to last 4 sts, k2tog—64 (66, 70, 72, 78, 80, 84, 84, 86, 88, 90, 94) sts remain. Work even until armhole measures 5½ (6, 6¼, 6½, 7, 7¼, 7½, 8, 8¼, 8¾, 9, 9½)" [14 (15, 16, 16.5, 18, 18.5, 19, 20.5, 21, 22, 23, 24) cm], ending with a WS row.

SHAPE NECK

NEXT ROW (RS): Work 12 (12, 13, 13, 14, 14, 15, 15, 15, 16, 16, 17) sts, join a second ball of yarn, BO center 40 (42, 44, 46, 50, 52, 54, 54, 56, 56, 58, 60) sts, work to end. Working both sides at the same time, decrease 1 st at each neck edge every RS row twice, as follows: On right neck edge, knit to last 3 sts, k2tog, k1; on left neck edge, k1, ssk, knit to end—10 (10, 11, 11, 12, 12, 13, 13, 13, 14, 14, 15) sts remain each shoulder. Work even until armhole measures 6½ (7, 7¼, 7½, 8, 8¼, 8½, 9, 9¼, 9¾, 10, 10½)" [16.5 (18, 18.5, 19, 20.5, 21, 21.5, 23, 23.5, 25, 25.5, 26.5) cm], ending with a WS row.

SHAPE SHOULDERS

BO 5 (5, 6, 6, 6, 6, 7, 7, 7, 7, 7, 8) sts at each armhole edge once, then 5 (5, 5, 5, 6, 6, 6, 6, 6, 7, 7, 7) sts once.

FRONT

Work as for Back until armhole measures 4 (4½, 4¾, 5, 5½, 5¾, 6, 6½, 6¾, 7¼, 7½, 8)" [10 (11.5, 12, 12.5, 14, 14.5, 15, 16.5, 17, 18.5, 19, 20.5) cm], ending with a WS row—64 (66, 70, 72, 78, 80, 84, 84, 86, 88, 90, 94) sts remain.

SHAPE NECK

Work 13 (13, 14, 14, 15, 15, 16, 16, 16, 17, 17, 18) sts, join a second ball of yarn, BO center 38 (40, 42, 44, 48, 50, 52, 52, 54, 54, 56, 58) sts, work to end. Working both sides at the same time, decrease 1 st at each neck edge every RS row 3 times, as follows: On right neck edge, knit to last 3 sts, k2tog, k1; on left neck edge, k1, ssk, knit to end—10 (10, 11, 11, 12, 12, 13, 13, 13, 14, 14, 15) sts remain each shoulder. Work even until armhole measures 6½ (7, 7¼, 7½, 8, 8¼, 8½, 9, 9¼, 9¾, 10, 10½)" [16.5 (18, 18.5, 19, 20.5, 21, 21.5, 23, 23.5, 25, 25.5, 26.5) cm], ending with a WS row.

SHAPE SHOULDERS

BO 5 (5, 6, 6, 6, 6, 7, 7, 7, 7, 7, 8) sts at each armhole edge once, then 5 (5, 5, 5, 6, 6, 6, 6, 6, 7, 7, 7) sts once.

FINISHING

Block pieces as desired. Sew shoulder seams. Sew side seams.

NECKBAND

With RS facing, using 24" (60 cm) circular needle and beginning at left Back shoulder, pick up and knit sts around neck shaping, picking up 1 st for each BO st, 3 sts for every 4 rows along vertical edges, and 4 sts for every 5 rows along diagonal edges, making sure to end with an even number of sts. Join for working in the rnd; pm for beginning of rnd. Begin 1x1 Rib; work even for ½" (1.5 cm). BO all sts in pattern.

ARMHOLE EDGING

With RS facing, using 16" (40 cm) circular needle and beginning at center underarm, pick up and knit sts around armhole shaping, picking up 1 st for each BO st, 3 sts for every 4 rows along vertical edges, and 4 sts for every 5 rows along diagonal edges, making sure to end with an even number of sts. Join for working in the rnd; pm for beginning of rnd. Purl 1 rnd. Knit 1 rnd. BO all sts purlwise.

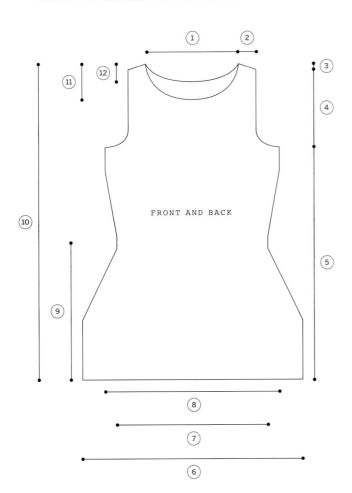

FRONT AND BACK

1 8 (8¼, 8¾, 9, 9¾, 10¼, 10½, 10½, 11, 11, 11¼, 11¾)"
   20.5 (21, 22, 23, 25, 26, 26.5, 26.5, 28, 28, 28.5, 30) cm

2 1¾ (1¾, 2, 2, 2¼, 2¼, 2¼, 2¼, 2¼, 2½, 2½, 2¾)"
   4.5 (4.5, 5, 5, 5.5, 5.5, 5.5, 5.5, 5.5, 6.5, 6.5, 7) cm

3 ½"/1.5 cm

4 6½ (7, 7¼, 7½, 8, 8¼, 8½, 9, 9¼, 9¾, 10, 10½)"
   16.5 (18, 18.5, 19, 20.5, 21, 21.5, 23, 23.5, 25, 25.5, 26.5) cm

5 19½ (19¾, 20, 20¼, 21½, 21¾, 22, 22, 22½, 22½, 22½, 22½)"
   49.5 (50, 51, 51.5, 54.5, 55, 56, 56, 57, 57, 57, 57) cm

6 19 (20, 21, 21¾, 23, 24, 25, 25¾, 27, 28, 29, 31)" hip
   48.5 (51, 53.5, 55, 58.5, 61, 63.5, 65.5, 68.5, 71, 73.5, 78.5) cm

7 13 (14¼, 15¼, 16, 17, 18¼, 19¼, 20, 21, 22¼, 23¼, 25)" waist
   33 (36, 38.5, 40.5, 43, 46.5, 49, 51, 53.5, 56.5, 59, 63.5) cm

8 15 (16, 17, 17¾, 19, 20, 21, 21¾, 23, 24, 25, 27)" bust
   38 (40.5, 43, 45, 48.5, 51, 53.5, 55, 58.5, 61, 63.5, 68.5) cm

9 12½ (12½, 12½, 12½, 13½, 13½, 13½, 13½, 13½, 13½, 13½, 13½)"
   32 (32, 32, 32, 34.5, 34.5, 34.5, 34.5, 34.5, 34.5, 34.5, 34.5) cm

10 26½ (27¼, 27¾, 28¼, 30, 30½, 31, 31½, 32¼, 32¾, 33, 33½)"
    67.5 (69, 70.5, 72, 76, 77.5, 78.5, 80, 82, 83, 84, 85) cm

11 3"/7.5 cm

12 1½"/4 cm

VESTS

WOODCUTTER VEST

Screw-in closure means no buttonholes!

Front and neck edgings worked separately

Woodcutter Vest

The Woodcutter Vest rounds out our collection, providing a style with a classic silhouette in a durable yarn with a funky closure. It offers a figure-flattering scoop neckline and makes a great layering piece for chillier days without being bulky or boxy. It's worked in three pieces from the bottom up, with edgings picked up and worked after seaming. The back and fronts include vertical dart waist shaping (see page 53) to keep things tailored. The closures can be found online and screw into the finished cardigan edges—no buttonholes or finishing required!

FINISHED
MEASUREMENTS
30½ (32½, 35, 37¾, 39¾, 41¾, 43¼, 45, 47, 49, 51½, 55¼)" [77.5 (82.5, 89, 96, 101, 106, 110, 114.5, 119.5, 124.5, 131, 140.5) cm] bust, closed

NOTE: Vest is intended to be worn with 2" (5 cm) ease in the bust.

YARN
Harrisville Designs WATERshed [100% wool; 110 yards (100 meters)/50 grams]: 5 (6, 6, 7, 7, 8, 8, 9, 9, 10, 10, 11) hanks Barn Door

NEEDLES
One pair straight needles size US 8 (5 mm)

One 24" (60 cm) long circular needle size US 8 (5 mm), for Neckband

One 16" (40 cm) long circular needle size US 8 (5 mm), for Armhole Edging

Change needle size if necessary to obtain correct gauge.

NOTIONS
Stitch markers; stitch holder; JUL closure (see Sources)

GAUGE
17 sts and 28 rows = 4" (10 cm) in St st

STITCH PATTERNS
1X1 RIB
(even number of sts; 1-row/rnd repeat)
ALL ROWS/RNDS: *K1, p1; repeat from * to end.

1X1 RIB
(odd number of sts; 1-row repeat)
ROW 1 (WS): *P1, k1; repeat from * to last st, p1.
ROW 2: Knit the knit sts and purl the purl sts as they face you.
Repeat Row 2 for 1x1 Rib.

BACK

CO 64 (68, 74, 78, 82, 86, 90, 94, 98, 102, 108, 116) sts. Begin 1x1 Rib; work even for 1½" (4 cm), ending with a WS row. Change to St st; work even for 1 row.
NEXT ROW (WS): P21 (23, 25, 26, 27, 29, 30, 31, 33, 34, 36, 39), pm, p22 (22, 24, 26, 28, 28, 30, 32, 32, 34, 36, 38), pm, purl to end.

SHAPE WAIST

DECREASE ROW (RS): Decrease 2 sts this row, then every 12 rows 3 times, as follows: Knit to 2 sts before first marker, ssk, sm, knit to next marker, sm, k2tog, knit to end—56 (60, 66, 70, 74, 78, 82, 86, 90, 94, 100, 108) sts remain. Work even until piece measures 8" (20.5 cm) from the beginning, ending with a WS row.

SHAPE BUST

INCREASE ROW (RS): Increase 2 sts this row, then every 10 rows 3 times, as follows: Knit to first marker, M1R, sm, knit to next marker, sm, M1L, knit to end—64 (68, 74, 78, 82, 86, 90, 94, 98, 102, 108, 116) sts. Work even, removing markers on first row, until piece measures 14½ (14¾, 15, 15¼, 15½, 15¾, 16, 16, 16½, 16½, 16½, 16½)" [37 (37.5, 38, 38.5, 39.5, 40, 40.5, 40.5, 42, 42, 42, 42) cm] from the beginning, ending with a WS row.

SHAPE ARMHOLES

BO 5 (6, 6, 6, 6, 6, 6, 6, 8, 8, 10) sts at beginning of next 2 rows, then 0 (0, 2, 2, 2, 2, 2, 2, 4, 4, 6, 6) sts at beginning of next 2 rows, then decrease 1 st each side every RS row 2 (2, 2, 3, 3, 4, 5, 6, 6, 5, 5, 5) times, as follows: K2, ssk, knit to last

4 sts, k2tog, k2—50 (52, 54, 56, 60, 62, 64, 66, 66, 68, 70, 74) sts remain. Work even until armhole measures 5½ (6, 6¼, 6½, 7, 7¼, 7½, 8, 8¼, 8¾, 9, 9½)" [14 (15, 16, 16.5, 18, 18.5, 19, 20.5, 21, 22, 23, 24) cm], ending with a WS row.

SHAPE NECK

NEXT ROW (RS): K16 (17, 17, 18, 19, 20, 20, 21, 21, 21, 22, 23), join a second ball of yarn, BO center 18 (18, 20, 20, 22, 22, 24, 24, 24, 26, 26, 28) sts, knit to end. Working both sides at the same time, decrease 1 st at each neck edge every RS row twice, as follows: On right neck edge, knit to last 2 sts, k2tog; on left neck edge, ssk, knit to end—14 (15, 15, 16, 17, 18, 18, 19, 19, 19, 20, 21) sts remain each shoulder. Work even until armhole measures 6½ (7, 7¼, 7½, 8, 8¼, 8½, 9, 9¼, 9¾, 10, 10½)" [16.5 (18, 18.5, 19, 20.5, 21, 21.5, 23, 23.5, 25, 25.5, 26.5) cm], ending with a WS row.

SHAPE SHOULDERS

BO 7 (8, 8, 8, 9, 9, 9, 10, 10, 10, 10, 11) sts at each armhole edge once, then 7 (7, 7, 8, 8, 9, 9, 9, 9, 9, 10, 10) sts once.

RIGHT FRONT

CO 30 (32, 34, 38, 40, 42, 44, 46, 48, 50, 52, 56) sts. Begin 1x1 Rib; work even for 1½" (4 cm), ending with a WS row. Change to St st; work even for 1 row.
NEXT ROW (WS): P15 (16, 17, 19, 20, 21, 22, 23, 24, 25, 26, 28), pm, purl to end.

SHAPE WAIST

DECREASE ROW (RS): Decrease 1 st this row, then every 12 rows 3 times, as follows: Knit to marker, sm, k2tog, knit to end—26 (28, 30, 34, 36, 38, 40, 42, 44, 46, 48, 52) sts remain. Work even until piece measures 8" (20.5 cm) from the beginning, ending with a WS row.

SHAPE BUST

INCREASE ROW (RS): Increase 1 st this row, then every 10 rows 3 times, as follows: Knit to marker, sm, M1L, knit to end—30 (32, 34, 38, 40, 42, 44, 46, 48, 50, 52, 56) sts. Work even, removing marker on first row, until piece measures 14½ (14¾, 15, 15¼, 15½, 15¾, 16, 16, 16½, 16½, 16½, 16½)" [37 (37.5, 38, 38.5, 39.5, 40, 40.5, 40.5, 42, 42, 42, 42) cm] from the beginning, ending with a RS row.

SHAPE ARMHOLE AND NECK

Note: Armhole and neck shaping are worked at the same time for some of the sizes; please read entire section through before beginning.

BO 5 (6, 6, 6, 6, 6, 6, 6, 8, 8, 10) sts at armhole edge once, then 0 (0, 2, 2, 2, 2, 2, 4, 4, 6, 6) sts once, then decrease

1 st at armhole edge every RS row 2 (2, 2, 3, 3, 4, 5, 6, 6, 5, 5, 5) times, as follows: Work to last 4 sts, k2tog, k2. AT THE SAME TIME, when armhole measures 1" (2.5 cm), ending with a WS row, shape neck as follows:

BO 5 (5, 5, 5, 6, 6, 6, 6, 7, 6, 7) sts at neck edge once, then decrease 1 st at neck edge every RS row 2 (2, 2, 3, 3, 3, 3, 3, 3, 3, 3) times, then every 4 rows 2 (2, 2, 3, 3, 4, 4, 4, 4, 4, 4) times, as follows: Ssk, work to end—14 (15, 15, 16, 17, 18, 18, 19, 19, 19, 20, 21) sts remain when all shaping is complete. Work even until armhole measures 6½ (7, 7¼, 7½, 8, 8¼, 8½, 9, 9¼, 9¾, 10, 10½)" [16.5 (18, 18.5, 19, 20.5, 21, 21.5, 23, 23.5, 25, 25.5, 26.5) cm, ending with a RS row.

SHAPE SHOULDER

BO 7 (8, 8, 8, 9, 9, 9, 10, 10, 10, 10, 11) sts at armhole edge once, then 7 (7, 7, 8, 8, 9, 9, 9, 9, 10, 10) sts once.

LEFT FRONT

CO 30 (32, 34, 38, 40, 42, 44, 46, 48, 50, 52, 56) sts. Begin 1x1 Rib; work even for 1½" (4 cm), ending with a WS row. Change to St st; work even for 1 row.
NEXT ROW (WS): P15 (16, 17, 19, 20, 21, 22, 23, 24, 25, 26, 28), pm, purl to end.

SHAPE WAIST

DECREASE ROW (RS): Decrease 1 st this row, then every 12 rows 3 times, as follows: Knit to 2 sts before marker, ssk, sm, knit to end—26 (28, 30, 34, 36, 38, 40, 42, 44, 46, 48, 52) sts remain. Work even until piece measures 8" (20.5 cm) from the beginning, ending with a WS row.

SHAPE BUST

INCREASE ROW (RS): Increase 1 st this row, then every 10 rows 3 times, as follows: Knit to marker, M1R, sm, knit to end—30 (32, 34, 38, 40, 42, 44, 46, 48, 50, 52, 56) sts. Work even until piece measures 14½ (14¾, 15, 15¼, 15½, 15¾, 16, 16, 16½, 16½, 16½, 16½)" [37 (37.5, 38, 38.5, 39.5, 40, 40.5, 40.5, 42, 42, 42, 42) cm] from the beginning, ending with a WS row.

SHAPE ARMHOLE AND NECK

Note: Armhole and neck shaping are worked at the same time for some of the sizes; please read entire section through before beginning.

BO 5 (6, 6, 6, 6, 6, 6, 6, 8, 8, 10) sts at armhole edge once, then 0 (0, 2, 2, 2, 2, 2, 4, 4, 6, 6) sts once, then decrease 1 st at armhole edge every RS row 2 (2, 2, 3, 3, 4, 5, 6, 6, 5, 5, 5) times, as follows: K2, ssk, work to end. AT THE SAME TIME, when armhole measures 1" (2.5 cm), ending with a RS row, shape neck as follows:

BO 5 (5, 5, 5, 6, 6, 6, 6, 7, 6, 7) sts at neck edge once, then

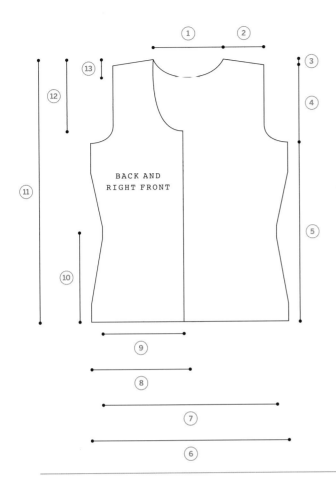

1   5¼ (5¼, 5¾, 5¾, 6, 6, 6½, 6½, 6½, 7, 7, 7½)"
13.5 (13.5, 14.5, 14.5, 15, 15, 16.5, 16.5, 16.5, 18, 18, 19) cm

2   3¼ (3½, 3½, 3¾, 4, 4¼, 4¼, 4½, 4½, 4½, 4¾, 5)"
8.5 (9, 9, 9.5, 10, 11, 11, 11.5, 11.5, 11.5, 12, 12.5) cm

3   ½"/1.5 cm

4   6½ (7, 7¼, 7½, 8, 8¼, 8½, 9, 9¼, 9¾, 10, 10½)"
16.5 (18, 18.5, 19, 20.5, 21, 21.5, 23, 23.5, 25, 25.5, 26.5) cm

5   14½ (14¾, 15, 15¼, 15½, 15¾, 16, 16, 16½, 16½, 16½, 16½)"
37 (37.5, 38, 38.5, 39.5, 40, 40.5, 40.5, 42, 42, 42, 42) cm

6   15 (16, 17½, 18¼, 19¼, 20¼, 21¼, 22, 23, 24, 25½, 27¼)" hip and bust
38 (40.5, 44.5, 46.5, 49, 51.5, 54, 56, 58.5, 61, 65, 69) cm

7   13¼ (14, 15½, 16½, 17½, 18¼, 19¼, 20¼, 21¼, 22, 23½, 25½)" waist
33.5 (35.5, 39.5, 42, 44.5, 46.5, 49, 51.5, 54, 56, 59.5, 65) cm

8   7 (7½, 8, 9, 9½, 10, 10¼, 10¾, 11¼, 11¾, 12¼, 13¼)"
18 (19, 20.5, 23, 24, 25.5, 26, 27.5, 28.5, 30, 31, 33.5) cm

9   6 (6½, 7, 8, 8½, 9, 9½, 10, 10¼, 10¾, 11¼, 12¼)"
15 (16.5, 18, 20.5, 21.5, 23, 24, 25.5, 26, 27.5, 28.5, 31) cm

10   7½"/19 cm

11   21½ (22¼, 22¾, 23¼, 24, 24½, 25, 25½, 26¼, 26¾, 27, 27½)"
54.5 (56.5, 58, 59, 61, 62, 63.5, 65, 66.5, 68, 68.5, 70) cm

12   6 (6½, 6¾, 7, 7½, 7¾, 8, 8½, 8¾, 9¼, 9½, 10)"
15 (16.5, 17, 18, 19, 19.5, 20.5, 21.5, 22, 23.5, 24, 25.5) cm

13   1½"/4 cm

---

decrease 1 st at neck edge every RS row 2 (2, 2, 3, 3, 3, 3, 3, 3, 3, 3) times, then every 4 rows 2 (2, 2, 3, 3, 3, 4, 4, 4, 4, 4, 4) times, as follows: Work to last 2 sts, k2tog—14 (15, 15, 16, 17, 18, 18, 19, 19, 19, 20, 21) sts remain when all shaping is complete. Work even until armhole measures 6½ (7, 7¼, 7½, 8, 8¼, 8½, 9, 9¼, 9¾, 10, 10½)" [16.5 (18, 18.5, 19, 20.5, 21, 21.5, 23, 23.5, 25, 25.5, 26.5) cm], ending with a WS row.

SHAPE SHOULDER

BO 7 (8, 8, 8, 9, 9, 9, 10, 10, 10, 10, 11) sts at armhole edge once, then 7 (7, 7, 8, 8, 9, 9, 9, 9, 10, 10) sts once.

FINISHING

Block pieces as desired. Sew shoulder seams. Sew side seams.

FRONT BANDS

With RS facing and beginning at lower Right Front edge, pick up and knit 3 sts for every 4 rows along Front edge, making sure to end with an odd number of sts.

ROW 1 (WS): P2, *k1, p1; repeat from * to last st, p1.

ROW 2: Knit the knit sts and purl the purl sts as they face you.

Repeat Row 2 until Band measures 1½" (4 cm). Repeat for Left Front, beginning at neck edge.

NECKBAND

With RS facing, using 24" (60 cm) circular needle and beginning at edge of Right Front, pick up and knit sts around neck shaping, picking up 1 st for every BO st, 3 sts for every 4 rows along vertical edges, and 4 sts for every 5 rows along diagonal edges, making sure to end with an odd number of sts. Begin 1x1 Rib; work even for 1" (2.5 cm). BO all sts in pattern somewhat snugly.

ARMHOLE EDGING

With RS facing, using 16" (40 cm) circular needle and beginning at center underarm, pick up and knit sts around armhole shaping, picking up 1 st for every BO st, 3 sts for every 4 rows along vertical edges, and 4 sts for every 5 rows along diagonal edges, making sure to end with an even number of sts. Join for working in the rnd; pm for beginning of rnd. Begin 1x1 Rib; work even for 2 rnds. BO all sts in pattern.

Attach closure to Right and Left Fronts as desired.

INTEGRATED SLEEVES

I'll be honest, here: I struggled to come up with a more clever name for the kinds of sweaters in this chapter. Often, they're knit in one piece, with the single seam falling under the arm, but not always. The one thing all these sweaters have in common is that the sleeves are knit at the same time as the body.

This technique makes for great, casual, comfortable sweaters that look good with minimal waist shaping. (Think "sweater sweatshirt" and you're on the right track!) I chose a soft cotton yarn for the Easygoing Sweatshirt Mini sweater on page 65, just right for a warm hug on a breezy day. In terms of technical specs, the fit for these garments should be relaxed. Aim for 4" (10 cm) or more of positive ease through the bust for the sweater to sit properly on your body.

Since they're worn looser than the set-in sleeve fitted sweaters from Chapter 9, drapey fabrics work best for these garments. I've chosen a number of fluid, comfortable fibers for the samples: An adult version of the mini sweatshirt is worked up in a hemp blend; a combination of wool, alpaca, and silk yarn makes for an incredibly luscious cuff-to-cuff cardigan; and a lighter-than-air cotton-alpaca blend works up into a sweet little cap-sleeve tee.

You'll learn lots of new things in this chapter, so please be sure to read each pattern carefully if you're unfamiliar with its construction! Take things one step at a time, and you'll end up with a sweater you like even more than your store-bought faves.

Simple
garter stitch
ornamentation

DIFFICULTY LEVEL:

INTEGRATED
SLEEVES

EASYGOING
SWEATSHIRT MINI

Minimal
seams

Easygoing Sweatshirt Mini

Integrated-sleeve sweaters can often cause a lot of head-scratching during the knitting process, as newer knitters struggle to imagine how the lumpy piece of fabric they're creating will ever turn into a sweater. Never fear! This mini gives you a quick, fun look at how one single piece of knitting can turn into a super-comfy garment. Worked in a soft, kind-to-the-hands cotton yarn, this child's sweatshirt features simple garter stitch trim and a fast gauge.

SIZES
To fit children 1 (2, 3/4, 5/6, 7/8, 9/10) year(s)

FINISHED MEASUREMENTS
20 (24, 26½, 28½, 30, 32½)" [51 (61, 67.5, 72.5, 76, 82.5) cm] chest

NOTE: Pullover is intended to be worn with at least 4" (10 cm) ease in the chest.

YARN
Rowan Softknit Cotton [92% cotton/8% polyamide; 115 yards (105 meters)/50 grams]: 4 (5, 6, 7, 8, 9) balls #570 Cream

NEEDLES
One 24" (60 cm) long or longer circular needle size US 7 (4.5 mm)

One set of five double-pointed needles (dpns) size US 7 (4.5 mm), for Cuffs

Change needle size if necessary to obtain correct gauge.

NOTIONS
Stitch markers

GAUGE
21 sts and 32 rows = 4" (10 cm) in St st

NOTE
This child's sweatshirt is worked in one piece from the front hem to the back hem, with sleeve stitches added (and later removed) in a series of cast-on and bind-off rows.

FRONT

CO 53 (63, 69, 75, 79, 85) sts. Begin Garter st (knit every row); work even for 1" (2.5 cm).

Change to St st; work even until piece measures 9 (9¾, 10¼, 12½, 13½, 14½)" [23 (25, 26, 32, 34.5, 37) cm] from the beginning, ending with a WS row.

NEXT ROW (RS): K26 (31, 34, 37, 39, 42), pm, k1, pm, knit to end.

SHAPE GARTER INSERT AND SLEEVES

Note: Garter insert and Sleeves will be shaped at the same time; please read entire section through before beginning.

NEXT ROW (WS): Purl to 1 st before first marker, pm, k1, remove marker, knit to next marker, remove marker, k1, pm, purl to end.

Knit 1 row.

Repeat last 2 rows to beginning of neck shaping. AT THE SAME TIME, beginning on first RS row of Garter insert shaping, work Sleeve shaping as follows:

Continuing to shape Garter insert, CO 6 (7, 7, 6, 7, 6) sts at beginning of next 10 (8, 6, 22, 10, 18) rows, then 5 (6, 6, 5, 6, 5) sts at beginning of next 8 (10, 14, 2, 14, 12) rows—153 (179, 195, 217, 233, 253) sts.

Work even until piece measures 11¾ (12½, 13¼, 16, 17, 18¾)" [30 (32, 33.5, 40.5, 43, 47.5) cm] from the beginning, ending with a WS row, removing markers on last row.

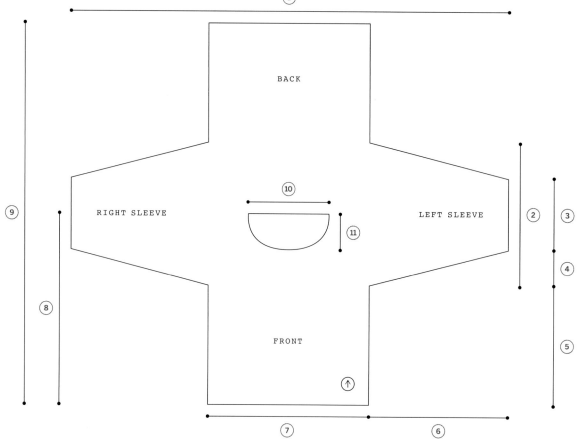

1 29 (34, 37¼, 41¼, 44½, 48¼)"
   73.5 (86.5, 94.5, 105, 113, 122.5) cm

2 9½ (10½, 11½, 12½, 13, 15)"
   24 (26.5, 29, 32, 33, 38) cm

3 5 (6, 6½, 6½, 7, 7½)"
   12.5 (15, 16.5, 16.5, 18, 19) cm

4 2¼ (2¼, 2½, 3, 3, 3¾)"
   5.5 (5.5, 6.5, 7.5, 7.5, 9.5) cm

5 9 (9¾, 10¼, 12½, 13½, 14½)"
   23 (25, 26, 32, 34.5, 37) cm

6 9½ (11, 12, 13½, 14¾, 16)"
   24 (28, 30.5, 34.5, 37.5, 40.5) cm

7 10 (12, 13¼, 14¼, 15, 16¼)"
   25.5 (30.5, 33.5, 36, 38, 41.5) cm

8 13¾ (15, 16, 18¾, 20, 22)"
   35 (38, 40.5, 47.5, 51, 56) cm

9 27½ (30, 32, 37½, 40, 44)"
   70 (76, 81.5, 95.5, 101.5, 112) cm

10 5¼ (5½, 6¼, 6¾, 7, 7¾)"
    13.5 (14, 16, 17, 18, 19.5) cm

11 2¼ (2¾, 3, 3, 3¼, 3½)"
    5.5 (7, 7.5, 7.5, 8.5, 9) cm

SHAPE NECK

NEXT ROW (RS): K65 (77, 84, 94, 101, 109), join a second ball of yarn and BO 23 (25, 27, 29, 31, 35) sts, knit to end. Working both sides at the same time, decrease 1 st at each neck edge every RS row 2 (2, 3, 3, 3, 3) times, as follows: On left neck edge, knit to last 2 sts, k2tog; on right neck edge, ssk, knit to end—63 (75, 81, 91, 98, 106) sts remain each shoulder/Sleeve. Work even until short (outside) edge of Sleeve measures 2½ (3, 3¼, 3¼, 3½, 3¾)" [6.5 (7.5, 8.5, 8.5, 9, 9.5) cm] from last CO row, ending with a WS row.

BACK

NEXT ROW (RS): Knit across left shoulder/Sleeve sts, CO 27 (29, 33, 35, 37, 41) sts for Back neck, knit across right shoulder/Sleeve sts with same ball of yarn (cut second ball of yarn)—153 (179, 195, 217, 233, 253) sts. Work even until short edge of Sleeve measures 5 (6, 6½, 6½, 7, 7½)" [12.5 (15, 16.5, 16.5, 18, 19) cm] from last Sleeve CO row, ending with a WS row.

SHAPE SLEEVE

BO 5 (6, 6, 5, 6, 5) sts at beginning of next 8 (10, 14, 2, 14, 12) rows, then 6 (7, 7, 6, 7, 6) sts at beginning of next 10 (8, 6, 22, 10, 18) rows—53 (63, 69, 75, 79, 85) sts remain. Work even until Back measures same as for Front from underarm to beginning of bottom Garter st edging, ending with a RS row.

Change to Garter st; work even for 1" (2.5 cm), ending with a WS row.

BO all sts.

FINISHING

Block piece as desired. Sew side and Sleeve seams.

NECKBAND

With RS facing, using circular needle and beginning at right shoulder, pick up and knit sts around neck shaping, picking up 1 st for every BO st, 3 sts for every 4 rows along vertical edges, and 4 sts for every 5 rows along diagonal edges. Join for working in the rnd; pm for beginning of rnd. Purl 1 rnd, knit 1 rnd, purl 1 rnd.

BO all sts.

CUFFS

With RS facing, using dpns, pick up and knit sts around Sleeve opening, picking up 3 sts for every 4 rows. Join for working in the rnd; pm for beginning of rnd. Purl 1 rnd, knit 1 rnd, purl 1 rnd.

BO all sts.

Rigging Sweatshirt

This ultra-comfortable adult take on the hem-to-hem one-piece construction was the first one I pulled into my own closet after the book's photography was complete. The ever-so-slightly dolman nature of the pullover is easygoing and comfy, and the hemp-blend yarn gives it a lovely drape. Simple lace stripes on the front of the sweater further emphasize the lines of this construction.

FINISHED MEASUREMENTS

35½ (36½, 39½, 40½, 43½, 44½, 47½, 48½, 51½, 52½, 56½, 60½)" [90 (92.5, 100.5, 103, 110.5, 113, 120.5, 123, 131, 133.5, 143.5, 153.5) cm bust

NOTE: Pullover is intended to be worn with 2–4" (5–10 cm) ease in the bust.

YARN

Elsebeth Lavold Hempathy [41% cotton/34% hemp/25% modal; 153 yards (140 meters)/50 grams]: 8 (8, 9, 9, 10, 10, 11, 11, 12, 13, 14, 15) balls #041 Hazy Blue

NEEDLES

One 24" (60 cm) long or longer circular needle size US 4 (3.5 mm)

One set of five double-pointed needles (dpns) size US 4 (3.5 mm), for Cuffs

Change needle size if necessary to obtain correct gauge.

GAUGE

24 sts and 36 rows = 4" (10 cm) in St st

NOTES

This sweater is worked in one piece from the front hem to the back hem, with sleeve stitches added (and later removed) in a series of cast-on and bind-off rows.

When shaping sleeves in Lace Stripe, don't work a yo without a corresponding k2tog, and vice versa.

STITCH PATTERNS

2X2 RIB FLAT
(multiple of 4 sts + 2; 1-row repeat)

ROW 1 (RS): *K2, p2; repeat from * to last 2 sts, k2.

ROW 2: Knit the knit sts and purl the purl sts as they face you. Repeat Row 2 for 2x2 Rib Flat.

2X2 RIB IN THE RND
(multiple of 4 sts; 1-rnd repeat)

ALL RNDS: *K2, p2; repeat from * to end.

LACE STRIPE

(even number of sts; 16-row repeat)

ROWS 1 AND 3 (RS): Knit.

ROWS 2 AND 4: Purl.

ROW 5: K1, *yo, k2tog; rep from * to last st, k1.

ROW 6: P1, *yo, k2tog; rep from * to last st, p1.

ROWS 7–16: Repeat Rows 1 and 2. Repeat Rows 1–16 for Lace Stripe.

FRONT

CO 106 (110, 118, 122, 130, 134, 142, 146, 154, 158, 170, 182) sts. Begin 2x2 Rib Flat; work even for 1½" (4 cm), ending with a WS row.

Change to Lace Stripe; work even until piece measures 13½ (13¾, 13¾, 13¾, 13½, 13¾, 14, 14, 14¼, 15, 15, 15)" [34.5 (35, 35, 35, 34.5, 35, 35.5, 35.5, 36, 38, 38, 38) cm] from the beginning, ending with a WS row.

SHAPE SLEEVES

CO 5 (5, 4, 4, 4, 4, 4, 3, 4, 3, 3) sts at beginning of next 10 (2, 24, 20, 4, 12, 12, 48, 44, 6, 44, 40) rows, then 4 (4, 3, 3, 3, 3, 3, 0, 2, 3, 2, 2) sts at beginning of next 22 (32, 14, 20, 42, 32, 32, 0, 6, 40, 6, 14) rows, working new sts in pattern—244 (248, 256, 262, 272, 278, 286, 290, 298, 302, 314, 330) sts. Work even until piece measures 18¾ (19½, 20¼, 20¾, 21¼, 21¾, 22¼, 22½, 23¼, 23½, 24¼, 24¾)" [47.5 (49.5, 51.5, 52.5, 54, 55, 56.5, 57, 59, 59.5, 61.5, 63) cm] from the beginning, ending with a WS row.

Simple
lace stripes
on front only

Straight shape,
drapey fabric

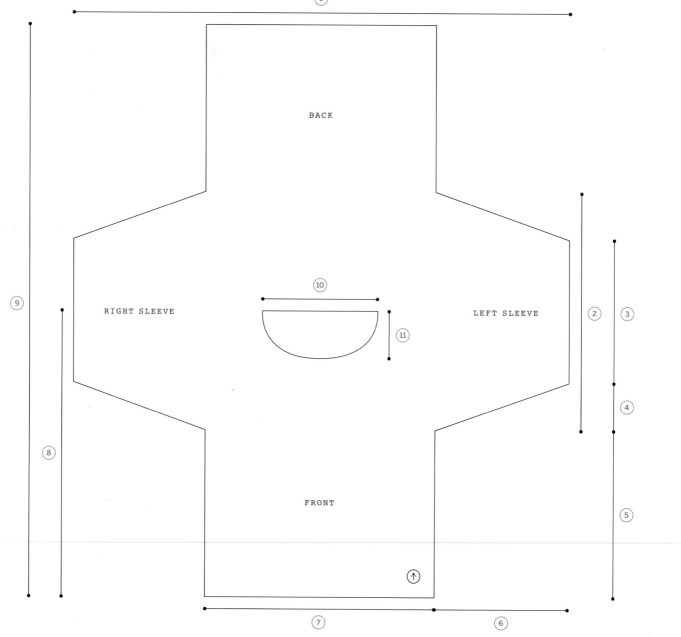

1 40¾ (41¼, 42¾, 43¾, 45¼, 46¼, 47¾, 48¼, 49¾, 50¼, 52¼, 54¾)"
103.5 (105, 108.5, 111, 115, 117.5, 121.5, 122.5, 126.5, 127.5, 132.5, 139) cm

2 18½ (19½, 21, 22, 23½, 24, 24½, 25, 26, 25, 26½, 27½)"
47 (49.5, 53.5, 56, 59.5, 61, 62, 63.5, 66, 63.5, 67.5, 70) cm

3 11½ (12, 12½, 13, 13½, 14, 14½, 14½, 15, 15, 15½, 15½)"
29 (30.5, 32, 33, 34.5, 35.5, 37, 37, 38, 38, 39.5, 39.5) cm

4 3½ (3¾, 4¼, 4½, 5, 5, 5, 5¼, 5½, 5, 5½, 6)"
9 (9.5, 11, 11.5, 12.5, 12.5, 12.5, 13.5, 14, 12.5, 14, 15) cm

5 13½ (13¾, 13¾, 13¾, 13½, 13¾, 14, 14, 14¼, 15, 15, 15)"
34.5 (35, 35, 35, 34.5, 35, 35.5, 35.5, 36, 38, 38, 38) cm

6 11½ (11½, 11½, 11¾, 11¾, 12, 12, 12, 12, 12, 12, 12¼)"
29 (29, 29, 30, 30, 30.5, 30.5, 30.5, 30.5, 30.5, 30.5, 31) cm

7 17¾ (18¼, 19¾, 20¼, 21¾, 22¼, 23¾, 24¼, 25¾, 26¼, 28¼, 30¼)"
45 (46.5, 50, 51.5, 55, 56.5, 60.5, 61.5, 65.5, 66.5, 72, 77) cm

8 22¾ (23½, 24¼, 24¾, 25¼, 25¾, 26¼, 26½, 27¼, 27½, 28¼, 28¾)"
58 (59.5, 61.5, 63, 64, 65.5, 66.5, 67.5, 69, 70, 72, 73) cm

9 45½ (47, 48½, 49½, 50½, 51½, 52½, 53, 54½, 55, 56½, 57½)"
115.5 (119.5, 123, 125.5, 128.5, 131, 133.5, 134.5, 138.5, 139.5, 143.5, 146) cm

10 9 (9¾, 10, 10¼, 10¾, 11, 11, 11¾, 12, 12, 12¾, 12¾)"
23 (25, 25.5, 26, 27.5, 28, 28, 30, 30.5, 30.5, 32.5, 32.5) cm

11 4"/10 cm

SHAPE NECK

NEXT ROW (RS): Work 105 (106, 110, 112, 116, 119, 123, 124, 127, 129, 134, 142) sts, join a second ball of yarn and BO 34 (36, 36, 38, 40, 40, 40, 42, 44, 44, 46, 46) sts, work to end. Working both sides at the same time, decrease 1 st at each neck edge every row 4 (4, 4, 4, 4, 5, 5, 5, 5, 6, 6) times, then every RS row 6 (7, 8, 8, 8, 8, 9, 9, 9, 9, 9) times, as follows: On left neck edge, work to last 2 sts, k2tog; on right neck edge, ssk, work to end—95 (95, 98, 100, 104, 106, 110, 110, 113, 115, 119, 127) sts remain each shoulder/Sleeve. Work even until short (outside) edge of Sleeve measures 5¾ (6, 6¼, 6½, 6¾, 7, 7¼, 7¼, 7½, 7½, 7¾, 7¾)" [14.5 (15, 16, 16.5, 17, 18, 18.5, 18.5, 19, 19, 19.5, 19.5) cm from last Sleeve CO row, ending with a WS row.

BACK

Change to St st for remainder of piece.

NEXT ROW (RS): Knit across left shoulder/Sleeve sts, CO 54 (58, 60, 62, 64, 66, 66, 70, 72, 72, 76, 76) sts, knit across right shoulder/Sleeve sts with same ball of yarn (cut second ball of yarn)—244 (248, 256, 262, 272, 278, 286, 290, 298, 302, 314, 330) sts. Work even until short edge of Sleeve measures 11½ (12, 12½, 13, 13½, 14, 14½, 14½, 15, 15, 15½, 15½)" / 29 (30.5, 32, 33, 34.5, 35.5, 37, 37, 38, 38, 39.5, 39.5) cm from last Sleeve CO row, ending with a WS row.

SHAPE SLEEVE

BO 4 (4, 3, 3, 3, 3, 3, 0, 2, 3, 2, 2) sts at beginning of next 22 (32, 14, 20, 42, 32, 32, 0, 6, 40, 6, 14) rows, then 5 (5, 4, 4, 4, 4, 4, 3, 3, 4, 3, 3) sts at beginning of next 10 (2, 24, 20, 4, 12, 12, 48, 44, 6, 44, 40) rows—106 (110, 118, 122, 130, 134, 142, 146, 154, 158, 170, 182) sts remain. Work even until Back measures same as for Front from underarm to beginning of ribbing, ending with a WS row.

Change to 2x2 Rib Flat; work even for 1½" (4 cm), ending with a WS row.

BO all sts in pattern.

FINISHING

Block piece as desired. Sew side and Sleeve seams.

NECKBAND

With RS facing, using circular needle and beginning at right Back shoulder, pick up and knit sts around neck shaping, picking up 1 st for every BO st, 3 sts for every 4 rows along vertical edges, and 4 sts for every 5 rows along diagonal edges. Join for working in the rnd; pm for beginning of rnd. Knit 8 rnds.

BO all sts, allowing edge to roll.

CUFFS

With RS facing, using dpns, pick up and knit sts around Sleeve opening, picking up 3 sts for every 4 rows, making sure to end with a multiple of 4 sts. Join for working in the rnd; pm for beginning of rnd.

Begin 2x2 Rib in the Rnd; work even for 1" (2.5 cm).

BO all sts in pattern.

DIFFICULTY LEVEL:

INTEGRATED
SLEEVES

BLAZE CARDIGAN

Worked
cuff-to-cuff

Drapey silk and
alpaca balance
larger gauge

Blaze Cardigan

Another way to knit the sleeves of a sweater at the same time as the body is to start at one cuff and work sideways across the garment to the other cuff. The fit is similar to hem-to-hem sweaters, but with more fun stitch patterning possibilities—can you imagine cables going horizontally from one side of the sweater to the other? Yum! Most of these sweaters don't have waist shaping, and hence rely on drapey, figure-flattering fabrics to work well. I've turned the drape up to 11 here, with a mix of alpaca and silk yarn.

FINISHED MEASUREMENTS

34 (36½, 38, 39½, 42, 44½, 46, 47½, 50, 52½, 56, 60)" [86.5 (92.5, 96.5, 100.5, 106.5, 113, 117, 120.5, 127, 133.5, 142, 152.5) cm] bust

NOTE: Cardigan is intended to be worn with 4" (10 cm) ease in the bust.

YARN

Shibui Knits Maai [70% superbaby alpaca/30% merino wool; 175 yards (160 meters)/50 grams]; 5 (6, 6, 7, 7, 8, 8, 8, 9, 9, 10, 11) skeins Brownstone **(A)**

Shibui Knits Staccato [70% superwash merino wool/30% silk; 191 yards (175 meters)/50 grams]; 5 (6, 6, 7, 7, 8, 8, 8, 9, 9, 10, 11) skeins Brownstone **(B)**

NEEDLES

One 24" (60 cm) long or longer circular needle size US 9 (5.5 mm)

Change needle size if necessary to obtain correct gauge.

NOTIONS

Stitch holder or waste yarn; removable stitch marker

GAUGE

18 sts and 28 rows = 4" (10 cm) in St st, using 1 strand each of A and B held together

STITCH PATTERNS

1X1 RIB

(even number of sts; 1-row repeat)

ALL ROWS: *K1, p1; repeat from * to end.

1X1 RIB

(odd number of sts; 1-row repeat)

ROW 1 (RS): *K1, p1; repeat from * to last st, k1.

ROW 2: Knit the knit sts and purl the purl sts as they face you. Repeat Row 2 for 1x1 Rib.

NOTES

This cardigan is worked in one piece from left cuff to right cuff.

Use 1 strand each of A and B held together throughout the entire piece.

LEFT SLEEVE

Using 1 strand each of A and B held together, CO 36 (36, 40, 40, 42, 42, 42, 44, 44, 46, 46, 48) sts. Begin 1x1 Rib; work even for 4" (10 cm), ending with a WS row.

Change to St st; work even for 2 rows.

SHAPE SLEEVE

INCREASE ROW (RS): Increase 1 st each side this row, then every 4 (4, 4, 4, 4, 2, 2, 2, 2, 2, 2, 2) rows 2 (8, 6, 15, 16, 1, 3, 7, 11, 10, 12, 14) times, then every 6 (6, 6, 6, 6, 4, 4, 4, 4, 4, 4, 4) rows 11 (7, 9, 3, 3, 20, 20, 18, 16, 17, 16, 15) times, as follows: K1, M1R, knit to last st, M1L, k1—64 (68, 72, 78, 82, 86, 90, 96, 100, 102, 104, 108) sts. Pm at beginning of final Increase Row. Work even until piece measures 16½ (16½, 17, 17, 17½, 17½, 18, 18, 18, 18½, 18½, 18½)" [42 (42, 43, 43, 44.5, 44.5, 45.5, 45.5, 45.5, 47, 47, 47) cm] from the beginning, ending with a WS row. Make a note of the number of rows worked after marker; you will need this number when working the Right Sleeve.

BACK/LEFT FRONT

CO 66 (67, 67, 67, 68, 68, 68, 68, 68, 68, 68, 68) sts at beginning of row, work across these CO sts, work across Sleeve sts, then CO 66 (67, 67, 67, 68, 68, 68, 68, 68, 68, 68, 68) sts at end of row—196 (202, 206, 212, 218, 222, 226, 232, 236, 238, 240, 244) sts. Work even until piece measures 5½ (6, 6¼, 6½, 7, 7½, 7¾, 8, 8½, 9, 9¾, 10¾)" [14 (15, 16, 16.5, 18, 19, 19.5, 20.5, 21.5, 23, 25, 27.5) cm] from Back/Left Front CO edge, ending with a WS row.

BACK

SHAPE BACK NECK

NEXT ROW (RS): K98 (101, 103, 106, 109, 111, 113, 116, 118, 119, 120, 122), place next 98 (101, 103, 106, 109, 111, 113, 116, 118, 119, 120, 122) sts on holder or waste yarn for Left Front.

DECREASE ROW: Working on Back sts only, decrease 1 st at neck edge this row, then every WS row 4 times, as follows: P1, ssp, purl to end—93 (96, 98, 101, 104, 106, 108, 111, 113, 114, 115, 117) sts remain. Work even until piece measures 10¾ (11½, 12, 12½, 13¼, 14, 14½, 15, 15¾, 16½, 17½, 18½)" [27.5 (29, 30.5, 32, 33.5, 35.5, 37, 38, 40, 42, 44.5, 47) cm] from Back/Left Front CO edge, ending with a WS row.

INCREASE ROW (RS): Increase 1 st at neck edge this row, then every RS row 4 times, as follows: Knit to last st, M1L, k1—98 (101, 103, 106, 109, 111, 113, 116, 118, 119, 120, 122) sts. Place sts on holder or waste yarn.

LEFT FRONT

Return Left Front sts to circular needle and rejoin 1 strand each of A and B at neck edge. With RS facing, CO 15 (15, 16, 16, 17, 18, 18, 19, 19, 20, 20, 20) sts at beginning of row for left Back collar, work across these CO sts, then work across Left Front sts—113 (116, 119, 122, 126, 129, 131, 135, 137, 139, 140, 142) sts.

Purl 1 row.

Begin 1x1 Rib; work even for 3 (3, 3, 3¼, 3½, 3½, 3½, 3¾, 4, 4, 4, 4)" [7.5 (7.5, 7.5, 8.5, 9, 9, 9, 9.5, 10, 10, 10, 10) cm].

BO all sts in pattern.

RIGHT FRONT

Using 1 strand each of A and B held together, CO 113 (116, 119, 122, 126, 129, 131, 135, 137, 139, 140, 142) sts. Begin 1x1 Rib; work even for 3 (3, 3, 3¼, 3½, 3½, 3½, 3¾, 4, 4, 4, 4)" [7.5 (7.5, 7.5, 8.5, 9, 9, 9, 9.5, 10, 10, 10, 10) cm], ending with a WS row.

NEXT ROW (RS): BO 15 (15, 16, 16, 17, 18, 18, 19, 19, 20, 20, 20) sts for right Back collar, knit to end—98 (101, 103, 106, 109, 111, 113, 116, 118, 119, 120, 122) sts remain.

NEXT ROW: Purl to end, then purl across Back sts from holder—196 (202, 206, 212, 218, 222, 226, 232, 236, 238, 240, 244) sts.

BACK/RIGHT FRONT

Work even until piece measures 17 (18¼, 19, 19¾, 21, 22¼, 23, 23¾, 25, 26¼, 28, 30)" [43 (46.5, 48.5, 50, 53.5, 56.5, 58.5, 60.5, 63.5, 66.5, 71, 76) cm] from Back/Left Front CO edge, ending with a WS row.

BO 66 (67, 67, 67, 68, 68, 68, 68, 68, 68, 68, 68) sts at beginning of next 2 rows—64 (68, 72, 78, 82, 86, 90, 96, 100, 102, 104, 108) sts remain.

RIGHT SLEEVE

Work even for 1 row less than number of rows that you worked after marker for Left Sleeve, ending with a WS row.

SHAPE SLEEVE

DECREASE ROW (RS): Decrease 1 st each side this row, then every 6 (6, 6, 6, 6, 4, 4, 4, 4, 4, 4, 4) rows 11 (7, 9, 3, 3, 20, 20, 18, 16, 17, 16, 15) times, then every 4 (4, 4, 4, 4, 2, 2, 2, 2, 2, 2, 2) rows 2 (8, 6, 15, 16, 1, 3, 7, 11, 10, 12, 14) time(s), as follows: K1, ssk, knit to last 3 sts, k2tog, k1—36 (36, 40, 40, 42, 42, 42, 44, 44, 46, 46, 48) sts remain. Work even for 3 rows.

Change to 1x1 Rib; work even for 4" (10 cm).

BO all sts in pattern.

FINISHING

Block as desired. Sew side and Sleeve seams. Sew ends of Back collar together, then sew to Back neck.

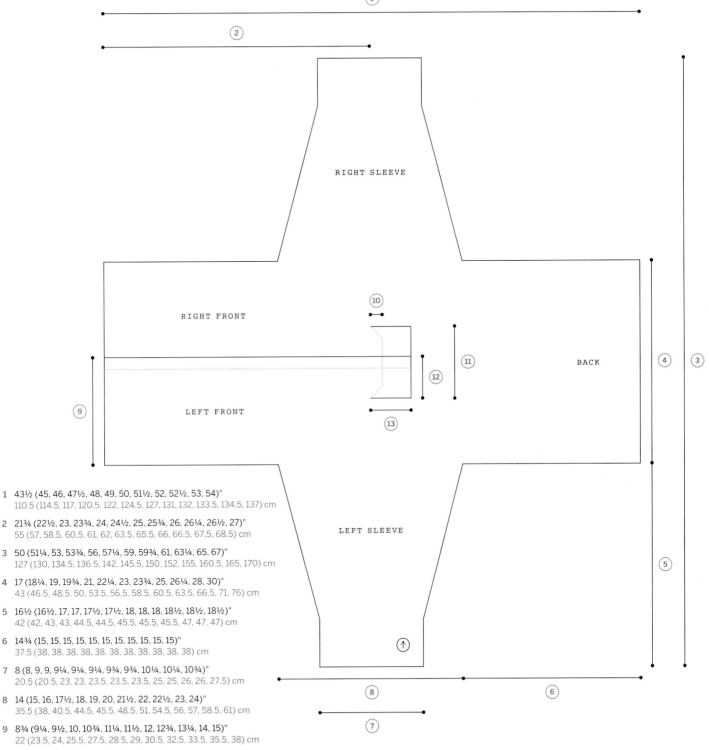

RIGHT SLEEVE

RIGHT FRONT

LEFT FRONT

LEFT SLEEVE

BACK

1   43½ (45, 46, 47½, 48, 49, 50, 51½, 52, 52½, 53, 54)"
    110.5 (114.5, 117, 120.5, 122, 124.5, 127, 131, 132, 133.5, 134.5, 137) cm

2   21¾ (22½, 23, 23¾, 24, 24½, 25, 25¾, 26, 26¼, 26½, 27)"
    55 (57, 58.5, 60.5, 61, 62, 63.5, 65.5, 66, 66.5, 67.5, 68.5) cm

3   50 (51¼, 53, 53¾, 56, 57¼, 59, 59¾, 61, 63¼, 65, 67)"
    127 (130, 134.5, 136.5, 142, 145.5, 150, 152, 155, 160.5, 165, 170) cm

4   17 (18¼, 19, 19¾, 21, 22¼, 23, 23¾, 25, 26¼, 28, 30)"
    43 (46.5, 48.5, 50, 53.5, 56.5, 58.5, 60.5, 63.5, 66.5, 71, 76) cm

5   16½ (16½, 17, 17, 17½, 17½, 18, 18, 18, 18½, 18½, 18½)"
    42 (42, 43, 43, 44.5, 44.5, 45.5, 45.5, 45.5, 47, 47, 47) cm

6   14¾ (15, 15, 15, 15, 15, 15, 15, 15, 15, 15, 15)"
    37.5 (38, 38, 38, 38, 38, 38, 38, 38, 38, 38, 38) cm

7   8 (8, 9, 9, 9¼, 9¼, 9¼, 9¾, 9¾, 10¼, 10¼, 10¾)"
    20.5 (20.5, 23, 23, 23.5, 23.5, 23.5, 25, 25, 26, 26, 27.5) cm

8   14 (15, 16, 17½, 18, 19, 20, 21½, 22, 22½, 23, 24)"
    35.5 (38, 40.5, 44.5, 45.5, 48.5, 51, 54.5, 56, 57, 58.5, 61) cm

9   8¾ (9¼, 9½, 10, 10¾, 11¼, 11½, 12, 12¾, 13¼, 14, 15)"
    22 (23.5, 24, 25.5, 27.5, 28.5, 29, 30.5, 32.5, 33.5, 35.5, 38) cm

10 1"/2.5 cm

11 6 (6¼, 6½, 6¾, 7, 7¼, 7½, 7¾, 8, 8¼, 8½, 8½)"
    15 (16, 16.5, 17, 18, 18.5, 19, 19.5, 20.5, 21, 21.5, 21.5) cm

12 3¼ (3¼, 3¼, 3½, 3¾, 3¾, 3¾, 4, 4¼, 4¼, 4¼, 4¼)"
    8.5 (8.5, 8.5, 9, 9.5, 9.5, 9.5, 10, 11, 11, 11, 11) cm

13 3¼ (3¼, 3½, 3½, 3¾, 4, 4, 4¼, 4¼, 4½, 4½, 4½)"
    8.5 (8.5, 9, 9, 9.5, 10, 10, 11, 11, 11.5, 11.5, 11.5) cm

Whisper Tee

Although this sweater is knit in two pieces rather than one, the cute cap sleeves are part of the front and back, with only shoulder and side seams holding the piece together. It's worked in a lightweight, alpaca-cotton blend that drapes beautifully and is exceptionally soft. The gathers at the neckline are formed with triple-decreases at the neck edge, combined with a firm hand when picking up stitches for the neckline. (Hint: You want the sweater to pucker here!) Waist shaping on the back of the sweater creates a nice silhouette and applied I-cord trim on the armholes keeps the focus on the lovely neckline.

FINISHED MEASUREMENTS
30½ (32, 34½, 36, 38½, 40, 42½, 44, 46½, 48, 50½, 54½)" [77.5 (81.5, 87.5, 91.5, 98, 101.5, 108, 112, 118, 122, 128.5, 138.5) cm] bust

NOTE: Pullover is intended to be worn with 2" (5 cm) ease in the bust. The Front neck decreases will gather the Front by approximately 2" (5 cm) at the center bust.

YARN
Manos del Uruguay Serena [60% baby alpaca/40% pima cotton; 170 yards (155 meters)/ 50 grams]: 3 (4, 4, 4, 5, 5, 5, 6, 6, 6, 7) hanks #S2262 Hare

NEEDLES
One pair straight needles size US 2 (2.75 mm)

One pair double-pointed needles (dpns) size US 2 (2.75 mm), for Armhole Edging

One 24" (60 cm) long circular needle size US 2 (2.75 mm), for Armhole Edging and Neckband

Change needle size if necessary to obtain correct gauge.

NOTIONS
Stitch markers

GAUGE
28 sts and 36 rows = 4" (10 cm) in St st

STITCH PATTERNS
2X2 RIB FLAT
(multiple of 4 sts + 2; 1-row repeat)
ROW 1 (RS): *K2, p2; repeat from * to last 2 sts, k2.
ROW 2: Knit the knit sts and purl the purl sts as they face you. Repeat Row 2 for 2x2 Rib Flat.

2X2 RIB IN THE RND
(multiple of 4 sts; 1-rnd repeat)
ALL RNDS: *K2, p2; repeat from * to end.

NOTES
This tee is worked in two pieces from the bottom up, with stitches increased for the cap sleeves.

BACK
CO 106 (114, 122, 126, 134, 142, 150, 154, 162, 170, 178, 190) sts. Begin 2x2 Rib Flat; work even for 1½" (4 cm), ending with a WS row.
Change to St st; work even, decreasing 0 (2, 2, 0, 0, 2, 2, 0, 0, 2, 2, 0) sts evenly on first row, until piece measures 2¼" (5.5 cm) from the beginning, ending with a RS row—106 (112, 120, 126, 134, 140, 148, 154, 162, 168, 176, 190) sts.
NEXT ROW (WS): P35 (37, 40, 42, 45, 47, 49, 51, 54, 56, 59, 63) sts, pm, p36 (38, 40, 42, 44, 46, 50, 52, 54, 56, 58, 64) sts, pm, purl to end.

SHAPE WAIST
DECREASE ROW (RS): Decrease 2 sts this row, then every 10 rows 5 times, as follows: Knit to 2 sts before first marker, ssk, sm, knit to next marker, sm, k2tog, knit to end—94 (100, 108, 114, 122, 128, 136, 142, 150, 156, 164, 178) sts remain. Work even until piece measures 9" (23 cm) from the beginning, ending with a WS row.

SHAPE BUST
INCREASE ROW (RS): Increase 2 sts this row, then every 8 rows 5 times, as follows: Knit to first marker, M1R, sm, knit to next marker, sm, M1L, knit to end—106 (112, 120, 126, 134, 140, 148, 154, 162, 168, 176, 190) sts. Work even, removing markers on first row, until piece measures 15½ (15¾, 16, 16¼, 16½, 16¾, 17, 17, 17½, 17½, 17½, 17½)" [39.5 (40, 40.5, 41.5, 42, 42.5, 43,

DIFFICULTY LEVEL:

INTEGRATED
SLEEVES

WHISPER TEE

Subtle, elegant
I-cord trim

Dart-style
waist shaping
on back only

43, 44.5, 44.5, 44.5, 44.5) cm] from the beginning, ending with a WS row.

SHAPE ARMHOLES

BO 8 (8, 8, 8, 8, 8, 8, 10, 12, 14, 14) sts at beginning of next 2 rows—90 (96, 104, 110, 118, 124, 132, 138, 142, 144, 148, 162) sts remain.

Knit 1 row.

NEXT ROW (WS): P29 (32, 35, 37, 39, 42, 45, 47, 49, 49, 51, 56), pm, p32 (32, 34, 36, 40, 40, 42, 44, 44, 46, 46, 50) sts, pm, purl to end.

SHAPE CAP SLEEVES

INCREASE ROW (RS): Increase 2 sts this row, then every RS row 10 (8, 7, 6, 4, 2, 1, 0, 2, 4, 6, 4) time(s), then every 4 rows 4 (6, 7, 8, 10, 12, 13, 14, 14, 14, 14, 16) times, as follows: K1, M1R, knit to last st, M1L, k1—120 (126, 134, 140, 148, 154, 162, 168, 176, 182, 190, 204) sts remain. Work even until armhole measures 5 (5½, 5¾, 6, 6½, 6¾, 7, 7½, 7¾, 8¼, 8½, 9)" [12.5 (14, 14.5, 15, 16.5, 17, 18, 19, 19.5, 21, 21.5, 23) cm], ending with a WS row.

SHAPE NECK

NEXT ROW (RS): Work to first marker, join a second ball of yarn and BO 32 (32, 34, 36, 40, 40, 42, 44, 44, 46, 46, 50) sts, work to end. Working both sides at the same time, decrease 1 st at each neck edge every RS row twice—42 (45, 48, 50, 52, 55, 58, 60, 64, 66, 70, 75) sts remain each shoulder when all shaping is complete. Work even until armhole measures 6 (6½, 6¾, 7, 7½, 7¾, 8, 8½, 8¾, 9¼, 9½, 10)" [15 (16.5, 17, 18, 19, 19.5, 20.5, 21.5, 22, 23.5, 24, 25.5) cm], ending with a WS row. BO all sts.

FRONT

CO 122 (126, 134, 142, 150, 154, 162, 170, 178, 182, 190, 206) sts. Begin 2x2 Rib Flat; work even for 1½" (4 cm), ending with a WS row.

Change to St st; work even, decreasing 2 (0, 0, 2, 2, 0, 0, 2, 2, 0, 0, 2) sts evenly on first row, until piece measures 13¼ (13¾, 14, 14¼, 14½, 14¾, 15, 15, 15½, 15½, 15½, 15½)" [34.5 (35, 35.5, 36, 37, 37.5, 38, 38, 39.5, 39.5, 39.5, 39.5) cm] from the beginning, ending with a WS row—120 (126, 134, 140, 148, 154, 162, 168, 176, 182, 190, 204) sts. Place marker between 2 center sts.

SHAPE NECK, ARMHOLES, AND CAP SLEEVES

Note: Neck, armhole, and cap Sleeve shaping are worked at the same time; please read entire section through before beginning.

DECREASE ROW 1 (RS): Knit to 3 sts before marker, sssk, join a second ball of yarn, k3tog, knit to end—58 (61, 65, 68, 72, 75, 79, 82, 86, 89, 93, 100) sts remain each side.

Purl 1 row.

DECREASE ROW 2: Decrease 2 sts each neck edge this row, then every RS row 5 times, as follows: On left neck edge, work to last 3 sts, sssk; on right neck edge, k3tog, work to end.

Purl 1 row.

DECREASE ROW 3: Decrease 1 st each neck edge this row, then every RS row 10 (10, 11, 12, 14, 14, 15, 16, 16, 17, 17, 19) times, as follows: On left neck edge, work to last 2 sts, ssk; on right neck edge, k2tog, work to end.

AT THE SAME TIME, when piece measures 15½ (15¾, 16, 16¼, 16½, 16¾, 17, 17, 17½, 17½, 17½, 17½)" [39.5 (40, 40.5, 41.5, 42, 42.5, 43, 43, 44.5, 44.5, 44.5, 44.5) cm] from the beginning, ending with a WS row, work armhole and cap Sleeve shaping as follows:

NEXT ROW (RS): Continuing to work neck shaping, BO 8 (8, 8, 8, 8, 8, 8, 10, 12, 14, 14) sts at each armhole edge once.

Work in St st for 2 rows.

INCREASE ROW (RS): Increase 1 st at each armhole edge this row, then every RS row 10 (8, 7, 6, 4, 2, 1, 0, 2, 4, 6, 4) time(s), then every 4 rows 4 (6, 7, 8, 10, 12, 13, 14, 14, 14, 14, 16) times, as follows: On left armhole edge, k1, M1R, work to end; on right armhole edge, work to last st, M1L, k1—42 (45, 48, 50, 52, 55, 58, 60, 64, 66, 70, 75) sts remain each shoulder when all shaping is complete. Work even until armhole measures 6 (6½, 6¾, 7, 7½, 7¾, 8, 8½, 8¾, 9¼, 9½, 10)" [15 (16.5, 17, 18, 19, 19.5, 20.5, 21.5, 22, 23.5, 24, 25.5) cm], ending with a WS row. BO all sts.

FABRIC AND YARN SUBSTITUTIONS FOR BOXY SWEATERS

Bonus Lesson

ANYONE WHO HAS been knitting sweaters for a while has a horror story about a sweater that made them look like a box. Generally, hand-knit fabrics are sturdier, thicker, and move less than store-bought fabrics, and as a rule, those stiffer fabrics require waist shaping (page 53) to keep you from looking totally lost (and square) in your sweater.

But you can look shapely in an unshaped sweater if you play your fibers right. You'll want a finished fabric with both drape and fluidity—that is, the finished fabric should hang somewhat heavily, ripple if you shake it, and compress pretty gracefully if you grab a handful and squeeze it tight. I've selected yarns that work well for the sweaters in this chapter, but if you'd like help with other sweaters, or with yarn substitutions, read on!

Here's a quick summary of the fibers you're looking for (you can check out the descriptions on pages 13–14 for more detail):

SILK adds drape, fluidity, and a beautiful sheen to hand-knit fabric. It's my top choice for fibers for unshaped garments. Check out the Blaze Cardigan on page 73, and the Revive Cardigan on page 93 for examples of garments made with silk-blend yarn.

LINEN AND HEMP are drapey and fluid without the shine of silk, and with a slightly rougher texture. They make great casual, beachy sweaters. The Rigging Sweatshirt (page 68) and Beachwalker pullover (page 97) are great examples.

ALPACA provides subtle drape and a soft, fuzzy halo to the sweaters it's used for. It's combined with cotton for the delicate cap sleeve Whisper Tee opposite, and works fabulously for the Cushy Pullover on page 89.

RAYON, VISCOSE, AND BAMBOO are your final great options for fibers for unshaped sweaters. They're slinky, shiny, and shimmery. The only caution I have for you is to make sure you knit them pretty tightly—that slinkiness can cause these fabrics to stretch out of shape while you wear them if knit too loosely.

FINISHING

Block pieces as desired. Sew shoulder seams. Sew side seams.

NECKBAND

With RS facing, using circular needle and beginning at right Back shoulder, pick up and knit sts around neck shaping, picking up 1 st for every BO st, 3 sts for every 4 rows along vertical edges, 4 sts for every 5 rows along diagonal edges, and 2 sts at bottom center of Front neck (placing marker between these 2 sts), making sure to end with a multiple of 4 sts for the total pick-up, and with a multiple of 4 sts + 2 to center Front marker. Join for working in the rnd; pm for beginning of rnd.

DECREASE RND: Work in 2x2 Rib in the Rnd to 2 sts before marker, k2tog, sm, ssk, work in 2x2 Rib, beginning with p2, to end—2 sts decreased.

Repeat Decrease Rnd until Neckband measures 1¼" (3 cm).

Knit 7 rnds.
BO all sts loosely, allowing edge to roll.

ARMHOLE EDGING

With RS facing, using circular needle, and beginning at center underarm, pick up and knit 1 st in every st and row around armhole opening. Cut yarn.

Using dpn, CO 3 sts. Slide sts back to right end of needle.

RND 1: *Pulling yarn tightly across back of work, k2, ssk (next I-cord st together with next st on circular needle); slide sts back to right end of needle.

RND 2: *Pulling yarn tightly across back of work, k3; slide sts back to right end of needle.

Repeat Rnds 1 and 2 until 3 sts remain.
BO all sts. Sew CO and BO edges together.

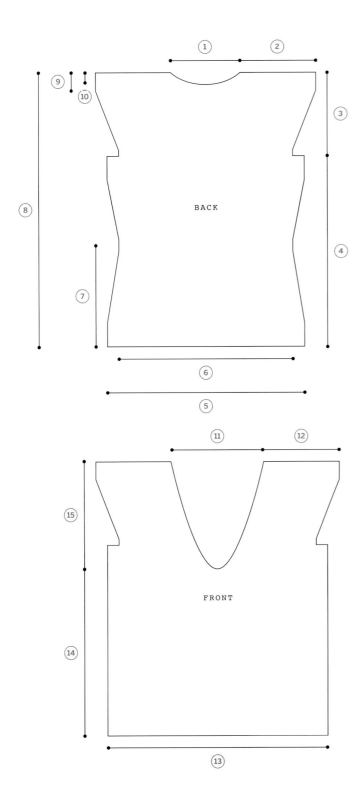

BACK

1. 5¼ (5¼, 5½, 5¾, 6¼, 6¼, 6½, 6¾, 6¾, 7¼, 7¼, 7¾)"
   13.5 (13.5, 14, 14.5, 16, 16, 16.5, 17, 17, 18.5, 18.5, 19.5) cm

2. 6 (6½, 6¾, 7¼, 7½, 7¾, 8¼, 8½, 9¼, 9½, 10, 10¾)"
   15 (16.5, 17, 18.5, 19, 19.5, 21, 21.5, 23.5, 24, 25.5, 27.5) cm

3. 6 (6½, 6¾, 7, 7½, 7¾, 8, 8½, 8¾, 9¼, 9½, 10)"
   15 (16.5, 17, 18, 19, 19.5, 20.5, 21.5, 22, 23.5, 24, 25.5) cm

4. 15½ (15¾, 16, 16¼, 16½, 16¾, 17, 17, 17½, 17½, 17½, 17½)"
   39.5 (40, 40.5, 41.5, 42, 42.5, 43, 43, 44.5, 44.5, 44.5, 44.5) cm

5. 15¼ (16, 17¼, 18, 19¼, 20, 21¼, 22, 23¼, 24, 25¼, 27¼)" hip and bust
   38.5 (40.5, 44, 45.5, 49, 51, 54, 56, 59, 61, 64, 69) cm

6. 13½ (14¼, 15½, 16¼, 17½, 18¼, 19½, 20¼, 21½, 22¼, 23½, 25½)" waist
   34.5 (36, 39.5, 41.5, 44.5, 46.5, 49.5, 51.5, 54.5, 56.5, 59.5, 65) cm

7. 8½"/21.5 cm

8. 21½ (22¼, 22¾, 23¼, 24, 24½, 25, 25½, 26¼, 26¾, 27, 27½)"
   54.5 (56.5, 58, 59, 61, 62, 63.5, 65, 66.5, 68, 68.5, 70) cm

9. 1½"/4 cm

10. 1"/2.5 cm

FRONT

11. 7¼ (7¼, 7½, 7¾, 8¼, 8¼, 8½, 8¾, 8¾, 9¼, 9¼, 9¾)"
    18.5 (18.5, 19, 19.5, 21, 21, 21.5, 22, 22, 23.5, 23.5, 25) cm

12. 6 (6½, 6¾, 7¼, 7½, 7¾, 8¼, 8½, 9¼, 9½, 10, 10¾)"
    15 (16.5, 17, 18.5, 19, 19.5, 21, 21.5, 23.5, 24, 25.5, 27.5) cm

13. 17¼ (18, 19¼, 20, 21¼, 22, 23¼, 24, 25¼, 26, 27¼, 29¼)"
    44 (45.5, 49, 51, 54, 56, 59, 61, 64, 66, 69, 74.5) cm

14. 13½ (13¾, 14, 14¼, 14½, 14¾, 15, 15, 15½, 15½, 15½, 15½)"
    34.5 (35, 35.5, 36, 37, 37.5, 38, 38, 39.5, 39.5, 39.5, 39.5) cm

15. 8 (8½, 8¾, 9, 9½, 9¾, 10, 10½, 10¾, 11¼, 11½, 12)"
    20.5 (21.5, 22, 23, 24, 25, 25.5, 26.5, 27.5, 28.5, 29, 30.5) cm

DROP SHOULDERS

Drop-shoulder sweaters are maybe the most well-known of all hand-knit sweaters. There's good reason for this: They're incredibly simple to knit and require only minimal shaping. This is great for stitch patterning, too—the drop-shoulder construction has given us the Guernsey, steeked Fair Isle pullovers and cardigans, and many heavily cabled designs.

Drop-shoulder sweaters went through a less-popular time in the 1990s and early 2000s, in my opinion largely due to their boxy nature and the yarn that was available then. But they're back with a vengeance—today, our yarn selection allows for some truly beautiful, wearable garments that weren't possible fifteen years ago.

In this chapter I've given you three silhouettes that reflect the current state of the drop-shoulder sweater. An incredibly soft, chainette construction yarn and simple ribbed detailing make the V-neck Cushy Pullover on page 89 one of the most comfortable hand-knits you'll ever wear; an alpaca-silk-wool blend with a nubby texture makes for a stylish, modern cardigan; and a traditional Guernsey is modernized with a crisp linen.

Much like hem-to-hem constructions, drop-shoulder sweaters need a lot of room for the fit to be comfortable. Make sure to take a look at the ease recommendations in each specific pattern before starting on your own.

I hope you'll give these drop-shoulder sweaters a try, and see just how comfortable and wearable they can be.

DIFFICULTY LEVEL:

DROP
SHOULDERS

PEBBLED CARDI MINI

Cardi buttons
on the
top only

Stitch pattern
on front and
back yoke

Pebbled Cardi Mini

Drop-shoulder sweaters offer great decorative opportunities, since the minimal shaping lets any stitch patterning stay intact. I've used a textured pattern on the top section of this adorable cardigan, which gives you the chance to practice all of the techniques you'll need in this chapter: picking up stitches, working buttonholes, working stitch patterning, and putting the sweater pieces together.

SIZES

To fit children 1 (2, 3/4, 5/6, 7/8, 9/10) year(s)

FINISHED MEASUREMENTS

21½ (24¾, 27, 28½, 31½, 32¼)" [54.5 (63, 68.5, 72.5, 80, 82) cm] chest, buttoned

NOTE: Cardigan is intended to be worn with 2–4" (5–10 cm) ease in the chest.

YARN

Berroco Vintage [52% acrylic, 40% wool, 8% nylon; 217 yards (198 meters)/100 grams]: 2 (3, 3, 4, 4, 5) hanks #5182 Black Currant

NEEDLES

One pair straight needles size US 7 (4.5 mm)

One 24" (60 cm) long circular needle size US 7 (4.5 mm), for Neckband

Change needle size if necessary to obtain correct gauge.

NOTIONS

Stitch markers; four ¾" (19 mm) buttons

GAUGE

20 sts and 28 rows = 4" (10 cm) in St st

STITCH PATTERNS

2X2 RIB

(multiple of 4 sts + 2; 1-row repeat)

ROW 1 (RS): *K2, p2; repeat from * to last 2 sts, k2.

ROW 2: Knit the knit sts and purl the purl sts as they face you. Repeat Row 2 for 2x2 Rib.

SEEDED RIB

(multiple of 4 sts + 3; 2-row repeat)

ROW 1 (RS): K3, *p1, k3; repeat from * to end.

ROW 2: K1, *p1, k3; repeat from * to last 2 sts, p1, k1. Repeat Rows 1 and 2 for Seeded Rib.

NOTES

Neck decreases should be worked to match the slant of the edge being shaped, as follows:

FOR LEFT-SLANTING EDGES:
On RS rows, k1, ssk, work to end; on WS rows, work to last 3 sts, ssp, p1.

FOR RIGHT-SLANTING EDGES:
On RS rows, work to last 3 sts, k2tog, k1; on WS rows, p1, p2tog, work to end.

BACK

CO 54 (62, 66, 74, 78, 82) sts. Begin 2x2 Rib; work even for 1½" (4 cm), ending with a WS row, and decreasing 1 st at end of final row—53 (61, 65, 73, 77, 81) sts remain.

Change to St st; work even until piece measures 9 (9¾, 10¼, 12½, 13½, 14½)" [23 (25, 26, 32, 34.5, 37) cm] from the beginning, ending with a WS row.

SHAPE ARMHOLES

NEXT ROW (RS): BO 5 sts, knit to end.

NEXT ROW: BO 5 sts, knit to end—43 (51, 55, 63, 67, 71) sts remain.

Change to Seeded Rib; work even until armhole measures 4 (4½, 5¼, 5½, 6, 7)" [10 (11.5, 13.5, 14, 15, 18) cm], ending with a WS row.

SHAPE NECK

NEXT ROW (RS): K10 (12, 13, 16, 17, 17) sts, join a second ball of yarn and BO center 23 (27, 29, 31, 33, 37) sts, knit to end. Working both sides at the same time, decrease 1 st at each neck edge once—9 (11, 12, 15, 16, 16) sts remain each shoulder. Work even until armhole measures 4½ (5, 5¾, 6, 6½, 7½)" [11.5 (12.5, 14.5, 15, 16.5, 19) cm], ending with a WS row.

SHAPE SHOULDERS

BO 5 (6, 6, 8, 8, 8) sts at each armhole edge once, then 4 (5, 6, 7, 8, 8) sts once.

RIGHT FRONT

CO 26 (30, 34, 34, 38, 38) sts. Begin 2x2 Rib; work even for

1½" (4 cm), ending with a WS row, and decreasing 1 st at end of final row—25 (29, 33, 33, 37, 37) sts remain.

Change to St st; work even until piece measures 9 (9¾, 10¼, 12½, 13½, 14½)" [23 (25, 26, 32, 34.5, 37) cm] from the beginning, ending with a RS row.

SHAPE ARMHOLE

NEXT ROW (WS): BO 5 sts, knit to end—20 (24, 28, 28, 32, 32) sts remain.

NEXT ROW: Work in Seeded Rib to last st, k1 (edge st, keep in St st). Work even until armhole measures 2¼ (2¼, 2¾, 3, 3¼, 4)" [5.5 (5.5, 7, 7.5, 8.5, 10) cm], ending with a WS row.

SHAPE NECK

BO 6 (7, 8, 7, 8, 8) sts at neck edge once, then decrease 1 st at neck edge every row 3 (3, 4, 3, 4, 4) times, then every RS row 2 (3, 4, 3, 4, 4) times—9 (11, 12, 15, 16, 16) sts remain. Work even until armhole measures 4½ (5, 5¾, 6, 6½, 7½)" [11.5 (12.5, 14.5, 15, 16.5, 19) cm], ending with a RS row.

SHAPE SHOULDER

BO 5 (6, 6, 8, 8, 8) sts at armhole edge once, then 4 (5, 6, 7, 8, 8) sts once.

LEFT FRONT

CO 26 (30, 34, 34, 38, 38) sts. Begin 2x2 Rib; work even for 1½" (4 cm), ending with a WS row, and decreasing 1 st at beginning of final row—25 (29, 33, 33, 37, 37) sts remain.

Change to St st; work even until piece measures 9 (9¾, 10¼, 12½, 13½, 14½)" [23 (25, 26, 32, 34.5, 37) cm] from the beginning, ending with a WS row.

SHAPE ARMHOLES

NEXT ROW (RS): BO 5 sts, knit to end—20 (24, 28, 28, 32, 32) sts. Knit 1 row.

NEXT ROW (RS): K1 (edge st, keep in St st), work in Seeded Rib to end. Work even until armhole measures 2¼ (2¼, 2¾, 3, 3¼, 4)" [5.5 (5.5, 7, 7.5, 8.5, 10) cm], ending with a RS row.

SHAPE NECK

NEXT ROW (WS): BO 6 (7, 8, 7, 8, 8) sts at neck edge once, then decrease 1 st at neck edge every row 3 (3, 4, 3, 4, 4) times, then every RS row 2 (3, 4, 3, 4, 4) times—9 (11, 12, 15, 16, 16) sts remain. Work even until armhole measures 4½ (5, 5¾, 6, 6½, 7½)" [11.5 (12.5, 14.5, 15, 16.5, 19) cm], ending with a WS row.

SHAPE SHOULDER

BO 5 (6, 6, 8, 8, 8) sts at armhole edge once, then 4 (5, 6, 7, 8, 8) sts once.

SLEEVES

CO 30 (34, 38, 38, 42, 46) sts. Begin 2x2 Rib; work even for 1" (2.5 cm), ending with a WS row.

Change to St st; work even for 2 rows.

SHAPE SLEEVE

INCREASE ROW (RS): Increase 2 sts this row, every 6 rows 7 (4, 7, 4, 4, 11) times, then every 0 (8, 8, 8, 8, 8) rows 0 (3, 2, 6, 7, 3) times, as follows: K2, M1R, knit to last 2 sts, M1L, k2—46 (50, 58, 60, 66, 76) sts. Work even until piece measures 9 (10, 11½, 13½, 14½, 16)" [23 (25.5, 29, 34.5, 37, 40.5) cm] from the beginning, ending with a WS row.
BO all sts.

FINISHING

Block as desired. Sew shoulder seams. Sew in Sleeves; sew side and Sleeve seams.

BUTTON BAND

With RS facing, and beginning at Left Front neck edge, pick up and knit 3 sts for every 4 rows along Front edge.
Knit 6 rows.
BO all sts.

BUTTONHOLE BAND

With RS facing, and beginning at lower Right Front edge, pick up and knit 3 sts for every 4 rows along Front edge. Place markers for 3 buttonholes, the first approximately 1½" (4 cm) below neck edge, and the next two 1¾" (4.5 cm) and 3½" (9 cm) below the first.
Knit 2 rows.
BUTTONHOLE ROW (WS): [Knit to 2 sts before marker, BO 3 sts] 3 times, knit to end.
NEXT ROW: Knit, CO 3 sts over BO sts from previous row.
Knit 3 rows.
BO all sts.

NECKBAND

With RS facing, using circular needle, and beginning at edge of Right Front band, pick up and knit sts around neck shaping, picking up 1 st for every BO st, 3 sts for every 4 rows along vertical edges, and 4 sts for every 5 rows along diagonal edges.
Knit 1 row.
BUTTONHOLE ROW (RS): K2, BO 3 sts, knit to end.
NEXT ROW: Knit, CO 3 sts over BO sts from previous row.
Knit 2 rows.
BO all sts.

Sew buttons opposite buttonholes.

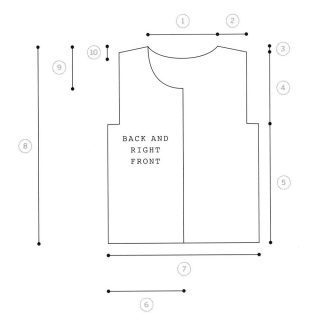

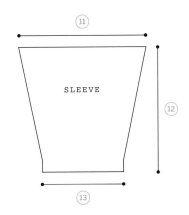

BACK AND RIGHT FRONT

1 5 (5¾, 6¼, 6½, 7, 7¾)"
   12.5 (14.5, 16, 16.5, 18, 19.5) cm

2 1¾ (2¼, 2½, 3, 3¼, 3¼)"
   4.5 (5.5, 6.5, 7.5, 8.5, 8.5) cm

3 ½"/1.5 cm

4 4½ (5, 5¾, 6, 6½, 7½)"
   11.5 (12.5, 14.5, 15, 16.5, 19) cm

5 9 (9¾, 10¼, 12½, 13½, 14½)"
   23 (25, 26, 32, 34.5, 37) cm

6 5 (5¾, 6½, 6½, 7½, 7½)"
   12.5 (14.5, 16.5, 16.5, 19, 19) cm

7 10½ (12¼, 13, 14½, 15½, 16¼)"
   26.5 (31, 33, 37, 39.5, 41.5) cm

8 14 (15¼, 16½, 19, 20½, 22½)"
   35.5 (38.5, 42, 48.5, 52, 57) cm

9 2¾ (3¼, 3½, 3½, 3¾, 4)"
   7 (8.5, 9, 9, 9.5, 10) cm

10 1"/2.5 cm

SLEEVE

11 9¼ (10, 11½, 12, 13¼, 15¼)"
   23.5 (25.5, 29, 30.5, 33.5, 38.5) cm

12 9 (10, 11½, 13½, 14½, 16)"
   23 (25.5, 29, 34.5, 37, 40.5) cm

13 6 (6¾, 7½, 7½, 8½, 9¼)"
   15 (17, 19, 19, 21.5, 23.5) cm

DIFFICULTY LEVEL:

DROP SHOULDERS

CUSHY PULLOVER

Modern silhouette:
slimmer arms,
looser body

Zero shaping

Cushy Pullover

As anyone who was knitting drop-shoulder sweaters with me in the 1980s can attest, drop shoulder + hand knitting doesn't always equal a great idea. The biggest key to making these sweaters attractive and comfortable to wear lies in their fabric, which needs to have enough movement and "crushability" to comfortably lie under the arms. This pullover has a more modern fit with slimmer arms, so to avoid a constraining fit, choose a size with at least 8" (20.5 cm) of positive ease at the bust. Sweaters this oversized need a lot of stability around the neck, so keep your neck edging nice and firm!

FINISHED MEASUREMENTS

38 (40, 42, 44, 46, 48, 50, 52, 54, 56, 60, 64)" [96.5 (101.5, 106.5, 112, 117, 122, 127, 132, 137, 142, 152.5, 162.5) cm] bust

NOTE: Pullover is intended to be worn with 8–12" (20.5–30.5 cm) ease in the bust.

YARN

Shibui Knits Maai [70% super-baby alpaca/30% fine merino wool; 175 yards (160 meters); 50 grams]: 7 (7, 8, 8, 9, 9, 10, 10, 11, 11, 12, 13) skeins Fjord

NEEDLES

One pair straight needles size US 6 (4 mm)

One 24" (60 cm) long circular needle size US 6 (4 mm), for Neckband

Change needle size if necessary to obtain correct gauge.

NOTIONS

Stitch markers; removable marker

GAUGE

24 sts and 32 rows = 4" (10 cm) in St st

STITCH PATTERN

1X1 RIB

(even number of sts; 1-row repeat)

ALL ROWS: *K1, p1; repeat from * to end.

NOTES

Neck decreases should be worked to match the slant of the edge being shaped, as follows:

FOR LEFT-SLANTING EDGES: On RS rows, k1, ssk, work to end; on WS rows, work to last 3 sts, ssp, p1.

FOR RIGHT-SLANTING EDGES: On RS rows, work to last 3 sts, k2tog, k1; on WS rows, p1, p2tog, work to end.

BACK

CO 114 (120, 126, 132, 138, 144, 150, 156, 162, 168, 180, 192) sts. Begin 1x1 Rib; work even for 1½" (4 cm), ending with a RS row.

NEXT ROW (RS): Work 12 (12, 12, 14, 14, 14, 16, 16, 16, 18, 18, 18) sts in rib as established, pm, knit to last 12 (12, 12, 14, 14, 14, 16, 16, 16, 18, 18, 18) sts, pm, work in rib as established to end. Work even, working sts between markers in St st, and remaining sts in rib, until piece measures 22½ (22¾, 23, 23½, 24, 24½, 25, 25½, 26, 26½, 27, 27)" [57 (58, 58.5, 59.5, 61, 62, 63.5, 65, 66, 67.5, 68.5, 68.5) cm] from the beginning, ending with a WS row.

SHAPE NECK

NEXT ROW (RS): Work 30 (33, 35, 36, 38, 39, 41, 44, 45, 48, 53, 59) sts, join a second ball of yarn and BO center 54 (54, 56, 60, 62, 66, 68, 68, 72, 72, 74, 74) sts, work to end. Working both sides at the same time, decrease 1 st at each neck edge every RS row twice—28 (31, 33, 34, 36, 37, 39, 42, 43, 46, 51, 57) sts remain each shoulder. Work even until piece measures 23½ (23¾, 24, 24½, 25, 25½, 26, 26½, 27, 27½, 28, 28)" [59.5 (60.5, 61, 62, 63.5, 65, 66, 67.5, 68.5, 70, 71, 71) cm] from the beginning, ending with a WS row.

SHAPE SHOULDERS

BO 14 (16, 17, 17, 18, 19, 20, 21, 22, 23, 26, 29) sts at each armhole edge once, then 14 (15, 16, 17, 18, 18, 19, 21, 21, 23, 25, 28) sts once.

FRONT

Work as for Back until piece measures 16¼ (16¼, 16, 16, 16, 16, 16, 16, 16, 16½, 17, 17)" [41.5 (41.5, 40.5, 40.5, 40.5, 40.5, 40.5, 40.5, 40.5, 42, 43, 43) cm] from the beginning, ending with a RS row.

SHAPE NECK

NEXT ROW (RS): Work 54 (57, 60, 63, 66, 69, 72, 75, 78, 81, 87, 93) sts, k2tog, k1, join a second ball of yarn, k1, ssk, work to end. Working both sides at the same time, decrease 1 st at each neck edge every RS row 28 (28, 29, 31, 32, 34, 35, 35, 37, 37, 38, 38) times—28 (31, 33, 34, 36, 37, 39, 42, 43, 46, 51, 57) sts remain each shoulder. Work even until piece measures 23½ (23¾, 24, 24½, 25, 25½, 26, 26½, 27, 27½, 28, 28)" [59.5 (60.5, 61, 62, 63.5, 65, 66, 67.5, 68.5, 70, 71, 71) cm] from the beginning, ending with a WS row.

SHAPE SHOULDERS

BO 14 (16, 17, 17, 18, 19, 20, 21, 22, 23, 26, 29) sts at each armhole edge once, then 14 (15, 16, 17, 18, 18, 19, 21, 21, 23, 25, 28) sts once.

SLEEVES

CO 54 (54, 58, 58, 58, 60, 60, 64, 66, 70, 72, 78) sts. Begin 1x1 Rib; work even for 2½" (6.5 cm), ending with a WS row.

SHAPE SLEEVE

Note: You will change to St st while working Sleeve shaping; please read entire section through before beginning.

INCREASE ROW (RS): Working new sts in pattern, increase 1 st each side this row, then every 10 (8, 6, 6, 4, 4, 4, 2, 2, 2, 4) rows 1 (8, 1, 11, 5, 11, 18, 21, 1, 3, 5, 25) time(s), then every 12 (10, 8, 8, 6, 6, 6, 6, 4, 4, 4, 6) rows 7 (3, 11, 4, 13, 9, 5, 3, 25, 24, 24, 1) time(s), as follows: K1, increase 1 st (M1R or M1P to keep in pattern), work to last st, increase 1 st (M1L or M1P to keep in pattern), k1—72 (78, 84, 90, 96, 102, 108, 114, 120, 126, 132, 132) sts. AT THE SAME TIME, when piece measures 6" (15 cm) from the beginning, change to St st across all sts. Work even until piece measures 15½ (15½, 15½, 16, 16, 16, 16½, 16½, 16½, 16½, 17, 17)" [39.5 (39.5, 39.5, 40.5, 40.5, 40.5, 42, 42, 42, 42, 43, 43) cm] from the beginning, ending with a WS row.
BO all sts.

FINISHING

Block pieces as desired. Sew shoulder seams. Place markers 6 (6½, 7, 7½, 8, 8½, 9, 9½, 10, 10½, 11, 11)" [15 (16.5, 18, 19, 20.5, 21.5, 23, 24, 25.5, 26.5, 28, 28) cm] down from shoulder seams on Front and Back. Sew Sleeves between markers. Sew side and Sleeve seams.

NECKBAND

With RS facing, using circular needle and beginning at right Back shoulder, pick up and knit sts around neck opening, picking up 1 st for every BO st, 2 sts for every 3 rows along vertical edges, 3 sts for every 4 rows along diagonal edges, and 1 st at base of center Front neck. End with an even number of sts, making sure that center Front neck st is an odd number from beginning of rnd. Join for working in the rnd; pm for beginning of rnd. Place removable marker on center Front st. Begin 1x1 Rib; work 1 rnd.

DECREASE RND: Decrease 2 sts this rnd, then every other rnd until Neckband measures ¾" (2 cm), as follows: Work to 1 st before marked center Front st, s2kp2, work to end.
BO all sts in pattern.

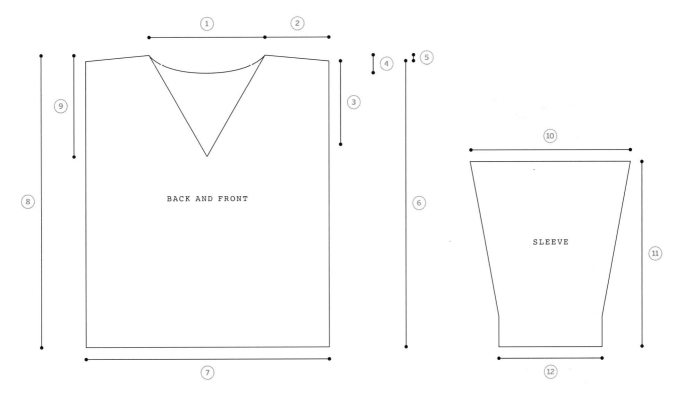

BACK AND FRONT

1 9¾ (9¾, 10, 10¾, 11, 11¾, 12, 12, 12¾, 12¾, 13, 13)"
   25 (25, 25.5, 27.5, 28, 30, 30.5, 30.5, 32.5, 32.5, 33, 33) cm

2 4¾ (5¼, 5½, 5¾, 6, 6¼, 6½, 7, 7¼, 7¾, 8½, 9½)"
   12 (13.5, 14, 14.5, 15, 16, 16.5, 18, 18.5, 19.5, 21.5, 24) cm

3 6 (6½, 7, 7½, 8, 8½, 9, 9½, 10, 10½, 11, 11)"
   15 (16.5, 18, 19, 20.5, 21.5, 23, 24, 25.5, 26.5, 28, 28) cm

4 1½"/4 cm

5 ½"/1.5 cm

6 23½ (23¾, 24, 24½, 25, 25½, 26, 26½, 27, 27½, 28, 28)"
   59.5 (60.5, 61, 62, 63.5, 65, 66, 67.5, 68.5, 70, 71, 71) cm

7 19 (20, 21, 22, 23, 24, 25, 26, 27, 28, 30, 32)"
   48.5 (51, 53.5, 56, 58.5, 61, 63.5, 66, 68.5, 71, 76, 81.5) cm

8 24 (24¼, 24½, 25, 25½, 26, 26½, 27, 27½, 28, 28½, 28½)"
   61 (61.5, 62, 63.5, 65, 66, 67.5, 68.5, 70, 71, 72.5, 72.5) cm

9 7¾ (8, 8½, 9, 9½, 10, 10½, 11, 11½, 11½, 11½, 11½)"
   19.5 (20.5, 21.5, 23, 24, 25.5, 26.5, 28, 29, 29, 29, 29) cm

SLEEVE

10 12 (13, 14, 15, 16, 17, 18, 19, 20, 21, 22, 22)"
    30.5 (33, 35.5, 38, 40.5, 43, 45.5, 48.5, 51, 53.5, 56, 56) cm

11 15½ (15½, 15½, 16, 16, 16, 16½, 16½, 16½, 16½, 17, 17)"
    39.5 (39.5, 39.5, 40.5, 40.5, 40.5, 42, 42, 42, 42, 43, 43) cm

12 8¼ (8¼, 9, 9, 9, 9¼, 9¼, 9¾, 10¼, 10¾, 11, 12)"
    21 (21, 23, 23, 23, 23.5, 23.5, 25, 26, 27.5, 28, 30.5) cm

DIFFICULTY LEVEL:

DROP SHOULDERS

REVIVE CARDIGAN

Cardigan
front ribbing
continues to form
back neck trim

Dart-style waist
shaping on back

Revive Cardigan

This cardigan is exceptionally comfortable, and represents some of the best of what I think drop-shoulder sweaters can be: The fit is exactly like the sweater I was knitting 20 years ago, but the materials and some slight waist shaping on the back turn it into a much more pleasurable garment to knit and wear. I chose an alpaca-silk-wool blend for this garment, with muted, neutral colors and a slightly nubby texture. The fit should be generous, but not exaggerated—you want to have room to move, without the sweater falling off your body.

FINISHED MEASUREMENTS
36½ (38¼, 40¼, 41½, 43½, 45¾, 47¼, 48½, 50½, 52¾, 56, 60¼)" [92.5 (97, 102, 105.5, 110.5, 116, 120, 123, 128.5, 134, 142, 153) cm] bust

NOTE: Cardigan is intended to be worn with 4" (10 cm) ease in the bust, with the Fronts open.

YARN
The Fibre Company Acadia [60% merino wool/20% baby alpaca/20% silk; 145 yards (133 meters)/50 grams]: 7 (8, 8, 9, 9, 10, 11, 11, 12, 13, 13, 14) hanks Moraine

NEEDLES
One pair straight needles size US 6 (4 mm)

Change needle size if necessary to obtain correct gauge.

NOTIONS
Stitch markers; stitch holders

GAUGE
22 sts and 32 rows = 4" (10 cm) in St st

STITCH PATTERN
2X2 RIB
(multiple of 4 sts + 2; 1-row repeat)
ROW 1 (RS): *K2, p2; repeat from * to last 2 sts, k2.
ROW 2: Knit the knit sts and purl the purl sts as they face you. Repeat Row 2 for 2x2 Rib.

BACK

CO 94 (102, 106, 110, 118, 122, 130, 134, 138, 146, 154, 166) sts. Begin 2x2 Rib; work even for 3" (7.5 cm), ending with a WS row.

Change to St st; work even for 3 rows, decreasing 0 (2, 0, 0, 2, 0, 2, 2, 0, 2, 0, 0) sts evenly on first row—94 (100, 106, 110, 116, 122, 128, 132, 138, 144, 154, 166) sts remain.

NEXT ROW (WS): P31 (33, 35, 36, 38, 40, 42, 44, 46, 48, 51, 55), pm, p32 (34, 36, 38, 40, 42, 44, 44, 46, 48, 52, 56) sts, pm, purl to end.

SHAPE WAIST

DECREASE ROW (RS): Decrease 2 sts this row, then every 8 rows 3 times, as follows: Knit to 2 sts before first marker, ssk, sm, knit to next marker, sm, k2tog, knit to end—86 (92, 98, 102, 108, 114, 120, 124, 130, 136, 146, 158) sts remain. Work even until piece measures 8½" (21.5 cm) from the beginning, ending with a WS row.

SHAPE BUST

INCREASE ROW (RS): Increase 2 sts this row, then every 8 rows 3 times, as follows: Knit to first marker, M1R, sm, knit to next marker, sm, M1L, knit to end—94 (100, 106, 110, 116, 122, 128, 132, 138, 144, 154, 166) sts. Work even, removing markers on first row, until piece measures 14½ (14¾, 14¾, 14¾, 15, 15, 15, 15, 15, 15¼, 15½, 15½)" [37 (37.5, 37.5, 37.5, 38, 38, 38, 38, 38, 38.5, 39.5, 39.5) cm] from the beginning, ending with a WS row.

SHAPE ARMHOLES

BO 6 sts at beginning of next 2 rows—82 (88, 94, 98, 104, 110, 116, 120, 126, 132, 142, 154) sts remain. Work even until armhole measures 7 (7½, 8, 8½, 9, 9½, 10, 10½, 11, 11¼, 11½, 12)" [18 (19, 20.5, 21.5, 23, 24, 25.5, 26.5, 28, 28.5, 29, 30.5) cm], ending with a WS row.

SHAPE NECK

NEXT ROW (RS): K26 (28, 31, 32, 34, 37, 39, 40, 43, 45, 49, 55), join a second ball of yarn and BO center 30 (32, 32, 34, 36, 36, 38, 40, 40, 42, 44, 44) sts, knit to end. Working both sides at the same time, decrease 1 st at each neck edge every RS row twice, as follows: On right neck edge, knit to last 3 sts, k2tog, k1; on left neck edge, k1, ssk, knit to end—24 (26, 29, 30, 32, 35, 37, 38, 41, 43, 47, 53) sts remain each shoulder. Work even until armhole measures 8 (8½, 9, 9½, 10, 10½, 11, 11½, 12, 12¼, 12½, 13)" [20.5 (21.5, 23, 24, 25.5, 26.5, 28, 29, 30.5, 31, 32, 33) cm], ending with a WS row.

SHAPE SHOULDERS

BO 12 (13, 15, 15, 16, 18, 19, 19, 21, 22, 24, 27) sts at each armhole edge once, then 12 (13, 14, 15, 16, 17, 18, 19, 20, 21, 23, 26) sts once.

RIGHT FRONT

CO 54 (54, 58, 58, 62, 66, 66, 66, 70, 74, 78, 82) sts. Begin 2x2 Rib; work even for 3" (7.5 cm), ending with a WS row.

NEXT ROW (RS): Work 22 sts in 2x2 Rib, pm, knit to end, decreasing 2 (0, 1, 0, 2, 3, 1, 0, 1, 3, 3, 1) st(s) evenly to end—52 (54, 57, 58, 60, 63, 65, 66, 69, 71, 75, 81) sts remain. Work even, working 22 neck edge sts in Rib and remaining sts in St st, until piece measures 14½ (14¾, 14¾, 14¾, 15, 15, 15, 15, 15, 15¼, 15½, 15½)" [37 (37.5, 37.5, 37.5, 38, 38, 38, 38, 38, 38.5, 39.5, 39.5) cm] from the beginning, ending with a RS row.

SHAPE ARMHOLE

NEXT ROW (WS): BO 6 sts, work to end—46 (48, 51, 52, 54, 57, 59, 60, 63, 65, 69, 75) sts remain. Work even until armhole measures 8 (8½, 9, 9½, 10, 10½, 11, 11½, 12, 12¼, 12½, 13)" [20.5 (21.5, 23, 24, 25.5, 26.5, 28, 29, 30.5, 31, 32, 33) cm], ending with a RS row.

SHAPE SHOULDER

BO 12 (13, 15, 15, 16, 18, 19, 19, 21, 22, 24, 27) sts at armhole edge once, then 12 (13, 14, 15, 16, 17, 18, 19, 20, 21, 23, 26) sts once—22 sts remain. Place sts on a holder.

LEFT FRONT

CO 54 (54, 58, 58, 62, 66, 66, 66, 70, 74, 78, 82) sts. Begin 2x2 Rib; work even for 3" (7.5 cm), ending with a WS row.

NEXT ROW (RS): Work to last 22 sts, decreasing 2 (0, 1, 0, 2, 3, 1, 0, 1, 3, 3, 1) st(s) evenly, pm, work in 2x2 Rib to end—52 (54, 57, 58, 60, 63, 65, 66, 69, 71, 75, 81) sts remain. Work even, working 22 neck edge sts in Rib and remaining sts in St st, until piece measures 14½ (14¾, 14¾, 14¾, 15, 15, 15, 15, 15, 15¼, 15½, 15½)" [37 (37.5, 37.5, 37.5, 38, 38, 38, 38, 38, 38.5, 39.5, 39.5) cm] from the beginning, ending with a WS row.

SHAPE ARMHOLE

NEXT ROW (RS): BO 6 sts, work to end—46 (48, 51, 52, 54, 57, 59, 60, 63, 65, 69, 75) sts remain. Work even until armhole measures 8 (8½, 9, 9½, 10, 10½, 11, 11½, 12, 12¼, 12½, 13)" [20.5 (21.5, 23, 24, 25.5, 26.5, 28, 29, 30.5, 31, 32, 33) cm], ending with a WS row.

SHAPE SHOULDER

BO 12 (13, 15, 15, 16, 18, 19, 19, 21, 22, 24, 27) sts at armhole edge once, then 12 (13, 14, 15, 16, 17, 18, 19, 20, 21, 23, 26) sts once—22 sts remain. Place sts on a holder.

SLEEVES

CO 58 (58, 58, 58, 62, 66, 66, 74, 78, 86, 90, 94) sts. Begin 2x2 Rib; work even for 2" (5 cm), ending with a WS row.

BEYOND THE BOXY SWEATSHIRT

Bonus Lesson

DROP-SHOULDER SWEATERS are enjoying a renaissance, and with good reason: They're easy to knit, and with the current selection of drapey, fluid yarns (see page 79 for more on this) they're super comfortable to wear.

There are a few "tech tips" that can keep your drop-shoulder sweaters comfortable to wear and not too boxy:

WAIST SHAPING. Drop-shoulder sweaters are a great place to experiment with adding a little waist shaping (page 53) on the back of your garment. The Revive Cardigan is written this way already, so check out page 93 for an idea of how it's done. Generally, you'll want to remove somewhere between 1 and 2" (2.5 and 5 cm) of stitches from the back of your sweater, and then add them back in, centered around your waist. Work the shaping away from the side seams to facilitate seaming.

TRADITIONALLY FIT DROP SHOULDERS. Any drop-shoulder sweater has a bicep measurement that's equal to twice the sweater's armhole depth—it's how the sweater is sewn together. In a more traditional fit like in the Revive Cardigan and Beachwalker Pullover, the armholes are generous—a couple of inches deeper, on average, than a set-in-sleeve armhole depth. For these sweaters, you'll need around 4 to 8" (10 to 20.5 cm) of positive ease in the bust of the sweater to ensure that the arms fall properly on your body. Any snugger than that and the armholes will be constricting.

MODERN DROP SHOULDERS. There's a new trend in drop-shoulder sweaters to have fairly snug arms that fit close to your own arm, with minimal positive ease in the bicep. This means that the armhole depth of the sweaters will be quite small—often less than a typical set-in-sleeve armhole. To avoid constricting, uncomfortable arms, you'll need the point where the sleeve joins the body to hit further down on your arm, perhaps all the way to the elbow. To achieve a good fit with a sweater like this (the Cushy Pullover is an example), choose a size with at least 8" (20.5 cm) of positive ease in the bust.

SHAPE SLEEVE

Note: You will change to St st while working Sleeve shaping; please read entire section through before beginning.

INCREASE ROW (RS): Working new sts in pattern, increase 1 st each side this row, then every 4 (2, 2, 2, 2, 2, 2, 2, 2, 2, 2, 2) rows 12 (4, 10, 12, 12, 14, 16, 14, 14, 8, 6, 8) times, then every 6 (4, 4, 4, 4, 4, 4, 4, 4, 4, 4) rows 2 (13, 10, 11, 11, 10, 11, 12, 12, 16, 17, 16) times, as follows: K1, increase 1 st (M1R or M1P to keep in pattern), work to last st, increase 1 st (M1L or M1P to keep in pattern), k1—88 (94, 100, 106, 110, 116, 122, 128, 132, 136, 138, 144) sts. AT THE SAME TIME, when piece measures 3" (7.5 cm) from the beginning, change to St st across all sts. Work even until piece measures 12 (12, 12, 13, 13, 13, 14, 14, 14, 14½, 14½, 14½)" [30.5 (30.5, 30.5, 33, 33, 33, 35.5, 35.5, 35.5, 37, 37, 37) cm] from the beginning, ending with a WS row. BO all sts.

FINISHING

Block piece as desired. Sew shoulder seams. Sew in Sleeves; sew side and Sleeve seams.

BACK COLLAR

With RS facing, transfer Right Front sts to needle. Join yarn at shoulder edge and work in pattern as established until piece, when slightly stretched, reaches center Back neck. BO all sts. Repeat for Left Front sts. Sew side edges to Back neck edge; sew BO edges together.

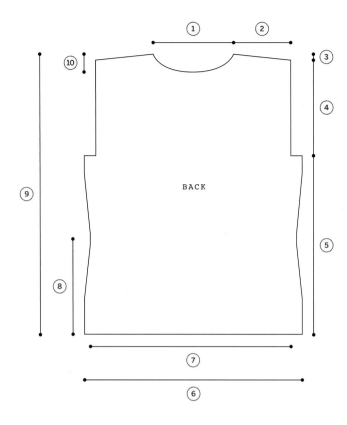

BACK

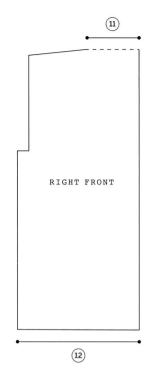

RIGHT FRONT

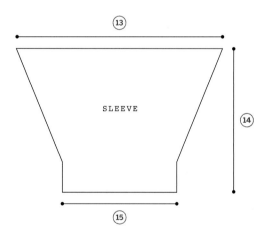

SLEEVE

BACK

1 6¼ (6½, 6½, 7, 7¼, 7¼, 7¾, 8, 8, 8¼, 8¾, 8¾)"
16 (16.5, 16.5, 18, 18.5, 18.5, 19.5, 20.5, 20.5, 21, 22, 22) cm

2 4¼ (4¾, 5¼, 5½, 5¾, 6¼, 6¾, 7, 7½, 7¾, 8½, 9¾)"
11 (12, 13.5, 14, 14.5, 16, 17, 18, 19, 19.5, 21.5, 25) cm

3 ½"/1.5 cm

4 8 (8½, 9, 9½, 10, 10½, 11, 11½, 12, 12¼, 12½, 13)"
20.5 (21.5, 23, 24, 25.5, 26.5, 28, 29, 30.5, 31, 32, 33) cm

5 14½ (14¾, 14¾, 14¾, 15, 15, 15, 15, 15, 15¼, 15½, 15½)"
37 (37.5, 37.5, 37.5, 38, 38, 38, 38, 38, 38.5, 39.5, 39.5) cm

6 17 (18¼, 19¼, 20, 21, 22¼, 23¼, 24, 25, 26¼, 28, 30¼)" hip and bust
43 (46.5, 49, 51, 53.5, 56.5, 59, 61, 63.5, 66.5, 71, 77) cm

7 15¾ (16¾, 17¾, 18½, 19¾, 20¾, 21¾, 22½, 23¾, 24¾, 26½, 28¾)" waist
40 (42.5, 45, 47, 50, 52.5, 55, 57, 60.5, 63, 67.5, 73) cm

8 8"/20.5 cm

9 23 (23¾, 24¼, 24¾, 25½, 26, 26½, 27, 27½, 28, 28½, 29)"
58.5 (60.5, 61.5, 63, 65, 66, 67.5, 68.5, 70, 71, 72.5, 73.5) cm

10 1½"/4 cm

RIGHT FRONT

11 4¼"/11 cm

12 9¾ (10, 10½, 10¾, 11¼, 11¾, 12, 12¼, 12¾, 13¼, 14, 15)"
25 (25.5, 26.5, 27.5, 28.5, 30, 30.5, 31, 32.5, 33.5, 35.5, 38) cm

SLEEVE

13 16 (17, 18¼, 19¼, 20, 21, 22¼, 23¼, 24, 24¾, 25, 26¼)"
40.5 (43, 46.5, 49, 51, 53.5, 56.5, 59, 61, 63, 63.5, 66.5) cm

14 12 (12, 12, 13, 13, 13, 14, 14, 14, 14½, 14½, 14½)"
30.5 (30.5, 30.5, 33, 33, 33, 35.5, 35.5, 35.5, 37, 37, 37) cm

15 10½ (10½, 10½, 10½, 11¼, 12, 12, 13½, 14¼, 15¾, 16¼, 17)"
26.5 (26.5, 26.5, 26.5, 28.5, 30.5, 30.5, 34.5, 36, 40, 41.5, 43) cm

Beachwalker

Sometimes, the only update a traditional garment needs is a new yarn choice. This classic Guernsey-inspired sweater is completely old-school in stitch patterning and construction. But it feels new and fresh, and decidedly unlike sweaters of old, thanks to the 100% linen yarn I used. Working with linen yarn can take some getting used to (translation: make a large swatch!), but the resulting garment is more than worth an unusual knitting experience. It softens with wear, has incredible sheen, and drapes beautifully, making a sweater that's *exactly* the kind of thing you'd want to throw on for a summer-night walk on the beach.

FINISHED MEASUREMENTS

33¾ (37, 38¾, 40¼, 41¾, 45, 46¾, 48¼, 49¾, 53, 56¼, 61)" [85.5 (94, 98.5, 102, 106, 114.5, 118.5, 122.5, 126.5, 134.5, 143, 155) cm] bust

NOTE: Pullover is intended to be worn with 4" (10 cm) ease in the bust.

YARN

Rowan Pure Linen [100% linen; 142 yards (130 meters); 50 grams]: 7 (7, 8, 8, 9, 9, 10, 10, 11, 12, 12, 13) skeins #395 Arizona

NEEDLES

One pair straight needles size US 6 (4 mm)

One 24" (60 cm) long circular needle size US 6 (4 mm), for Turtleneck

One 24" (60 cm) long circular needle size US 7 (4.5 mm), for Turtleneck

Change needle size if necessary to obtain correct gauge.

NOTIONS

Stitch markers

GAUGE

20 sts and 32 rows = 4" (10 cm) in St st

STITCH PATTERNS

2X2 RIB FLAT

(multiple of 4 sts + 2; 1-row repeat)

ROW 1 (RS): *K2, p2; repeat from * to last 2 sts, k2.

ROW 2: Knit the knit sts and purl the purl sts as they face you. Repeat Row 2 for 2x2 Rib Flat.

2X2 RIB IN THE RND

(multiple of 4 sts; 1-row repeat)

ALL RNDS: *K2, p2; repeat from * to end.

MOSS STITCH

(even number of sts; 4-row repeat)

ROW 1 (RS): *K1, p1; repeat from * to end.

ROW 2: Knit the knit sts and purl the purl sts as they face you.

ROW 3: *P1, k1; repeat from * to end.

ROW 4: Repeat Row 2. Repeat Rows 1–4 for Moss Stitch.

NOTES

Neck decreases should be worked to match the slant of the edge being shaped, as follows:

FOR LEFT-SLANTING EDGES: On RS rows, k1, ssk, work to end; on WS rows, work to last 3 sts, ssp, p1.

FOR RIGHT-SLANTING EDGES: On RS rows, work to last 3 sts, k2tog, k1; on WS rows, p1, p2tog, work to end.

You may work Chevron Panel, Jacob's Ladder, and Diamond Panel from text or Chart.

BACK

CO 86 (94, 98, 102, 106, 114, 118, 122, 126, 134, 142, 154) sts. Begin 2x2 Rib Flat; work even for 2½" (6.5 cm), ending with a RS row.

NEXT ROW (WS): Knit, decreasing 2 sts evenly across—84 (92, 96, 100, 104, 112, 116, 120, 124, 132, 140, 152) sts remain.

Change to St st; work even until piece measures 3½" (9 cm) from the beginning, ending with a RS row.

NEXT ROW (WS): P28 (30, 32, 33, 34, 37, 38, 40, 41, 44, 46, 50), pm, p28 (32, 32, 34, 36, 38, 40, 40, 42, 44, 48, 52), pm, purl to end.

DIFFICULTY LEVEL:

DROP SHOULDERS

BEACHWALKER

Traditional yoke patterning

100% linen yarn for a crisp, updated feel

SHAPE WAIST

DECREASE ROW (RS): Decrease 2 sts this row, then every 10 rows 3 times, as follows: Knit to 2 sts before first marker, ssk, sm, knit to next marker, sm, k2tog, knit to end—76 (84, 88, 92, 96, 104, 108, 112, 116, 124, 132, 144) sts remain. Work even until piece measures 8" (20.5 cm) from the beginning, ending with a WS row.

SHAPE BUST

INCREASE ROW (RS): Increase 2 sts this row, then every 10 rows 3 times, as follows: Knit to first marker, M1R, sm, knit to next marker, sm, M1L, knit to end—84 (92, 96, 100, 104, 112, 116, 120, 124, 132, 140, 152) sts remain. Work even, removing markers on first row, until piece measures 14½ (14½, 15, 14¾, 15, 15, 15, 15, 15, 15¼, 15½, 15)" [37 (37, 38, 37.5, 38, 38, 38, 38, 38, 38.5, 39.5, 38) cm from the beginning, ending with a WS row.

SHAPE ARMHOLES

BO 5 sts at beginning of next 2 rows—74 (82, 86, 90, 94, 102, 106, 110, 114, 122, 130, 142) sts remain. Work even until piece measures 20½ (21, 22, 22¼, 23, 23½, 24, 24½, 25, 25½, 26, 26)" [52 (53.5, 56, 56.5, 58.5, 59.5, 61, 62, 63.5, 65, 66, 66) cm from the beginning, ending with a WS row.

SHAPE NECK

NEXT ROW (RS): K20 (23, 25, 26, 27, 31, 32, 33, 35, 38, 42, 46), join a second ball of yarn and BO center 34 (36, 36, 38, 40, 40, 42, 44, 44, 46, 46, 50) sts, knit to end. Working both sides at the same time, decrease 1 st at each neck edge every RS row twice—18 (21, 23, 24, 25, 29, 30, 31, 33, 36, 40, 44) sts remain each shoulder. Work even until armhole measures 7 (7½, 8, 8½, 9, 9½, 10, 10½, 11, 11¼, 11½, 12)" [18 (19, 20.5, 21.5, 23, 24, 25.5, 26.5, 28, 28.5, 29, 30.5) cm, ending with a WS row.

SHAPE SHOULDERS

BO 9 (11, 12, 12, 13, 15, 15, 16, 17, 18, 20, 22) sts at each armhole edge once, then 9 (10, 11, 12, 12, 14, 15, 15, 16, 18, 20, 22) sts once.

FRONT

CO 86 (94, 98, 102, 106, 114, 118, 122, 126, 134, 142, 154) sts. Begin 2x2 Rib Flat; work even for 2½" (6.5 cm), ending with a RS row.

NEXT ROW (WS): Knit, decreasing 1 st—85 (93, 97, 101, 105, 113, 117, 121, 125, 133, 141, 153) sts remain.

Change to St st; work even until piece measures 14½ (14½, 15, 14¾, 15, 15, 15, 15, 15, 15¼, 15½, 15)" [37 (37, 38, 37.5, 38, 38, 38, 38, 38, 38.5, 39.5, 38) cm from the beginning, ending with a WS row.

SHAPE ARMHOLES AND BEGIN YOKE PATTERN

BO 5 sts at beginning of next 2 rows—75 (83, 87, 91, 95, 103, 107, 111, 115, 123, 131, 143) sts remain.
Knit 1 row.

SIZES 33¾, 37, 38¾, 40¼, AND 41¾" (85.5, 94, 98.5, 102, AND 106 CM) ONLY

SET-UP ROW (RS): Work Moss st over 11 (15, 17, 19, 21, -, -, -, -, -, -, -) sts, pm, work Chevron Panel (see page 100) over 9 sts, pm, work Jacob's Ladder (see page 100) over 11 sts, pm, work Diamond Panel (see page 100) over 13 sts, pm, work Jacob's Ladder over 11 sts, pm, work Chevron Panel over 9 sts, pm, work Moss st to end.

SIZES 45, 46¾, 48¼, 49¾, 53, 56¼, AND 61" (114.5, 118.5, 122.5, 126.5, 134.5, 143, AND 155 CM) ONLY

SET-UP ROW (RS): Work Moss st over - (-, -, -, -, 12, 14, 16, 18, 22, 26, 32) sts, pm, work Chevron Panel (see page 100) over 9 sts, pm, work Jacob's Ladder (see page 100) over 11 sts, pm, work Diamond Panel (see page 100) over 13 sts (beginning with Row 11), pm, work Diamond Panel over 13 sts (beginning with Row 1), pm, work Diamond Panel over 13 sts (beginning with Row 11), pm, work Jacob's Ladder over 11 sts, pm, work Chevron Panel over 9 sts, pm, work Moss st to end.

ALL SIZES

Work even until armhole measures 4 (4½, 5, 5½, 5½, 6, 6½, 7, 7, 7¼, 7½, 8)" [10 (11.5, 12.5, 14, 14, 15, 16.5, 18, 18, 18.5, 19, 20.5) cm, ending with a WS row.

SHAPE NECK

NEXT ROW (RS): Work 28 (32, 34, 35, 37, 41, 42, 44, 46, 50, 54, 59) sts, join a second ball of yarn and BO center 19 (19, 19, 21, 21, 21, 23, 23, 23, 23, 23, 25) sts, work to end. Working both sides at the same time, decrease 1 st at each neck edge every row 6 (8, 8, 8, 8, 8, 8, 8, 10, 10, 10) times, then every RS row 4 (3, 3, 3, 4, 4, 4, 5, 5, 4, 4, 5) times—18 (21, 23, 24, 25, 29, 30, 31, 33, 36, 40, 44) sts remain each shoulder. Work even until armhole measures 7 (7½, 8, 8½, 9, 9½, 10, 10½, 11, 11¼, 11½, 12)" [18 (19, 20.5, 21.5, 23, 24, 25.5, 26.5, 28, 28.5, 29, 30.5) cm from the beginning, ending with a WS row.

SHAPE SHOULDERS

BO 9 (11, 12, 12, 13, 15, 15, 16, 17, 18, 20, 22) sts at each armhole edge once, then 9 (10, 11, 12, 12, 14, 15, 15, 16, 18, 20, 22) sts once.

TURTLENECK

With RS facing, using smaller circular needle and beginning at right Back shoulder, pick up and knit sts around neck opening, picking up 1 st for every BO st, 2 sts for every 3 rows along vertical edges, and 3 sts for every 4 rows along diagonal edges, making sure to end with a multiple of 4 sts. Join for working in the rnd; pm for beginning of rnd. Begin 2x2 Rib in the Rnd; work evenfor 4" (10 cm). Change to larger circular needle; work even until Turtleneck measures 8" (20.5 cm) from pick-up rnd.

BO all sts in pattern.

CHEVRON PANEL (see Chart)
(panel of 9 sts; 6-row repeat)

ROW 1 (RS): K4, p1, k4.
ROW 2: P3, k3, p3.
ROW 3: K2, p2, k1, p2, k2.
ROW 4: P1, k2, p3, k2, p1.
ROW 5: K1, p1, k5, p1, k1.
ROW 6: Purl.
Repeat Rows 1–6 for Chevron Panel.

JACOB'S LADDER (see Chart)
(panel of 11 sts; 6-row repeat)

ROWS 1, 3, AND 5 (RS): P1, k1-tbl, p1, k5, p1, k1-tbl, p1.
ROWS 2 AND 4: K1, p1-tbl, k1, p5, k1, p1-tbl, k1.
ROW 6: K1, p1-tbl, k7, p1-tbl, k1.
Repeat Rows 1–6 for Jacob's Ladder.

DIAMOND PANEL (see Chart)
(panel of 13 sts; 20-row repeat)

ROW 1 (RS): K6, p1, k6.
ROW 2 AND ALL WS ROWS: Knit the knit sts and purl the purl sts as they face you.
ROW 3: K5, p1, k1, p1, k5.
ROW 5: K4, p1, [k1, p1] twice, k4.
ROW 7: K3, p1, [k1, p1] 3 times, k3.
ROW 9: K2, p1, k1, p1, k3, p1, k1, p1, k2.
ROW 11: [K1, p1] twice, k5, [p1, k1] twice.
ROW 13: Repeat Row 9.
ROW 15: Repeat Row 7.
ROW 17: Repeat Row 5.
ROW 19: Repeat Row 3.
ROW 20: Repeat Row 2.
Repeat Rows 1–20 for Diamond Panel.

CHEVRON PANEL

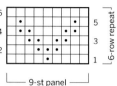

9-st panel / 6-row repeat

JACOB'S LADDER

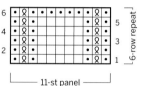

11-st panel / 6-row repeat

DIAMOND PANEL

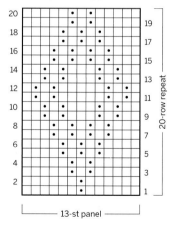

13-st panel / 20-row repeat

☐ Knit on RS, purl on WS.

• Purl on RS, knit on WS.

Ⓠ K1-tbl on RS, p1-tbl on WS.

SLEEVES

CO 46 (46, 50, 50, 54, 54, 58, 58, 58, 58, 62, 62) sts. Begin 2x2 Rib Flat; work even for 2½" (6.5 cm), ending with a WS row.

NEXT ROW (WS): Knit, decrease 2 sts evenly across—44 (44, 48, 48, 52, 52, 56, 56, 56, 56, 60, 60) sts remain.

Change to St st; work even for 2 rows.

SHAPE SLEEVE

INCREASE ROW (RS): Increase 1 st each side this row, then every 8 (6, 6, 4, 4, 4, 4, 4, 4, 4, 4, 2) rows 12 (12, 12, 2, 2, 11, 9, 18, 24, 28, 25, 2) times, then every 0 (6, 6, 4, 4, 4, 4, 4, 4, 0, 4, 2) rows 0 (3, 3, 16, 16, 10, 12, 6, 2, 0, 2, 27) times, as follows: K2, M1R, knit to last 2 sts, M1L, k2—70 (76, 80, 86, 90, 96, 100, 106, 110, 114, 116, 120) sts. Work even until piece measures 16 (16, 16, 17, 17, 17, 17½, 17½, 17½, 18, 18, 18)" [40.5 (40.5, 40.5, 43, 43, 43, 44.5, 44.5, 44.5, 45.5, 45.5, 45.5) cm] from the beginning, ending with a WS row.
BO all sts.

FINISHING

Block pieces as desired. Sew shoulder seams. Sew in Sleeves; sew side and Sleeve seams.

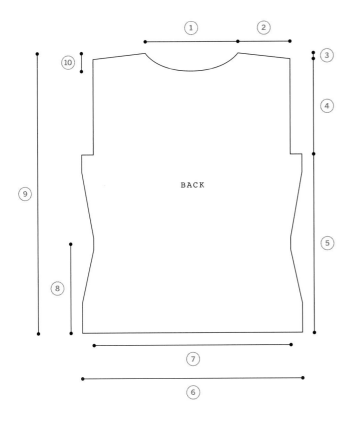

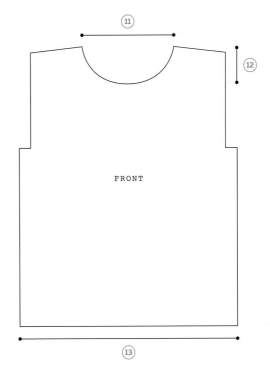

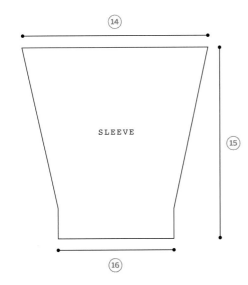

BACK

1. 7½ (8, 8, 8½, 8¾, 8¾, 9¼, 9½, 9½, 10, 10, 10¾)"
19 (20.5, 20.5, 21.5, 22, 22, 23.5, 24, 24, 25.5, 25.5, 27.5) cm

2. 3½ (4¼, 4½, 4¾, 5, 5¾, 6, 6¼, 6½, 7¼, 8, 8¾)"
9 (11, 11.5, 12, 12.5, 14.5, 15, 16, 16.5, 18.5, 20.5, 22) cm

3. ½"/1.5 cm

4. 7 (7½, 8, 8½, 9, 9½, 10, 10½, 11, 11¼, 11½, 12)"
18 (19, 20.5, 21.5, 23, 24, 25.5, 26.5, 28, 28.5, 29, 30.5) cm

5. 14½ (14½, 15, 14¾, 15, 15, 15, 15, 15, 15¼, 15½, 15)"
37 (37, 38, 37.5, 38, 38, 38, 38, 38, 38.5, 39.5, 38) cm

6. 16¾ (18½, 19¼, 20, 20¾, 22½, 23¼, 24, 24¾, 26½, 28, 30½)" hip and bust
42.5 (47, 49, 51, 52.5, 57, 59, 61, 63, 67.5, 71, 77.5) cm

7. 15¼ (16¾, 17½, 18½, 19¼, 20¾, 21½, 22½, 23¼, 24¾, 26½, 28¾)" waist
38.5 (42.5, 44.5, 47, 49, 52.5, 54.5, 57, 59, 63, 67.5, 73) cm

8. 7½"/19 cm

9. 22 (22½, 23½, 23¾, 24½, 25, 25½, 26, 26½, 27, 27½, 27½)"
56 (57, 59.5, 60.5, 62, 63.5, 65, 66, 67.5, 68.5, 70, 70) cm

10. 1½"/4 cm

FRONT

11. 7¾ (8¼, 8¼, 8½, 9, 9, 9½, 9¾, 9¾, 10¼, 10¼, 11)"
19.5 (21, 21, 21.5, 23, 23, 24, 25, 25, 26, 26, 28) cm

12. 3½ (3½, 3½, 3½, 4, 4, 4, 4, 4½, 4½, 4½, 4½)"
9 (9, 9, 9, 10, 10, 10, 10, 11.5, 11.5, 11.5, 11.5) cm

13. 17 (18½, 19½, 20¼, 21, 22½, 23½, 24¼, 25, 26½, 28¼, 30½)"
43 (47, 49.5, 51.5, 53.5, 57, 59.5, 61.5, 63.5, 67.5, 72, 77.5) cm

SLEEVE

14. 14 (15¼, 16, 17¼, 18, 19¼, 20, 21¼, 22, 22¾, 23¼, 24)"
35.5 (38.5, 40.5, 44, 45.5, 49, 51, 54, 56, 58, 59, 61) cm

15. 16 (16, 16, 17, 17, 17, 17½, 17½, 17½, 18, 18, 18)"
40.5 (40.5, 40.5, 43, 43, 43, 44.5, 44.5, 44.5, 45.5, 45.5, 45.5) cm

16. 8¾ (8¾, 9½, 9½, 10½, 10½, 11¼, 11¼, 11¼, 11¼, 12, 12)"
22 (22, 24, 24, 26.5, 26.5, 28.5, 28.5, 28.5, 28.5, 30.5, 30.5) cm

CHAPTER

7

Projects

PUDDLE JUMPING
CARDIGAN MINI

HEUBLEIN PULLOVER

SPEEDSTER RAGLAN

ENTANGLED RAGLAN

Techniques Learned

RAGLAN ARMHOLE
SHAPING AND FIT

SEAMING STRIPES

TEXTURED STITCH
PATTERNS WITH
SEMI-SOLID YARNS

MULTIPLE
AT-THE-SAME-TIME
INSTRUCTIONS

Bonus Lesson

RAGLAN TIPS AND TRICKS

RAGLANS

Legend has it that raglans came about when a clever tailor adjusted the fit of his lord's clothes to accommodate the increased range of motion required after the loss of an arm. At their heart, raglans are sportswear—the straight angles of the armhole-to-shoulder shaping allow for lots of movement with comfort. (Think baseball jersey!)

And yes, that increased range of motion should come with a more relaxed fit through the shoulders for the raglan lines to sit properly on your body. Generally speaking, you want around 3–4" (7.5–10 cm) of positive ease through the bust with a raglan, and the armhole depth of the sweater as worn should be an inch or two longer than your set-in-sleeve armhole depth.

You've got lots of stitch options with raglans, and I've given you sweaters that explore that freedom! Our mini this time is the Puddle Jumping Cardigan Mini (page 105), a wide-striped long-line cardi with buttons at the top of the sweater. The Heublein Pullover (page 108) makes for a perfect weekend sweater, comfortable while still being polished thanks to subtle waist shaping. The Speedster Raglan (page 113) riffs on the classic baseball jersey with a luxe yarn, and the Entangled Raglan (page 118) pairs a soft merino wool with lovely cables.

Feel free to use these sweaters as a jumping-off point, adjusting the shaping on the raglan lines to be more or less visible as described on page 26, or even adding stitch patterning to the raglan shaping. You can get lots of great looks out of this construction!

Buttons on
top only for
easy movement

DIFFICULTY LEVEL:

RAGLANS

PUDDLE JUMPING
CARDIGAN MINI

Stripes offer
great seaming
practice

Puddle Jumping Cardigan Mini

This long-line raglan cardigan has buttons only at the top, working with the seams to add stability in this important part of the sweater and keeping movement free through the body. Cute stripes take advantage of the raglan construction, and allow you to use up the smaller amounts of yarn that seem to hang around every knitter's house.

SIZES
To fit children 1 (2, 3/4, 5/6, 7/8, 9/10) year(s)

FINISHED MEASUREMENTS
23¼ (25¾, 26¾, 29½, 31½, 33)" [59 (65.5, 68, 75, 80, 84) cm] chest, buttoned

NOTE: Cardigan is intended to be worn with 2–4" (5–10 cm) ease in the chest.

YARN
Rowan Pure Wool Superwash DK [100% superwash merino wool; 137 yards (125 meters)/ 50 grams]: 2 (2, 3, 3, 4, 4) skeins each #102 Boulder **(A)** and #013 Enamel **(B)**

NEEDLES
One pair straight needles size US 6 (4 mm)

Change needle size if necessary to obtain correct gauge.

NOTIONS
Stitch holders; removable stitch markers; four ½" (13 mm) buttons

GAUGE
23 sts and 32 rows = 4" (10 cm) in St st

STITCH PATTERNS

1X1 RIB
(even number of sts; 1-row repeat)

ROW 1 (RS): *K1, p1; repeat from * to end.

ROW 2: Knit the knit sts and purl the purl sts as they face you. Repeat Row 2 for 1x1 Rib.

1X1 RIB
(odd number of sts; 1-row repeat)

ROW 1 (RS): *K1, p1; repeat from * to last st, k1.

ROW 2: Knit the knit sts and purl the purl sts as they face you. Repeat Row 2 for 1x1 Rib.

STRIPE PATTERN
(any number of sts; 16-row repeat)
*Work 8 rows in A, then 8 rows in B; repeat from * for Stripe Pattern.

BACK

Using A, CO 64 (70, 74, 80, 86, 92) sts. Begin 1x1 Rib; work even for 1¼" (3 cm), ending with a WS row.

Change to St st; work even for 4 rows.

Continuing in St st, begin Stripe Pattern; work even until piece measures 10 (10, 11, 12, 12½, 13)" [25.5 (25.5, 28, 30.5, 32, 33) cm] from the beginning, ending with a WS row. Make note of what row of Stripe Pattern you end with; you will need to end with the same row for Fronts and Sleeves.

SHAPE RAGLAN

BO 6 sts at beginning of next 2 rows—52 (58, 62, 68, 74, 80) sts remain.

DECREASE ROW (RS): Decrease 1 st each side this row, then every RS row 3 (2, 0, 0, 3, 3) times, then every 4 rows 5 (8, 11, 12, 11, 12) times, then every RS row 1 (0, 0, 0, 1, 1) time(s), as follows: K2, ssk, knit to last 4 sts, k2tog, k2—32 (36, 38, 42, 42, 46) sts remain. Purl 1 row. You should have worked 32 (40, 48, 52, 56, 60) rows from beginning of raglan shaping; raglan should measure approximately 4 (5, 6, 6½, 7, 7½)" [10 (12.5, 15, 16.5, 18, 19) cm].

Place sts on holder.

RIGHT FRONT

Using A, CO 32 (36, 38, 42, 44, 46) sts. Begin 1x1 Rib; work even for 1¼" (3 cm), ending with a WS row.

Change to St st; work even for 4 rows.

Continuing in St st, begin Stripe Pattern; work even until piece measures 10 (10, 11, 12, 12½, 13)" [25.5 (25.5, 28, 30.5, 32, 33) cm] from the beginning, ending with 1 more row of Stripe Pattern than for Back.

SHAPE RAGLAN

NEXT ROW (WS): BO 6 sts, knit to end—26 (30, 32, 36, 38, 40) sts remain.

DECREASE ROW (RS): Decrease 1 st this row, then every RS row 3 (2, 0, 0, 3, 3) times, then every 4 rows 5 (8, 11, 12, 11, 12) times, then every RS row 1 (0, 0, 0, 1, 1) time(s), as follows: Knit to last 4 sts, k2tog, k2—16 (19, 20, 23, 22, 23) sts remain. Purl 1 row. You should have worked 31 (39, 47, 51, 55, 59) rows from beginning of raglan shaping; raglan should measure approximately 4 (5, 6, 6½, 7, 7½)" [10 (12.5, 15, 16.5, 18, 19) cm]. Place sts on holder.

LEFT FRONT

Using A, CO 32 (36, 38, 42, 44, 46) sts. Begin 1x1 Rib; work even for 1¼" (3 cm), ending with a WS row.
Change to St st; work even for 4 rows.
Continuing in St st, begin Stripe Pattern; work even until piece measures 10 (10, 11, 12, 12½, 13)" [25.5 (25.5, 28, 30.5, 32, 33) cm] from the beginning, ending with same row of Stripe Pattern as for Back.

SHAPE RAGLAN

NEXT ROW (RS): BO 6 sts, knit to end—26 (30, 32, 36, 38, 40) sts remain.
Purl 1 row.

DECREASE ROW (RS): Decrease 1 st this row, then every RS row 3 (2, 0, 0, 3, 3) times, then every 4 rows 5 (8, 11, 12, 11, 12) times, then every RS row 1 (0, 0, 0, 1, 1) time(s), as follows: K2, ssk, knit to end—16 (19, 20, 23, 22, 23) sts remain. Purl 1 row. You should have worked 32 (40, 48, 52, 56, 60) rows from beginning of raglan shaping; raglan should measure approximately 4 (5, 6, 6½, 7, 7½)" [10 (12.5, 15, 16.5, 18, 19) cm].
Place sts on holder.

SLEEVES

Using B (A, A, B, A, B), CO 28 (28, 32, 36, 36, 40) sts. Begin 1x1 Rib; work even for 6 (6, 2, 6, 2, 6) rows.
Continuing in 1x1 Rib, begin Stripe Pattern; work even until piece measures 1¼" (3 cm) from the beginning, ending with a WS row.
Continuing in Stripe Pattern, begin St st; work even for 2 rows.

SHAPE SLEEVE

INCREASE ROW (RS): Increase 1 st each side this row, every 4 (4, 4, 8, 8, 8) rows 4 (6, 1, 9, 10, 6) time(s), then every 6 (6, 6, 0, 0, 10) rows 4 (4, 8, 0, 0, 4) times, as follows: K1, M1R, knit to last st, M1L, knit to end—46 (50, 52, 56, 58, 62) sts. Work even until piece measures approximately 9 (10, 10½, 13, 14, 15)" [23 (25.5, 26.5, 33, 35.5, 38) cm] from the beginning, ending with same row of Stripe Pattern as for Back.

SHAPE RAGLAN

BO 6 sts at beginning of next 2 rows—34 (38, 40, 44, 46, 50) sts remain.

DECREASE ROW (RS): Decrease 1 st each side every RS row 4 (3, 1, 1, 4, 4) time(s), then every 4 rows 2 (5, 9, 9, 10, 11) times, then every RS row 7 (6, 4, 6, 3, 3) times, as follows: K2, ssk, knit to last 4 sts, k2tog, k2—8 (10, 12, 12, 12, 14) sts remain. You should have worked 32 (40, 48, 52, 56, 60) rows from beginning of raglan shaping; raglan should measure approximately 4 (5, 6, 6½, 7, 7½)" [10 (12.5, 15, 16.5, 18, 19) cm]. Place sts on holder.

FINISHING

Block pieces as desired. Sew raglan seams. Sew side and Sleeve seams.

NECKBAND

Place 80 (94, 102, 112, 110, 120) held sts on needle. With RS facing and beginning at Right Front neck edge, work 1x1 Rib across all sts, working 2 sts together in pattern on each side of raglan seams. Work even until piece measures ¾" (2 cm) from pick-up row. BO all sts in pattern.

BUTTON BAND

With RS facing, beginning at Left Front neck edge, pick up and knit approximately 3 sts for every 4 rows along Left Front, ending with an odd number of sts. Begin 1x1 Rib; work even for 8 rows. BO all sts in pattern.

BUTTONHOLE BAND

With RS facing, beginning at lower Right Front neck edge, pick up and knit same number of sts as for Button Band. Begin 1x1 Rib; work even for 3 rows. Place markers for 4 buttonholes, the first 6 sts from neck edge and the remaining three spaced 12 sts apart.

BUTTONHOLE ROW (RS): [Work to marker, yo, ssk] 4 times, work to end.
Work even for 4 rows. BO all sts in pattern.
Sew buttons opposite buttonholes.

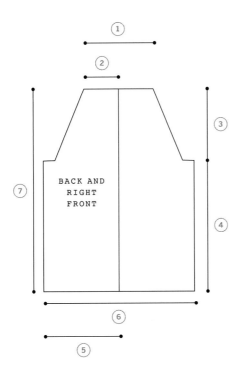

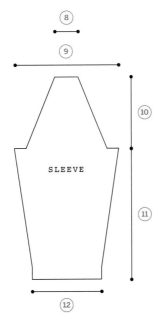

BACK AND RIGHT FRONT

1 5½ (6¼, 6½, 7¼, 7¼, 8)"
   14 (16, 16.5, 18.5, 18.5, 20.5) cm

2 2¾ (3¼, 3½, 4, 3¾, 4)"
   7 (8.5, 9, 10, 9.5, 10) cm

3 4 (5, 6, 6½, 7, 7½)"
   10 (12.5, 15, 16.5, 18, 19) cm

4 10 (10, 11, 12, 12½, 13)"
   25.5 (25.5, 28, 30.5, 32, 33) cm

5 5½ (6¼, 6½, 7¼, 7¾, 8)"
   14 (16, 16.5, 18.5, 19.5, 20.5) cm

6 11¼ (12¼, 12¾, 14, 15, 16)"
   28.5 (31, 32.5, 35.5, 38, 40.5) cm

7 14 (15, 17, 18½, 19½, 20½)"
   35.5 (38, 43, 47, 49.5, 52) cm

SLEEVE

8 1½ (1¾, 2, 2, 2, 2½)"
   4 (4.5, 5, 5, 5, 6.5) cm

9 8 (8¾, 9, 9¾, 10, 10¾)"
   20.5 (22, 23, 25, 25.5, 27.5) cm

10 4 (5, 6, 6½, 7, 7½)"
    10 (12.5, 15, 16.5, 18, 19) cm

11 9 (10, 11, 13, 14, 15)"
    23 (25.5, 28, 33, 35.5, 38) cm

12 4¾ (4¾, 5½, 6¼, 6¼, 7)"
    12 (12, 14, 16, 16, 18) cm

Heublein Pullover

The Heublein Tower is at the end of a gorgeous hike near where I live in Connecticut, and visiting it offers breathtaking views and often-chilly winds. This sweater is exactly what I want to wear on that hike: Warm, soft yarn that will be durable for decades; a construction that allows for an athletic range of movement as I scramble up rocks after my kids; and a not-too-long, not-too-short length that neither rides up nor gets in the way.

FINISHED MEASUREMENTS

32½ (34½, 36½, 38, 40, 42, 43½, 45½, 47½, 52½, 56½, 60)" [82.5 (87.5, 92.5, 96.5, 101.5, 106.5, 110.5, 115.5, 120.5, 133.5, 143.5, 152.5) cm] bust

NOTE: Pullover is intended to be worn with 3–4" (7.5–10 cm) ease in the bust.

YARN

Green Mountain Spinnery Alpaca Elegance [50% Targee wool/50% fine alpaca; 180 yards (164 meters)/2 ounces]: 6 (7, 7, 8, 8, 9, 9, 10, 10, 11, 12, 12) hanks #99955 Earl Grey

NEEDLES

One pair straight needles size US 5 (3.75 mm)

One 24" (60 cm) circular needle size US 5 (3.75 mm), for Neckband

Change needle size if necessary to obtain correct gauge.

NOTIONS

Stitch markers; stitch holders

GAUGE

22 sts and 30 rows = 4" (10 cm) in St st

STITCH PATTERNS

3X2 RIB FLAT

(multiple of 5 sts + 2; 1-row repeat)

ROW 1 (RS): K4, *p2, k3; repeat from * to last 3 sts, p2, k1.

ROW 2: Knit the knit sts and purl the purl sts as they face you. Repeat Row 2 for 3x2 Rib Flat.

3X2 RIB IN THE RND

(multiple of 5 sts; 1-rnd repeat)

ALL RNDS: *K3, p2; repeat from * to end.

NOTES

Raglan decreases should be worked to match the slant of the edge being shaped, as follows:

FOR LEFT-SLANTING EDGES:
On RS rows, k3, ssk, work to end; on WS rows, work to last 5 sts, ssp, p3.

FOR RIGHT-SLANTING EDGES:
On RS rows, work to last 5 sts, k2tog, k3; on WS rows, p3, p2tog, work to end.

Front neck decreases should be worked to match the slant of the edge being shaped, as follows:

FOR LEFT-SLANTING EDGES:
On RS rows, k1, ssk, work to end.

FOR RIGHT-SLANTING EDGES:
On RS rows, work to last 3 sts, k2tog, k1.

During the Front raglan and neck shaping, when 6 sts remain on each side, you will need to shift the raglan and neck decreases 1 or more sts toward the edges on each decrease row in order to complete the decreases.

BACK

CO 92 (97, 102, 107, 112, 117, 122, 127, 132, 147, 157, 167) sts. Begin 3x2 Rib Flat; work even for 2¼" (5.5 cm), ending with a WS row.

Change to St st; work even until piece measures 3" (7.5 cm), decreasing 2 sts evenly spaced on first row, and ending with a WS row—90 (95, 100, 105, 110, 115, 120, 125, 130, 145, 155, 165) sts remain.

NEXT ROW (WS): P30 (31, 33, 35, 36, 38, 40, 41, 43, 48, 51, 55), pm, p30 (33, 34, 35, 38, 39, 40, 43, 44, 49, 53, 55), pm, purl to end.

SHAPE WAIST

DECREASE ROW (RS): Decrease 2 sts this row, then every 6 rows 5 times, as follows: Knit to 2 sts before first marker, ssk, sm, knit to next marker, sm, k2tog, knit to end—78 (83, 88, 93, 98, 103, 108, 113, 118, 133, 143, 153) sts remain. Work even until piece measures 8 (8, 8¼, 8¼, 8½, 8½, 8½, 8¾, 8¾, 8¾, 9, 9)" [20.5 (20.5, 21, 21, 21.5, 21.5, 21.5, 22, 22, 22, 23, 23) cm] from the beginning, ending with a WS row.

Simple ribbed
trim

Slight waist
shaping

Decrease 1 st each side this row, then every RS row 6 (7, 8, 9, 10, 12, 11, 11, 13, 22, -, -) times, then every 4 rows 7 (7, 7, 7, 7, 6, 8, 8, 7, 1, -, -) time(s), then every RS row 3 (3, 3, 4, 4, 5, 4, 5, 5, 9, -, -) times, ending with a WS row—44 (47, 50, 51, 54, 55, 56, 59, 62, 63, -, -) sts remain. You should have worked 50 (52, 54, 58, 60, 62, 66, 68, 68, 70, -, -) rows from beginning of raglan shaping; raglan should measure approximately 6¾ (7, 7¼, 7¾, 8, 8¼, 8¾, 9, 9, 9¼, -, -)" [17 (18, 18.5, 19.5, 20.5, 21, 22, 23, 23, 23.5, -, -) cm].

Decrease 1 st each side this row, then every row - (-, -, -, -, -, -, -, -, -, 1, 4) time(s), then every RS row - (-, -, -, -, -, -, -, -, -, 33, 31) times, then every row - (-, -, -, -, -, -, -, -, -, 2, 5) times, ending with a WS row— - (-, -, -, -, -, -, -, -, -, 65, 67) sts remain. You should have worked - (-, -, -, -, -, -, -, -, -, 72, 74) rows from beginning of raglan shaping; raglan should measure approximately - (-, -, -, -, -, -, -, -, -, 9½, 9¾)" [- (-, -, -, -, -, -, -, -, -, 24, 25) cm].

ALL SIZES
Place sts on holder.

FRONT

Work as for Back until you have worked 28 (30, 32, 36, 38, 40, 44, 46, 46, 48, 50, 52) raglan shaping rows. Place marker either side of center 30 (33, 36, 37, 40, 41, 42, 45, 48, 49, 51, 53) sts.

SHAPE NECK

Note: When 6 sts remain on each side, you will need to shift the raglan and neck decreases 1 or more st(s) toward the edges on decrease rows in order to complete the decreases.

NEXT ROW (RS): Continuing to work raglan shaping as established, work to marker, place center sts on holder, join a second ball of yarn, work to end. Working both sides at the same time, decrease 1 st at each neck edge every RS row 4 times, then every 4 rows twice.

Work even at neck edge for 3 rows. Fasten off remaining st.

SLEEVES

CO 47 (47, 52, 52, 57, 57, 57, 62, 62, 62, 62, 67) sts. Begin 3x2 Rib Flat; work even for 2" (5 cm), ending with a WS row.

SHAPE SLEEVE

Note: You will change to St st while working Sleeve shaping; please read entire section through before beginning.

SHAPE BUST

INCREASE ROW (RS): Increase 2 sts this row, then every 6 rows 5 times, as follows: Knit to first marker, M1R, sm, knit to next marker, sm, M1L, knit to end—90 (95, 100, 105, 110, 115, 120, 125, 130, 145, 155, 165) sts. Work even, removing shaping markers on first row, until piece measures 15¼ (15¼, 15½, 15½, 16, 16, 16, 16¼, 16½, 16½, 16¾, 16¾)" [38.5 (38.5, 39.5, 39.5, 40.5, 40.5, 40.5, 41.5, 42, 42, 42.5, 42.5) cm] from the beginning, ending with a WS row.

SHAPE RAGLAN

BO 6 (6, 6, 6, 6, 8, 8, 8, 8, 8, 8) sts at beginning of next 2 rows—78 (83, 88, 93, 98, 103, 104, 109, 114, 129, 139, 149) sts remain.

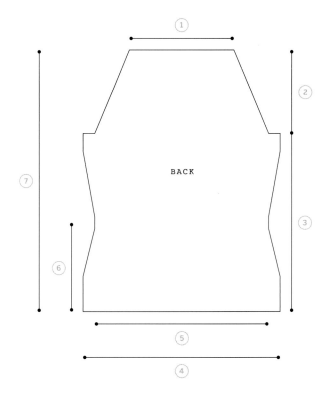

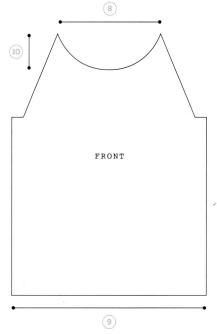

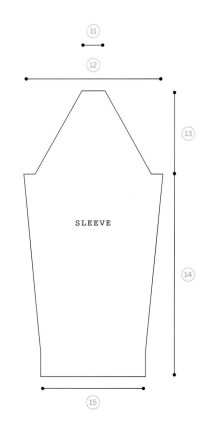

BACK

1 8 (8½, 9, 9¼, 9¾, 10, 10¼, 10¾, 11¼, 11½, 11¾, 12¼)"
20.5 (21.5, 23, 23.5, 25, 25.5, 26, 27.5, 28.5, 29, 30, 31) cm

2 6¾ (7, 7¼, 7¾, 8, 8¼, 8¾, 9, 9, 9¼, 9½, 9¾)"
17 (18, 18.5, 19.5, 20.5, 21, 22, 23, 23, 23.5, 24, 25) cm

3 15¼ (15¼, 15½, 15½, 16, 16, 16, 16¼, 16½, 16½, 16¾, 16¾)"
38.5 (38.5, 39.5, 39.5, 40.5, 40.5, 40.5, 41.5, 42, 42, 42.5, 42.5) cm

4 16¼ (17¼, 18¼, 19, 20, 21, 21¾, 22¾, 23¾, 26¼, 28¼, 30)" hip and bust
41.5 (44, 46.5, 48.5, 51, 53.5, 55, 58, 60.5, 66.5, 72, 76) cm

5 14¼ (15, 16, 17, 17¾, 18¾, 19¾, 20½, 21½, 24¼, 26, 27¾)" waist
36 (38, 40.5, 43, 45, 47.5, 50, 52, 54.5, 61.5, 66, 70.5) cm

6 7½ (7½, 7¾, 7¾, 8, 8, 8, 8¼, 8¼, 8¼, 8½, 8½)"
19 (19, 19.5, 19.5, 20.5, 20.5, 20.5, 21, 21, 21, 21.5, 21.5) cm

7 22 (22¼, 22¾, 23¼, 24, 24¼, 24¾, 25¼, 25½, 25¾, 26¼, 26½)"
56 (56.5, 58, 59, 61, 61.5, 63, 64, 65, 65.5, 66.5, 67.5) cm

FRONT

8 8 (8½, 9, 9¼, 9¾, 10, 10¼, 10¾, 11¼, 11½, 11¾, 12¼)"
20.5 (21.5, 23, 23.5, 25, 25.5, 26, 27.5, 28.5, 29, 30, 31) cm

9 16¼ (17¼, 18¼, 19, 20, 21, 21¾, 22¾, 23¾, 26¼, 28¼, 30)"
41.5 (44, 46.5, 48.5, 51, 53.5, 55, 58, 60.5, 66.5, 72, 76) cm

10 3"/7.5 cm

SLEEVE

11 2¾ (2¾, 2½, 2½, 3, 3, 3, 3¼, 3¾, 3¾, 3¾, 3¾)"
7 (7, 6.5, 6.5, 7.5, 7.5, 7.5, 8.5, 9.5, 9.5, 9.5, 9.5) cm

12 11 (12¼, 13, 14¼, 15, 16¼, 17¼, 18¼, 19¼, 20, 21, 22)"
28 (31, 33, 36, 38, 41.5, 44, 46.5, 49, 51, 53.5, 56) cm

13 6¾ (7, 7¼, 7¾, 8, 8¼, 8¾, 9, 9, 9¼, 9½, 9¾)"
17 (18, 18.5, 19.5, 20.5, 21, 22, 23, 23, 23.5, 24, 25) cm

14 17 (17, 17, 18, 18, 18, 18, 18, 18, 17½, 17, 16½)"
43 (43, 43, 45.5, 45.5, 45.5, 45.5, 45.5, 45.5, 44.5, 43, 42) cm

15 8¼ (8¼, 9, 9, 10, 10, 10, 11, 11, 11, 11, 11¾)"
21 (21, 23, 23, 25.5, 25.5, 25.5, 28, 28, 28, 28, 30) cm

INCREASE ROW (RS): Working new sts in pattern, increase 1 st each side this row, then every 12 (8, 8, 8, 8, 6, 4, 4, 4, 4, 2, 2) rows 1 (2, 2, 13, 13, 12, 5, 5, 14, 22, 6, 8) time(s), then every 14 (10, 10, 0, 0, 8, 6, 6, 6, 6, 4, 4) rows 6 (8, 8, 0, 0, 4, 14, 14, 8, 2, 21, 19) times, as follows: K1, increase 1 st (M1R or M1P to keep in pattern), work to last st, increase 1 st (M1L or M1P to keep in pattern), k1.

AT THE SAME TIME, when piece measures 7" (18 cm) from the beginning, change to St st, decreasing 2 sts evenly across first row—61 (67, 72, 78, 83, 89, 95, 100, 106, 110, 116, 121) sts remain when all shaping is complete. Work even until piece measures 17 (17, 17, 18, 18, 18, 18, 18, 18, 17½, 17, 16½)" [43 (43, 43, 45.5, 45.5, 45.5, 45.5, 45.5, 45.5, 44.5, 43, 42) cm] from the beginning, ending with a WS row.

SHAPE RAGLAN

BO 6 (6, 6, 6, 6, 6, 8, 8, 8, 8, 8, 8) sts at beginning of next 2 rows—49 (55, 60, 66, 71, 77, 79, 84, 90, 94, 100, 105) sts remain.

SIZES 32½, 34½, 36½, 38, 40, 42, 43½, AND 45½" (82.5, 87.5, 92.5, 96.5, 101.5, 106.5, 110.5, AND 115.5 CM) ONLY

Decrease 1 st each side this row, then every RS row 6 (7, 8, 9, 10, 12, 11, 11, -, -, -, -) times, then every 4 rows 7 (5, 3, 2, 2, 0, 1, 0, -, -, -, -) time(s), then every RS row 3 (7, 11, 14, 14, 17, 18, 21, -, -, -, -) times, ending with a WS row—15 (15, 14, 14, 17, 17, 17, 18, -, -, -, -) sts remain. You should have worked 50 (52, 54, 58, 60, 62, 66, 68, -, -, -, -) rows from beginning of raglan shaping; raglan should measure approximately 6¾ (7, 7¼, 7¾, 8, 8¼, 8¾, 9, -, -, -, -)" [17 (18, 18.5, 19.5, 20.5, 21, 22, 23, -, -, -, -) cm].

SIZES 47½, 52½, 56½, AND 60" (120.5, 133.5, 143.5, AND 152.5 CM) ONLY

Decrease 1 st each side this row, then every row - (-, -, -, -, -, -, -, 1, 2, 4, 5) time(s), then every RS row - (-, -, -, -, -, -, -, 31, 31, 30, 30) times, then every row - (-, -, -, -, -, -, -, 2, 3, 5, 6) times, ending with a WS row— - (-, -, -, -, -, -, -, 20, 20, 20, 21) sts remain. You should have worked - (-, -, -, -, -, -, -, 68, 70, 72, 74) rows from beginning of raglan shaping; raglan should measure approximately - (-, -, -, -, -, -, -, 9, 9¼, 9½, 9¾)" [- (-, -, -, -, -, -, -, 23, 23.5, 24, 25) cm].

ALL SIZES

Place sts on holder.

Block pieces as desired. Sew raglan seams. Sew side and Sleeve seams.

NECKBAND

With RS facing, using circular needle and beginning at right Back shoulder, and working 2 sts together in pattern on each side of all seams, knit across held Back and Left Sleeve sts, pick up and knit 19 (19, 19, 18, 17, 19, 18, 19, 19, 18, 18, 18) sts along left Front neck edge, knit across held Front neck sts, pick up and knit 20 (19, 20, 19, 18, 19, 18, 19, 19, 18, 19, 18) sts along right Front neck edge—135 (140, 145, 145, 155, 160, 160, 170, 180, 180, 185, 190) sts. Join for working in the rnd; pm for beginning of rnd. Begin 3x2 Rib in the Rnd; work even until piece measures 3" (7.5 cm) from pick-up rnd. BO all sts in pattern.

Speedster Raglan

Raglans don't always have to be rustic and loose, and this sweater
is proof. A slick, sleek wool-silk blend combines with
hand-dyed loveliness and a subtle texture pattern to make a raglan
that definitely says "sportswear," but in a more refined way.
The raglan is worked with seams for stability, and I urge you to keep
your focus while knitting the neckband: It should be structured
and firm to help the garment lie properly on your body.

FINISHED MEASUREMENTS
32 (34½, 35½, 38, 40½, 42, 44½, 45½, 48, 51½, 56½, 60½)" [81.5 (87.5, 90, 96.5, 103, 106.5, 113, 115.5, 122, 131, 143.5, 153.5) cm] bust

NOTE: Pullover is intended to be worn with 2–3" (5–7.5 cm) ease in the bust.

YARN
Mrs. Crosby Loves to Play Hat Box [75% superwash merino wool/15% silk/10% cashmere; 317 yards (290 meters)/100 grams]: 3 (4, 4, 4, 5, 5, 5, 6, 6, 6, 7, 7) hanks Roasted Chestnut

NEEDLES
One pair straight needles size US 3 (3.25 mm)

One 24" (60 cm) long circular needle size US 3 (3.25 mm), for Neckband

Change needle size if necessary to obtain correct gauge.

NOTIONS
Stitch markers

GAUGE
26 sts and 36 rows = 4" (10 cm) in St st

STITCH PATTERN
2X2 RIB
(multiple of 4 sts + 2; 1-row repeat)

ROW 1 (RS): *K2, p2; repeat from * to last 2 sts, k2.

ROW 2: Knit the knit sts and purl the purl sts as they face you. Repeat Row 2 for 2x2 Rib.

NOTES
Raglan decreases should be worked to match the slant of the edge being shaped, as follows:

FOR LEFT-SLANTING EDGES:
On RS rows, k2, ssk, work to end; on WS rows, work to last 4 sts, ssp, p2.

FOR RIGHT-SLANTING EDGES:
On RS rows, work to last 4 sts, k2tog, k2; on WS rows, p2, p2tog, work to end.
Front neck decreases should be worked to match the slant of the edge being shaped, as follows:

FOR LEFT-SLANTING EDGES:
On RS rows, ssk, work to end.

FOR RIGHT-SLANTING EDGES:
On RS rows, work to last 2 sts, k2tog.

You may work Purl Texture Pattern from text or Chart.

BACK
CO 106 (114, 118, 126, 134, 138, 146, 150, 158, 170, 186, 198) sts. Begin 2x2 Rib; work even for 2" (5 cm), ending with a WS row.
Change to St st; work even until piece measures 3 (3, 3½, 3½, 3½, 3½, 3½, 4, 4, 4, 4)" [7.5 (7.5, 9, 9, 9, 9, 9, 9, 10, 10, 10, 10) cm] from the beginning, decreasing 2 sts evenly spaced on first row, and ending with a RS row—104 (112, 116, 124, 132, 136, 144, 148, 156, 168, 184, 196) sts remain.

NEXT ROW (WS): P34 (37, 38, 41, 44, 45, 48, 49, 52, 56, 61, 65), pm, p36 (38, 40, 42, 44, 46, 48, 50, 52, 56, 62, 66), pm, purl to end.

SHAPE WAIST

DECREASE ROW (RS): Decrease 2 sts this row, then every 6 rows 5 times, as follows: Knit to 2 sts before first marker, ssk, sm, knit to next marker, sm, k2tog, knit to end—92 (100, 104, 112, 120, 124, 132, 136, 144, 156, 172, 184) sts remain. Work even until piece measures 7 (7, 7½, 7½, 7½, 7¾, 7¾, 7¾, 8, 8, 8, 8)" [18 (18, 19, 19, 19, 19.5, 19.5, 19.5, 20.5, 20.5, 20.5, 20.5) cm] from the beginning, ending with a WS row.

SHAPE BUST

INCREASE ROW (RS): Increase 2 sts this row, then every 6 rows 5 times, as follows: Knit to first marker, M1R, sm, knit to next marker, sm, M1L, knit to end—104 (112, 116, 124, 132, 136, 144, 148, 156, 168, 184, 196) sts. Work even, removing markers on first row, until piece measures 14¼ (14¼, 14¾, 14¾, 15, 15½, 15½, 15¾, 16, 16, 16¼, 16)" [36 (36, 37.5, 37.5, 38, 39.5, 39.5, 40, 40.5, 40.5, 41.5, 40.5) cm] from the beginning, ending with a WS row.

DIFFICULTY LEVEL:

RAGLANS

SPEEDSTER RAGLAN

Textured front
breaks up
variegated yarn

Sport weight
yarn makes a
luscious fabric

RAGLAN TIPS AND TRICKS

Bonus Lesson

THERE ARE ABOUT a billion raglan patterns out there right now, and while these sweaters are pretty simple to make, generally speaking, there are some important tips to wearing them successfully:

SEAMS ARE BETTER. Raglan sweaters are more successful when seamed for two big reasons: First, the nature of a raglan is that the weight of the garment rests on a small bit of Stockinette—not the most structural thing around. Seams will help the sweater stay in place well on your body. Second, knitting a raglan in pieces, like these sweaters are, allows you to shape the sleeves and body (and front and back, if you like!) differently, without concerns of the fabric puckering or "whirlpooling" along the raglan lines.

RAGLANS NEED STRUCTURED FABRIC! The raglan construction is the least structural on its own, so these sweaters require fabric that's dense, springy, and generally passes all the fabric tests on page 12. Pullovers are a little more structured than cardigans, and you can get away with a bit more there. But any raglan that's open in the front needs all the help it can get.

RAGLANS NEED STRONG FINISHING, TOO. This lack of structure means that the finishing on your raglan does important work to keep things neat and tidy through wear. Make sure your line of picked-up stitches is strong and sturdy, and consider strengthening your button bands and/or back neck edges, too—lining them with grosgrain ribbon is quick to hand-sew and does wonders!

SHAPE RAGLAN

BO 8 (8, 8, 8, 8, 8, 10, 10, 10, 10, 10) sts at beginning of next 2 rows, then decrease 1 st each side every RS row 3 (5, 5, 8, 11, 11, 14, 12, 14, 19, 30, 34) times, then every 4 rows 13 (12, 12, 11, 10, 11, 10, 12, 11, 8, 1, 0) time(s), then every RS row 0 (1, 2, 3, 4, 4, 5, 4, 5, 8, 12, 14) time(s)—56 (60, 62, 64, 66, 68, 70, 72, 76, 78, 78, 80) sts remain. You should have worked 60 (62, 64, 68, 72, 76, 80, 82, 84, 88, 90, 98) rows from beginning of raglan shaping; raglan should measure approximately 6¾ (7, 7, 7½, 8, 8½, 9, 9, 9¼, 9¾, 10, 11)" [17 (18, 18, 19, 20.5, 21.5, 23, 23, 23.5, 25, 25.5, 28) cm].
BO all sts.

FRONT

CO 106 (114, 118, 126, 134, 138, 146, 150, 158, 170, 186, 198) sts. Begin 2x2 Rib; work even for 2" (5 cm), ending with a WS row.
Change to St st; work even for 2 rows, decreasing 2 sts evenly spaced on first row—104 (112, 116, 124, 132, 136, 144, 148, 156, 168, 184, 196) sts remain.
NEXT ROW (RS): K1 (2, 1, 2, 0, 2, 0, 2, 0, 0, 2, 2), work Purl Texture Pattern (see page tk) to last 1 (2, 1, 2, 0, 2, 0, 2, 0, 0, 2, 2) st(s), knit to end.
Work even, working 1 (2, 1, 2, 0, 2, 0, 2, 0, 0, 2, 2) st(s) at beginning and end of row in St st, and remaining sts in Purl Texture Pattern, until piece measures 14¼ (14¼, 14¾, 14¾, 15, 15½, 15½, 15¾, 16, 16, 16¼, 16)" [36 (36, 37.5, 37.5, 38, 39.5, 39.5, 40, 40.5, 40.5, 41.5, 40.5) cm] from the beginning, ending with a RS row.

SHAPE RAGLAN AND NECK

Note: Raglan and neck shaping will be worked at the same time; please read entire section through before beginning. When 6 sts remain on each side, you will need to shift the raglan and neck decreases 1 or more sts toward the edges on decrease rows in order to complete the decreases. On non-decrease rows, work the first and last 3 sts in St st.

BO 8 (8, 8, 8, 8, 8, 10, 10, 10, 10, 10) sts at beginning of next 2 rows, then decrease 1 st each side every RS row 3 (5, 5, 8, 11, 11, 14, 12, 14, 19, 30, 34) times, then every 4 rows 13 (12, 12, 11, 10, 11, 10, 12, 11, 8, 1, 0) time(s), then every RS row 0 (1, 2, 3, 4, 4, 5, 4, 5, 8, 12, 14) time(s).

AT THE SAME TIME, when you have worked 32 (34, 36, 40, 44, 48, 52, 54, 56, 60, 62, 70) raglan shaping rows, begin neck shaping. Place marker either side of center 38 (42, 44, 46, 48, 50, 52, 54, 58, 60, 60, 62) sts.

NEXT ROW (RS): Continuing to work raglan shaping as established, work to marker, join a second ball of yarn, BO center sts, work to end. Working both sides at the same time, decrease 1 st at each neck edge every other row 5 times, then every 4 rows 3 times.

Work even at neck edge for 3 rows. Fasten off remaining st. You should have worked 60 (62, 64, 68, 72, 76, 80, 82, 84, 88, 90, 98) rows from beginning of raglan shaping; raglan should measure approximately 6¾ (7, 7, 7½, 8, 8½, 9, 9, 9¼, 9¾, 10, 11)" [17 (18, 18, 19, 20.5, 21.5, 23, 23, 23.5, 25, 25.5, 28) cm].

SLEEVES

CO 62 (66, 70, 74, 82, 86, 86, 98, 106, 114, 114, 114) sts. Begin 2x2 Rib; work even for 1" (2.5 cm), ending with a WS row. Change to St st; work even for 2 rows, decreasing 2 sts evenly spaced on first row—60 (64, 68, 72, 80, 84, 84, 96, 104, 112, 112, 112) sts.

SHAPE SLEEVE

INCREASE ROW (RS): Increase 1 st each side this row, then every 20 (12, 10, 8, 10, 8, 4, 4, 4, 4, 2, 2) rows 2 (1, 4, 5, 5, 5, 2, 5, 2, 2, 3, 12) time(s), then every 0 (14, 0, 10, 0, 10, 6, 6, 6, 6, 4, 4) rows 0 (2, 0, 1, 0, 1, 7, 5, 7, 6, 9, 3) time(s), as follows: K1, M1R, knit to last st, M1L, knit to end—66 (72, 78, 86, 92, 98, 104, 118, 124, 130, 138, 144) sts. Work even until piece measures 8 (8, 8, 9, 9, 9, 9, 9, 8½, 8, 7½)" [20.5 (20.5, 20.5, 23, 23, 23, 23, 23, 23, 21.5, 20.5, 19) cm] from the beginning, ending with a WS row.

SHAPE RAGLAN

BO 8 (8, 8, 8, 8, 8, 8, 10, 10, 10, 10, 10) sts at beginning of next 2 rows—50 (56, 62, 70, 76, 82, 88, 98, 104, 110, 118, 124) sts remain.

SIZES 32, 34½, 35½, 38, 40½, 42, 44½, AND 45½" (81.5, 87.5, 90, 96.5, 103, 106.5, 113, AND 115.5 CM) ONLY
Decrease 1 st each side this row, then every RS row 2 (4, 4, 7, 10, 10, 13, 11, -, -, -, -) times, then every 4 rows 13 (11, 9, 7, 6, 5, 5, 1, -, -, -, -) time(s), then every RS row 0 (3, 8, 11, 12, 16, 15, 26, -, -, -, -) times, ending with a WS row—18 (18, 18, 18, 18, 18, 20, 20, -, -, -, -) sts remain when all shaping is complete. You should have worked 60 (62, 64, 68, 72, 76, 80, 82, -, -, -, -) rows from beginning of raglan shaping; raglan should measure approximately 6¾ (7, 7, 7½, 8, 8½, 9, 9, -, -, -, -)" [17 (18, 18, 19, 20.5, 21.5, 23, 23, -, -, -, -) cm].

SIZES 48, 51½, 56½, AND 60½" (122, 131, 143.5, AND 153.5 CM) ONLY
Decrease 1 st each side this row, then every row - (-, -, -, -, -, -, -, 0, 1, 3, 1) time(s), then every RS row - (-, -, -, -, -, -, -, 40, 41, 40, 46) times, then every row - (-, -, -, -, -, -, -, 1, 2, 4, 2) time(s), ending with a WS row— - (-, -, -, -, -, -, -, 20, 20, 22, 24) sts remain when all shaping is complete. You should have worked - (-, -, -, -, -, -, -, 84, 88, 90, 98) rows from beginning of raglan shaping; raglan should measure approximately - (-, -, -, -, -, -, -, 9¼, 9¾, 10, 11)" [- (-, -, -, -, -, -, -, 23.5, 25, 25.5, 28) cm].

ALL SIZES
BO all sts.

FINISHING

Block pieces as desired. Sew raglan seams. Sew side and Sleeve seams.

NECKBAND

With RS facing, beginning at right Back shoulder seam, pick up and knit 54 (58, 60, 62, 64, 66, 68, 70, 74, 76, 76, 78) sts across Back neck, 16 (16, 16, 16, 16, 16, 18, 18, 18, 18, 20, 22) sts across Left Sleeve, 22 sts along left Front neck edge, 38 (42, 44, 46, 48, 50, 52, 54, 58, 60, 60, 62) sts across center Front BO sts, 22 sts along right Front neck edge, then 16 (16, 16, 16, 16, 16, 18, 18, 18, 18, 20, 22) sts along Right Sleeve—168 (176, 180, 184, 188, 192, 200, 204, 212, 216, 220, 228) sts. *Note: Exact st count is not essential, but be sure to end with a multiple of 4 sts.* Join for working in the rnd; pm for beginning of rnd. Begin 2x2 Rib; work even for ¾" (2 cm). BO all sts in pattern.

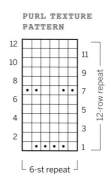

PURL TEXTURE PATTERN
(multiple of 6 sts;
12-row repeat)

ROW 1 (RS): *K1, p4, k1; repeat from * to end.

ROWS 2–6: Work in St st.

ROW 7: *P2, k2, p2; repeat from * to end.

ROWS 8–12: Work in St st. Repeat Rows 1–12 for Purl Texture Pattern.

☐ Knit on RS, purl on WS.

⊡ Purl on RS, knit on WS.

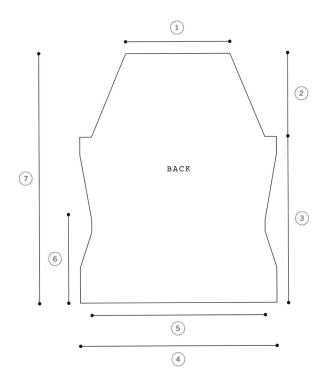

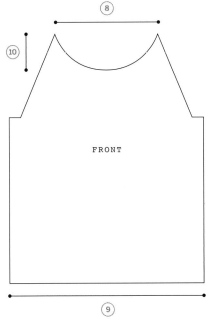

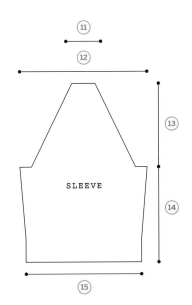

BACK

1 8½ (9¼, 9½, 9¾, 10¼, 10½, 10¾, 11, 11¾, 12, 12, 12¼)"
   21.5 (23.5, 24, 25, 26, 26.5, 27.5, 28, 30, 30.5, 30.5, 31) cm

2 6¾ (7, 7, 7½, 8, 8½, 9, 9, 9¼, 9¾, 10, 11)"
   17 (18, 18, 19, 20.5, 21.5, 23, 23, 23.5, 25, 25.5, 28) cm

3 14¼ (14¼, 14¾, 14¾, 15, 15½, 15½, 15¾, 16, 16, 16¼, 16)"
   36 (36, 37.5, 37.5, 38, 39.5, 39.5, 40, 40.5, 40.5, 41.5, 40.5) cm

4 16 (17¼, 17¾, 19, 20¼, 21, 22¼, 22¾, 24, 25¾, 28¼, 30¼)" hip and bust
   40.5 (44, 45, 48.5, 51.5, 53.5, 56.5, 58, 61, 65.5, 72, 77) cm

5 14¼ (15½, 16, 17¼, 18½, 19, 20¼, 21, 22¼, 24, 26½, 28¼)" waist
   36 (39.5, 40.5, 44, 47, 48.5, 51.5, 53.5, 56.5, 61, 67.5, 72) cm

6 6½ (6½, 7, 7, 7, 7¼, 7¼, 7¼, 7½, 7½, 7½, 7½)"
   16.5 (16.5, 18, 18, 18, 18.5, 18.5, 18.5, 19, 19, 19, 19) cm

7 21 (21¼, 21¾, 22¼, 23, 24, 24½, 24¾, 25¼, 25¾, 26¼, 27)"
   53.5 (54, 55, 56.5, 58.5, 61, 62, 63, 64, 65.5, 66.5, 68.5) cm

FRONT

8 8½ (9¼, 9½, 9¾, 10¼, 10½, 10¾, 11, 11¾, 12, 12, 12¼)"
   21.5 (23.5, 24, 25, 26, 26.5, 27.5, 28, 30, 30.5, 30.5, 31) cm

9 16 (17¼, 17¾, 19, 20¼, 21, 22¼, 22¾, 24, 25¾, 28¼, 30¼)"
   40.5 (44, 45, 48.5, 51.5, 53.5, 56.5, 58, 61, 65.5, 72, 77) cm

10 3"/7.5 cm

SLEEVE

11 2¾ (2¾, 2¾, 2¾, 2¾, 2¾, 3, 3, 3, 3, 3½, 3¾)"
   7 (7, 7, 7, 7, 7, 7.5, 7.5, 7.5, 7.5, 9, 9.5) cm

12 10¼ (11, 12, 13¼, 14¼, 15, 16, 18¼, 19, 20, 21¼, 22¼)"
   26 (28, 30.5, 33.5, 36, 38, 40.5, 46.5, 48.5, 51, 54, 56.5) cm

13 6¾ (7, 7, 7½, 8, 8½, 9, 9, 9¼, 9¾, 10, 11)"
   17 (18, 18, 19, 20.5, 21.5, 23, 23, 23.5, 25, 25.5, 28) cm

14 8 (8, 8, 9, 9, 9, 9, 9, 8½, 8, 7½)"
   20.5 (20.5, 20.5, 23, 23, 23, 23, 23, 21.5, 20.5, 19) cm

15 9¼ (9¾, 10½, 11, 12¼, 13, 13, 14¾, 16, 17¼, 17¼, 17¼)"
   23.5 (25, 26.5, 28, 31, 33, 33, 37.5, 40.5, 44, 44, 44) cm

Entangled Raglan

One of the most exciting things about the raglan construction, from a designer's perspective, is that the raglan lines offer a beautiful chance to show off stitch patterning. In this cardigan, I combined a smooth, lovely wool with beautiful cables that I used to adorn the seams of the garments. Those seams are important for stability (cables are heavy!), as are the buttons at the top of the cardigan. As you knit, make sure your neck edge is strong, since much of the weight of the sweater is supported by it. You'll be rewarded by a stunning garment that's also comfortable to wear.

FINISHED MEASUREMENTS

33¼ (35½, 37, 38, 41, 41¾, 44, 47½, 49¾, 53¼, 57, 61½)" [84.5 (90, 94, 96.5, 104, 106, 112, 120.5, 126.5, 135.5, 145, 156) cm] bust, buttoned

NOTE: Pullover is intended to be worn with 3–4" (7.5–10 cm) ease in the bust.

YARN

Swans Island Yarns Washable Wool Merino DK Weight [100% washable merino wool; 140 yards (128 meters)/50 grams]: 8 (9, 9, 10, 11, 11, 12, 13, 14, 15, 16, 17) hanks Pumpkin

NEEDLES

One pair straight needles size US 6 (4 mm)

One 24" circular needle size US 6 (4 mm), for Neckband

One pair double pointed needles (dpns), size US 5 (3.75 mm), for I-cord

Change needle size if necessary to obtain correct gauge.

NOTIONS

Stitch markers; removable stitch markers; stitch holders; cable needle; three 1½" (4 cm) toggle-style buttons

GAUGE

22 sts and 32 rows = 4" (10 cm) in St st

NOTES

Front neck decreases should be worked to match the slant of the edge being shaped, as follows:

FOR LEFT-SLANTING EDGES:
On RS rows, ssk, work to end; on WS rows, work to last 2 sts, ssp.

FOR RIGHT-SLANTING EDGES:
On RS rows, work to last 2 sts, k2tog; on WS rows, p2tog, work to end.

You may work Right and Left Baluster Cables from text or Charts.

BACK

CO 92 (96, 104, 108, 116, 120, 124, 132, 136, 148, 160, 168) sts.

SET-UP ROW (RS): K1 (1, 1, 3, 3, 3, 1, 1, 1, 1, 1), [p2, k2] 2 (2, 2, 2, 2, 2, 3, 3, 3, 3, 3) times, pm, work Left Baluster Cable (see page 122) over 8 sts, pm, k2, *p2, k2; repeat from * to last 17 (17, 17, 19, 19, 19, 19, 21, 21, 21, 21, 21) sts, pm, work Right Baluster Cable (see page 122) over 8 sts, pm, [k2, p2] 2 (2, 2, 2, 2, 2, 3, 3, 3, 3, 3) times, knit to end.

NEXT ROW: P1 (1, 1, 3, 3, 3, 1, 1, 1, 1, 1), [k2, p2] 2 (2, 2, 2, 2, 2, 3, 3, 3, 3, 3) times, sm, work Right Baluster Cable to marker, sm, p2, *k2, p2; repeat from * to marker, sm, work Left Baluster Cable to marker, sm, [p2, k2] 2 (2, 2, 2, 2, 2, 3, 3, 3, 3, 3) times, purl to end.

Work even until piece measures 2" (5 cm) from the beginning, ending with a WS row.

Work even, working in St st between center markers, and in patterns as established on remaining sts, until piece measures 2½ (2½, 2¾, 2¾, 3, 3, 3, 3¼, 3¼, 3¼, 3¼, 3¼)" [6.5 (6.5, 7, 7, 7.5, 7.5, 7.5, 8.5, 8.5, 8.5, 8.5, 8.5) cm], ending with a RS row.

NEXT ROW (WS): Work 30 (32, 34, 36, 38, 40, 41, 44, 45, 49, 53, 56) sts, place shaping marker, p32 (32, 36, 36, 40, 40, 42, 44, 46, 50, 54, 56), place shaping marker, work to end.

SHAPE WAIST

DECREASE ROW (RS): Decrease 1 st each side this row, then every 8 rows 4 times, as follows: Work to 2 sts before first shaping marker, ssk, sm, work to next shaping marker, sm,

Cables and shaping at the same time

Gorgeous hand-dyed superwash wool

k2tog, work to end—82 (86, 94, 98, 106, 110, 114, 122, 126, 138, 150, 158) sts remain. Work even until piece measures 7½ (7½, 7¾, 7¾, 8, 8, 8¼, 8¼, 8¼, 8¼, 8¼)" [19 (19, 19.5, 19.5, 20.5, 20.5, 20.5, 21, 21, 21, 21, 21) cm] from the beginning, ending with a WS row.

SHAPE BUST

INCREASE ROW (RS): Increase 1 st each side this row, then every 10 rows 4 times, as follows: Work to first shaping marker, M1R, sm, work to next shaping marker, sm, M1L, work to end—92 (96, 104, 108, 116, 120, 124, 132, 136, 148, 160, 168) sts remain. Work even, removing shaping markers on first row, until piece measures 15¼ (15¼, 15½, 15½, 16, 16¼, 16¼, 16¾, 17, 16¾, 16¾, 16¾)" [38.5 (38.5, 39.5, 39.5, 40.5, 41.5, 41.5, 42.5, 43, 42.5, 42.5, 42.5) cm] from the beginning, ending with a WS row.

SHAPE RAGLAN

BO 6 (6, 6, 8, 8, 8, 10, 10, 10, 10, 10) sts at beginning of next 2 rows, then decrease 1 st along inside edge of cable panels every RS row 7 (7, 10, 7, 11, 12, 12, 12, 13, 19, 25, 29) times, then every 4 rows 8 (8, 7, 10, 8, 8, 9, 9, 9, 6, 2, 0) times, then every RS row 2 (3, 3, 2, 4, 4, 4, 5, 5, 7, 10, 12) times, as follows: K3, sm, work to marker, sm, k1, ssk, knit to last 14 sts, k2tog, k1, sm, work to marker, sm, k3—46 (48, 52, 54, 54, 56, 58, 60, 62, 64, 66, 66) sts remain. You should have worked 52 (54, 56, 60, 64, 66, 70, 72, 74, 78, 80, 84) rows from beginning of raglan shaping; raglan should measure approximately 6½ (6¾, 7, 7½, 8, 8¼, 8¾, 9, 9¼, 9¾, 10, 10½)" [16.5 (17, 18, 19, 20.5, 21, 22, 23, 23.5, 25, 25.5, 26.5) cm]. Make note of last row of Cable patterns worked.

BO all sts in pattern.

RIGHT FRONT

CO 50 (54, 54, 56, 60, 60, 64, 70, 74, 78, 82, 90) sts.

SET-UP ROW (RS): K3, pm, work Left Baluster Cable over 8 sts, pm, k2, *p2, k2; repeat from * to last 17 (17, 17, 19, 19, 19, 19, 21, 21, 21, 21, 21) sts, pm, work Right Baluster Cable over 8 sts, pm, [k2, p2] 2 (2, 2, 2, 2, 2, 2, 3, 3, 3, 3, 3) times, knit to end.

NEXT ROW: P1 (1, 1, 3, 3, 3, 3, 1, 1, 1, 1, 1), [k2, p2] 2 (2, 2, 2, 2, 2, 2, 3, 3, 3, 3, 3) times, sm, work Right Baluster Cable to marker, sm, p2, *k2, p2; repeat from * to marker, sm, work Left Baluster Cable to marker, sm, purl to end.

Work even until piece measures 2" (5 cm), ending with a WS row.

NEXT ROW (RS): Work in patterns as established to second marker, sm, knit to next marker, sm, work in patterns as established to end.

Work even, working in St st between center markers, and in patterns as established on remaining sts, until piece mea-

sures 15¼ (15¼, 15½, 15½, 16, 16¼, 16¼, 16¾, 17, 16¾, 16¾, 16¾)" [38.5 (38.5, 39.5, 39.5, 40.5, 41.5, 41.5, 42.5, 43, 42.5, 42.5, 42.5) cm], ending with a RS row.

SHAPE RAGLAN AND NECK

Note: Raglan and neck shaping will be worked at the same time; please read entire section through before beginning. When 14 sts remain, you will need to shift the raglan decreases 1 or more sts toward the armhole edge on decrease rows in order to complete the decreases.

NEXT ROW (WS): BO 6 (6, 6, 8, 8, 8, 10, 10, 10, 10, 10) sts, work to end—44 (48, 48, 48, 52, 52, 56, 60, 64, 68, 72, 80) sts remain.

DECREASE ROW (RS): Decrease 1 st this row, then every RS row 6 (6, 9, 6, 10, 11, 11, 11, 12, 18, 24, 28) times, then every 4 rows 8 (8, 7, 10, 8, 8, 9, 9, 9, 6, 2, 0) times, then every RS row 2 (3, 3, 2, 4, 4, 4, 5, 5, 7, 10, 12) times, as follows: Work to last 14 sts, k2tog, k1, sm, work to end.

AT THE SAME TIME, when you have worked 28 (30, 32, 36, 40, 42, 46, 48, 50, 54, 56, 60) raglan shaping rows, begin neck shaping.

NEXT ROW (RS): Work 11 sts and place on holder (including markers), work to end.

Work even for 1 row.

DECREASE ROW (RS): Continuing to work raglan shaping as established, decrease 1 st at neck edge this row, then every 4 (0, 0, 3, 3, 0, 2, 0, 1, 1, 1, 1) row(s) 1 (0, 0, 4, 4, 0, 3, 0, 6, 4, 2, 10) time(s), then every 5 (3, 4, 4, 4, 4, 3, 2, 2, 2, 2, 2) rows 3 (7, 5, 2, 2, 5, 5, 11, 8, 9, 10, 6) times, ending with a WS row—11 sts remain when all shaping is complete. You should have worked 52 (54, 56, 60, 64, 66, 70, 72, 74, 78, 80, 84) rows from beginning of raglan shaping; raglan should measure approximately 6½ (6¾, 7, 7½, 8, 8¼, 8¾, 9, 9¼, 9¾, 10, 10½)" [16.5 (17, 18, 19, 20.5, 21, 22, 23, 23.5, 25, 25.5, 26.5) cm]. Make note of last row of Cable patterns worked.

BO all sts in pattern.

LEFT FRONT

CO 50 (54, 54, 56, 60, 60, 64, 70, 74, 78, 82, 90) sts.

SET-UP ROW (RS): K1 (1, 1, 3, 3, 3, 3, 1, 1, 1, 1, 1), [p2, k2] 2 (2, 2, 2, 2, 2, 2, 3, 3, 3, 3, 3) times, pm, work Left Baluster Cable over 8 sts, pm, k2, *p2, k2; repeat from * to last 11 sts, pm, work Right Baluster Cable over 8 sts, pm, knit to end.

NEXT ROW: P3, sm, work Right Baluster Cable to marker, sm, p2, *k2, p2; repeat from * to marker, sm, work Left Baluster Cable to marker, sm, [p2, k2] 2 (2, 2, 2, 2, 2, 2, 3, 3, 3, 3, 3) times, purl to end.

Work even until piece measures 2" (5 cm), ending with a WS row.

NEXT ROW (RS): Work in patterns as established to second marker, sm, knit to next marker, sm, work in patterns as established to end.

Work even, working in St st between center markers, and in patterns as established on remaining sts, until piece measures 15¼ (15¼, 15½, 15½, 16, 16¼, 16¼, 16¾, 17, 16¾, 16¾, 16¾)" [38.5 (38.5, 39.5, 39.5, 40.5, 41.5, 41.5, 42.5, 43, 42.5, 42.5, 42.5) cm], ending with a RS row.

SHAPE RAGLAN AND NECK

Note: Raglan and neck shaping will be worked at the same time; please read entire section through before beginning. When 14 sts remain, you will need to shift the raglan decreases 1 or more sts toward the armhole edge on decrease rows in order to complete the decreases.

NEXT ROW (RS): BO 6 (6, 6, 8, 8, 8, 8, 10, 10, 10, 10, 10) sts, work to end—44 (48, 48, 48, 52, 52, 56, 60, 64, 68, 72, 80) sts remain. Work even for 1 row.

DECREASE ROW (RS): Decrease 1 st this row, then every RS row 6 (6, 9, 6, 10, 11, 11, 11, 12, 18, 24, 28) times, then every 4 rows 8 (8, 7, 10, 8, 8, 9, 9, 9, 6, 2, 0) times, then every RS row 2 (3, 3, 2, 4, 4, 4, 5, 5, 7, 10, 12) times, as follows: Work to second marker, sm, k1, ssk, work to end.

AT THE SAME TIME, when you have worked 28 (30, 32, 36, 40, 42, 46, 48, 50, 54, 56, 60) raglan shaping rows, begin neck shaping.

NEXT ROW (RS): Work to end. Cut yarn, place last 11 sts on holder (including markers). Rejoin yarn.

Work even for 1 row.

DECREASE ROW (RS): Continuing to work raglan shaping as established, decrease 1 st at neck edge this row, then every 4 (0, 0, 3, 3, 0, 2, 0, 1, 1, 1, 1) row(s) 1 (0, 0, 4, 4, 0, 3, 0, 6, 4, 2, 10) time(s), then every 5 (3, 4, 4, 4, 4, 3, 2, 2, 2, 2, 2) rows 3 (7, 5, 2, 2, 5, 5, 11, 8, 9, 10, 6) times, ending with a WS row—11 sts remain when all shaping is complete. You should have worked 52 (54, 56, 60, 64, 66, 70, 72, 74, 78, 80, 84) rows from beginning of raglan shaping; raglan should measure approximately 6½ (6¾, 7, 7½, 8, 8¼, 8¾, 9, 9¼, 9¾, 10, 10½)" [16.5 (17, 18, 19, 20.5, 21, 22, 23, 23.5, 25, 25.5, 26.5) cm]. Make note of last row of Cable patterns worked.

BO all sts in pattern.

SLEEVES

CO 52 (56, 56, 60, 60, 60, 68, 76, 80, 88, 88, 88) sts.

SET-UP ROW (RS): K1 (1, 1, 3, 3, 3, 3, 1, 1, 1, 1, 1), [p2, k2] 2 (2, 2, 2, 2, 2, 2, 3, 3, 3, 3, 3) times, pm, work Left Baluster Cable over 8 sts, pm, k2, *p2, k2; repeat from * to last 17 (17, 17, 19, 19, 19, 19, 21, 21, 21, 21, 21) sts, pm, work Right Baluster Cable over 8 sts, pm, [k2, p2] 2 (2, 2, 2, 2, 2, 2, 3, 3, 3, 3, 3) times, knit to end.

NEXT ROW: P1 (1, 1, 3, 3, 3, 3, 1, 1, 1, 1, 1), [k2, p2] 2 (2, 2, 2, 2, 2, 2, 3, 3, 3, 3, 3) times, sm, work Right Baluster Cable to marker, sm, p2, *k2, p2; repeat from * to marker, sm, work Left Baluster Cable to marker, sm, [p2, k2] 2 (2, 2, 2, 2, 2, 2, 3, 3, 3, 3, 3) times, purl to end.

Work even until piece measures 2" (5 cm), ending with a WS row.

NEXT ROW (RS): Work in patterns as established to second marker, sm, knit to next marker, sm, work in patterns as established to end.

Work even for 2 rows, working in St st between center markers, and in patterns as established on remaining sts.

SHAPE SLEEVE

INCREASE ROW (RS): Increase 1 st each side this row, then every 10 (8, 4, 6, 4, 4, 4, 2, 2, 2, 2, 2) rows 1 (2, 1, 9, 6, 14, 13, 4, 7, 2, 6, 10) time(s), then every 12 (10, 6, 0, 6, 0, 0, 4, 4, 4, 4, 4) rows 3 (3, 7, 0, 5, 0, 0, 10, 8, 11, 9, 7) times, as follows: Work to second marker, sm, k1, M1R, knit to 1 st before next marker, M1L, k1, sm, work to end—62 (68, 74, 80, 84, 90, 96, 106, 112, 116, 120, 124) sts. Work even until sleeve measures 10 (10, 10, 11, 11, 11, 10½, 10, 10, 10, 10, 10)" [25.5 (25.5, 25.5, 28, 28, 28, 26.5, 25.5, 25.5, 25.5, 25.5, 25.5) cm] from the beginning, ending with a WS row.

SHAPE RAGLAN

BO 6 (6, 6, 8, 8, 8, 8, 10, 10, 10, 10, 10) sts at beginning of next 2 rows, then decrease 1 st each side every RS row 1 (7, 10, 7, 11, 12, 12, 12, 13, 19, 25, 29) time(s), then every 4 rows 11 (9, 7, 8, 8, 6, 6, 4, 2, 2, 2, 2) times, then every RS row 2 (1, 3, 6, 4, 8, 10, 15,

19, 15, 10, 8) time(s), as follows: K3, sm, work to marker, sm, k1, ssk, knit to last 14 sts, k2tog, k1, sm, work to marker, sm, k3—50 (56, 62, 64, 68, 74, 80, 86, 92, 96, 100, 104) sts remain. You should have worked 52 (54, 56, 60, 64, 66, 70, 72, 74, 78, 80, 84) rows from beginning of raglan shaping; raglan should measure approximately 6½ (6¾, 7, 7½, 8, 8¼, 8¾, 9, 9¼, 9¾, 10, 10½)" [16.5 (17, 18, 19, 20.5, 21, 22, 23, 23.5, 25, 25.5, 26.5) cm]. Make note of last row of Cable patterns worked. BO all sts in pattern.

FINISHING

Block pieces as desired. Sew raglan seams. Sew side and Sleeve seams.

NECKBAND

With RS facing, using circular needle and beginning at Right Front neck edge, work across 11 held Right Front sts, pick up and knit 18 (18, 18, 18, 18, 18, 18, 22, 22, 22, 22, 22) sts along Front neck shaping edge; picking up 1 st in each BO st (and omitting seam sts), pick up and knit 10 Front sts to raglan seam, 20 (20, 20, 20, 20, 20, 22, 22, 22, 22, 24, 24) Right Sleeve sts to raglan seam, 44 (46, 50, 52, 52, 54, 56, 58, 60, 62, 64, 64) Back sts to raglan seam, 20 (20, 20, 20, 20, 20, 22, 22, 22, 22, 24, 24) Left Sleeve sts to raglan seam, then 10 sts to top of Left Front neck shaping; pick up and knit 18 (18, 18, 18, 18, 18, 18, 22, 22, 22, 22, 22) sts along Front neck shaping edge, then work across 11 held Left Front sts—162 (164, 168, 170, 170, 172, 178, 188, 190, 192, 198, 198) sts.

SET-UP ROW (WS): *Note: When working Cable patterns, begin with next WS row following last row worked before binding off.* P3, sm, work Left Baluster Cable over 8 sts, sm, k2, [p2, k2] 4 (4, 4, 4, 4, 4, 4, 5, 5, 5, 5, 5) times, pm, work Right Baluster Cable over 8 sts, pm, k4, pm, work Left Baluster Cable over 8 sts, pm, k0 (0, 0, 0, 0, 0, 2, 2, 2, 2, 4, 4), work Right Baluster Cable over 8 sts, pm, k4, pm, work Left Baluster Cable over 8 sts, pm, k3 (2, 2, 3, 3, 2, 3, 2, 3, 2, 3, 3), [p2, k2] 5 (6, 7, 7, 7, 8, 8, 9, 9, 10, 10, 10) times, k1 (0, 0, 1, 1, 0, 1, 0, 1, 0, 1, 1), work Left Baluster Cable over 8 sts, pm, k4, pm, work Left Baluster Cable over 8 sts, pm, k0 (0, 0, 0, 0, 0, 2, 2, 2, 2, 4, 4), work Right Baluster Cable over 8 sts, pm, k4, pm, work Left Baluster Cable over 8 sts, pm, k2, [p2, k2] 4 (4, 4, 4, 4, 4, 4, 5, 5, 5, 5, 5) times, sm, work Right Baluster Cable over 8 sts, sm, p3.

NEXT ROW: Work Cable patterns between markers as established; on all other sts, knit the knit sts and purl the purl sts as they face you.

Work even until piece measures 1" (2.5 cm) from pick-up row. BO all sts in pattern.

I-CORD BUTTON BAND

With RS facing, using circular needle and beginning at Left Front neck edge, pick up and knit 1 st in each row along Left Front edge. Cut yarn. Slide sts to opposite end of needle. Using dpn, CO 3 sts. *K2, skp (1 st from I-cord together with 1 st from circ needle), slide sts to opposite end of dpn; repeat from * until all sts on circ needle have been worked. BO I-cord sts.

I-CORD BUTTONHOLE BAND

Place markers for 3 buttonholes along Right Front, the first 1¼" (3 cm) down from neck edge, and the second and third buttons each 1¼" (3 cm) below the previous. With RS facing, using circular needle and beginning at lower Right Front neck edge, pick up and knit 1 st in each row along Right Front edge, skipping 3 rows at each marker to create buttonhole. Work I-cord as for Button Band, working 3 plain I-cord rows at each buttonhole, as follows: [K3, slide sts to opposite end of dpn]. Sew buttons opposite buttonholes.

LEFT BALUSTER CABLE   RIGHT BALUSTER CABLE

8-st panel   8-st panel

☐ Knit on RS, purl on WS.   ▪ Purl on RS, knit on WS.

▱ C4B: Slip 2 sts to cable needle, hold to back, k2, k2 from cable needle.

▱ C4F: Slip 2 sts to cable needle, hold to front, k2, k2 from cable needle.

LEFT BALUSTER CABLE
(panel of 8 sts; 18-row repeat)

ROW 1 (RS): P2, k4, p2.
ROW 2: Knit the knit sts and purl the purl sts as they face you.
ROWS 3, 7, AND 11: P2, C4F, p2.
ROWS 4–6, 8–10, AND 12–18: Repeat Row 2.
Repeat Rows 1–18 for Left Baluster Cable.

RIGHT BALUSTER CABLE
(panel of 8 sts; 18-row repeat)

ROW 1 (RS): P2, k4, p2.
ROW 2: Knit the knit sts and purl the purl sts as they face you.
ROWS 3, 7, AND 11: P2, C4B, p2.
ROWS 4–6, 8–10, AND 12–18: Repeat Row 2.
Repeat Rows 1–18 for Right Baluster Cable.

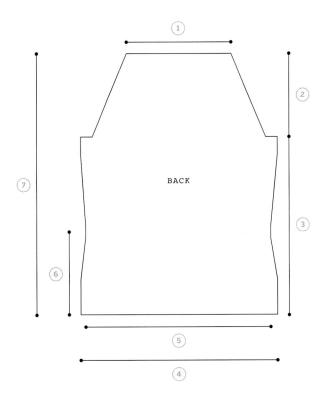

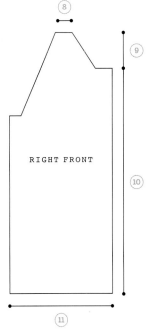

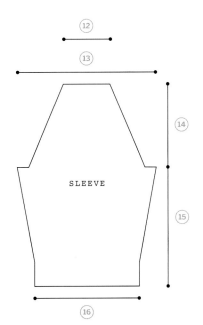

BACK

1 8¼ (8¾, 9½, 9¾, 9¾, 10¼, 10½, 11, 11¼, 11¾, 12, 12)"
   21 (22, 24, 25, 25, 26, 26.5, 28, 28.5, 30, 30.5, 30.5) cm

2 6½ (6¾, 7, 7½, 8, 8¼, 8¾, 9, 9¼, 9¾, 10, 10½)"
   16.5 (17, 18, 19, 20.5, 21, 22, 23, 23.5, 25, 25.5, 26.5) cm

3 15¼ (15¼, 15½, 15½, 16, 16¼, 16¼, 16¾, 17, 16¾, 16¾, 16¾)"
   38.5 (38.5, 39.5, 39.5, 40.5, 41.5, 41.5, 42.5, 43, 42.5, 42.5, 42.5) cm

4 16 (16¾, 18¼, 18¾, 20¼, 21, 21¾, 23¼, 24, 26, 28¼, 29¾)" hip and bust
   40.5 (42.5, 46.5, 47.5, 51.5, 53.5, 55, 59, 61, 66, 72, 75.5) cm

5 14¼ (15, 16½, 17, 18½, 19¼, 20, 21¼, 22, 24¼, 26½, 28)" waist
   36 (38, 42, 43, 47, 49, 51, 54, 56, 61.5, 67.5, 71) cm

6 7 (7, 7¼, 7¼, 7½, 7½, 7½, 7¾, 7¾, 7¾, 7¾, 7¾)"
   18 (18, 18.5, 18.5, 19, 19, 19, 19.5, 19.5, 19.5, 19.5, 19.5) cm

7 21¾ (22, 22½, 23, 24, 24½, 25, 25¾, 26¼, 26½, 26¾, 27¼)"
   55 (56, 57, 58.5, 61, 62, 63.5, 65.5, 66.5, 67.5, 68, 69) cm

RIGHT FRONT

8 1¾"/4.5 cm

9 3"/7.5 cm

10 18¾ (19, 19½, 20, 21, 21½, 22, 22¾, 23¼, 23½, 23¾, 24¼)"
    47.5 (48.5, 49.5, 51, 53.5, 54.5, 56, 58, 59, 59.5, 60.5, 61.5) cm

11 8½ (9¼, 9¼, 9½, 10¼, 10¼, 11, 12, 12¾, 13½, 14¼, 15¾)"
    21.5 (23.5, 23.5, 24, 26, 26, 28, 30.5, 32.5, 34.5, 36, 40) cm

SLEEVE

12 3½ (3½, 3½, 3½, 3½, 3½, 4, 4, 4, 4, 4¼, 4¼)"
    9 (9, 9, 9, 9, 9, 10, 10, 10, 10, 11, 11) cm

13 10½ (11¾, 12¾, 13¾, 14½, 15½, 16¾, 18½, 19½, 20¼, 21, 21¾)"
    26.5 (30, 32.5, 35, 37, 39.5, 42.5, 47, 49.5, 51.5, 53.5, 55) cm

14 6½ (6¾, 7, 7½, 8, 8¼, 8¾, 9, 9¼, 9¾, 10, 10½)"
    16.5 (17, 18, 19, 20.5, 21, 22, 23, 23.5, 25, 25.5, 26.5) cm

15 10 (10, 10, 11, 11, 11, 10½, 10, 10, 10, 10, 10)"
    25.5 (25.5, 25.5, 28, 28, 28, 26.5, 25.5, 25.5, 25.5, 25.5, 25.5) cm

16 8¾ (9½, 9½, 10¼, 10¼, 10¼, 11¾, 13, 13¾, 15, 15, 15)"
    22 (24, 24, 26, 26, 26, 30, 33, 35, 38, 38, 38) cm

YOKES

Yoked sweaters were an integral part of my childhood in chilly Maine. They're the go-to construction if you want to make a sweater with stranded colorwork, and that double- or triple-thick fabric keeps the wind out like no other. They're comfortable, cozy, and always make me want a cup of hot cocoa.

Yokes have gotten a modern do-over lately, with some shorter yoke depths, snugger fits, and stitch patterning like lace or cables (or both!) in place of, or in addition to, the color patterns of my youth. This chapter gives you some great freedom to explore all your options, starting with a classic stranded colorwork mini, Zellige (page 127), where the color patterning reminds me of Moroccan tilework.

Generally speaking, fit-wise, the deeper the yoke depth, the more generous you'll want your fit to be. For a short yoke depth like the cabled pullover on page 135, you can go with a relatively close fit of 2-4" (5-10 cm) ease if you wish; for something with a more generous yoke, like the Snowdrift Pullover on page 142, give yourself at least 4" (10 cm) of room.

I've also given you a plain option with the Clearsight Pullover (page 130), worked in a polished, modern superwash merino, and a lusciously cabled choice with the Maypole pullover (page 135), in a heathered and cozy wool-alpaca blend.

While these sweaters might look a bit fancier than some of the others in this book, they're really not all that scary—so go ahead and give them a try! I promise you'll love wearing the result.

Stranded color work

Easy-care,
kid-friendly
yarn

Zellige Yoke Mini

Zellige is the name of beautifully-intricate Morroccan mosaic tilework, often painted in shades of blue and white. I could think of nothing else when I swatched the pattern on this yoke, and I am excited to create an adult version for myself. In miniature, this sweater gives you all of the techniques you need to make a stunning yoke sweater—and a gift for someone else that's sure to wow—in a fraction of the time a larger garment would take.

SIZES
To fit children 1 (2, 3/4, 5/6, 7/8, 9/10) year(s)

FINISHED MEASUREMENTS
22 (24, 26, 28, 30, 32)" [56 (61, 66, 71, 76, 81.5) cm] chest

NOTE: Pullover is intended to be worn with 2–4" (5–10 cm) positive ease in the chest.

YARN
Berroco Vintage DK [52% acrylic/40% wool/8% nylon; 288 yards (263 meters); 100 grams]: 2 (2, 3, 3, 4, 4) hanks #2192 Chana Dal (MC); 1 hank each #2143 Dark Denim **(A)**, #2194 Breezeway **(B)**, and #2101 Mochi **(C)**

NEEDLES
One 20–24" (50–60 cm) long (depending on bust size) circular needle size US 5 (3.75 mm)

One set of five double-pointed needles (dpns) size US 5 (3.75 mm)

Change needle size if necessary to obtain correct gauge.

NOTIONS
Stitch markers; stitch holders or waste yarn

GAUGE
24 sts and 32 rnds = 4" (10 cm) in St st
24 sts and 32 rnds = 4" (10 cm) in Fair Isle pattern from Yoke Chart

NOTE: Be sure to swatch the Fair Isle pattern; you may need to change the needle size for the Fair Isle sections.

NOTES
The Body of this pullover is worked in the round from the bottom to the underarm, then set aside while the Sleeves are worked in the round from the bottom to the underarm. The Body and Sleeves are then joined and the Yoke is worked to the neck, with circular Yoke shaping; the Back neck is shaped using short rows.

BODY
Using circular needle and MC, CO 132 (144, 156, 168, 180, 192) sts. Join for working in the rnd, being careful not to twist sts; pm for beginning of rnd and after 66 (72, 78, 84, 90, 96) sts for side. Begin Garter st (purl 1 rnd, knit 1 rnd); work even for ¾" (2 cm), ending with a purl rnd.

Change to St st; work even until piece measures 10 (10, 11, 12, 12½, 13)" [25.5 (25.5, 28, 30.5, 32, 33) cm] from the beginning.

NEXT RND: [Knit to 5 (6, 6, 6, 7, 7) sts before marker, BO 10 (12, 12, 12, 14, 14) sts (removing marker)] twice—56 (60, 66, 72, 76, 82) sts remain each for Front and Back. Place sts on holder or waste yarn and set aside; do not cut yarn.

SLEEVES
Using dpns and MC, CO 34 (34, 36, 40, 42, 46) sts. Join for working in the rnd, being careful not to twist sts; pm for beginning of rnd. Begin Garter st; work even for ¾" (2 cm), ending with a purl rnd.

Change to St st; knit 2 rnds.

SHAPE SLEEVE

INCREASE RND: Increase 2 sts this rnd, then every 8 (7, 8, 10, 11, 12) rnds 6 (8, 8, 8, 8, 8) times, as follows: K2, M1R, knit to last 2 sts, M1L, knit to end—48 (52, 54, 58, 60, 64) sts. Work even until piece measures 9 (10, 11, 13, 14, 15)" [23 (25.5, 28, 33, 35.5, 38) cm], ending last rnd 5 (6, 6, 6, 7, 7) sts before beginning-of-rnd marker.

NEXT RND: BO 10 (12, 12, 12, 14, 14) sts (removing marker), knit to end—38 (40, 42, 46, 46, 50) sts remain. Place sts on holder for first Sleeve and set aside; leave sts on needles for second Sleeve.

YOKE

With RS facing, using yarn attached to Back, k28 (30, 33, 36, 38, 41) Back sts, pm for beginning of rnd, knit to end of Back, knit across Left Sleeve sts, pm, knit across Front sts, pm, knit across Right Sleeve sts, knit to beginning of rnd—188 (200, 216, 236, 244, 264) sts.

SHAPE YOKE

Note: Change to dpns when necessary for number of sts on needle.

SIZES 22, 24, AND 28" (56, 61, AND 71 CM) ONLY

DECREASE RND: Working decreases as k2tog, decrease 2 (2, -, 2, -, -) sts evenly across Back—186 (198, -, 234, -, -) sts remain.

SIZE 30" (76 CM) ONLY

INCREASE RND: Working increases as M1L, increase - (-, -, -, 2, -) sts evenly across Back—246 sts.

ALL SIZES

Knit 0 (1, 9, 13, 17, 21) rnd(s).

SHAPE BACK NECK

Note: Back neck is shaped using short rows (see Special Techniques, page 174).

SHORT ROW 1 (RS): Knit to 1 st before first marker, w&t.

SHORT ROW 2 (WS): Purl to 1 st before second marker, w&t.

SHORT ROW 3: Knit to 6 sts before wrapped st from previous RS row, w&t.

SHORT ROW 4: Purl to 6 sts before wrapped st from previous WS row, w&t.

SHORT ROWS 5–8: Repeat Short Rows 3 and 4.

SHORT ROW 9: Knit to end.

Knit 2 (2, 2, 5, 5, 5) rnds, knitting wraps together with wrapped sts as you come to them, and removing all markers except beginning-of-rnd marker.

Work Rnds 1–30 of Yoke Chart, working decreases as indicated in Chart—93 (99, 108, 117, 123, 132) sts remain.
Knit 1 rnd.

SIZE 22" (56 CM) ONLY

DECREASE RND: [(K1, k2tog) 7 times, k3] 3 times, [k1, k2tog] 6 times, k3—66 sts remain.

SIZE 24" (61 CM) ONLY

DECREASE RND: *[K1, k2tog] 4 times, k3, [k1, k2tog] 5 times, k3; repeat from * to end—72 sts remain.
Knit 2 rnds.

SIZE 26" (66 CM) ONLY

DECREASE RND: *[K1, k2tog] 5 times, k3; repeat from * to end—78 sts remain.
Knit 2 rnds.

SIZE 28" (71 CM) ONLY

DECREASE RND: *[K1, k2tog] 5 times, k3, [k1, k2tog] 6 times, k3]; repeat from * to end—84 sts remain.
Knit 2 rnds.

SIZE 30" (76 CM) ONLY

DECREASE RND: [(K1, k2tog) 6 times, k3] 5 times, [k1, k2tog] 5 times, k3—88 sts remain.
Knit 2 rnds.

SIZE 32" (81.5 CM) ONLY

DECREASE RND: [K1, k2tog] 7 times, k3, [(k1, k2tog) 6 times, k3] 4 times, [k1, k2tog] 7 times, k3—94 sts remain.
Knit 2 rnds.

ALL SIZES

Work even if necessary until Yoke measures 5½ (5¾, 6¾, 7¼, 7¾, 8¼)" [14 (14.5, 17, 18.5, 19.5, 21) cm] at center Back neck.

Change to Garter st; work even for ½" (1.5 cm), ending with a purl rnd.
BO all sts.

FINISHING

Block piece as desired. Sew underarm seams.

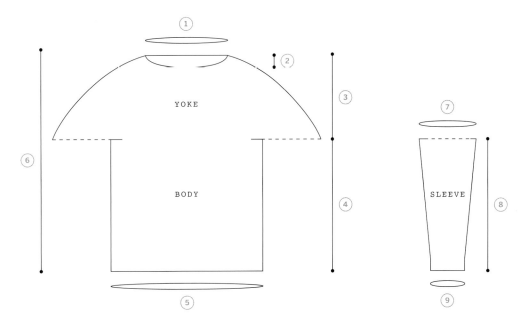

YOKE AND BODY

1 11 (12, 13, 14, 14¾, 15¾)"
   28 (30.5. 33, 35.5, 37.5, 40) cm

2 1"/2.5 cm

3 6 (6¼, 7¼, 7¾, 8¼, 8¾)"
   15 (16, 18.5, 19.5, 21, 22) cm

4 10 (10, 11, 12, 12½, 13)"
   25.5 (25.5, 28, 30.5, 32, 33) cm

5 22 (24, 26, 28, 30, 32)"
   56 (61, 66, 71, 76, 81.5) cm

6 16 (16¼, 18¼, 19¾, 20¾, 21¾)"
   40.5 (41.5, 46.5, 50, 52.5, 55) cm

SLEEVE

7 8 (8¾, 9, 9¾, 10, 10¾)"
   20.5 (22, 23, 25, 25.5, 27.5) cm

8 9 (10, 11, 13, 14, 15)"
   23 (25.5, 28, 33, 35.5, 38) cm

9 5¾ (5¾, 6, 6¾, 7, 7¾)"
   14.5 (14.5, 15, 17, 18, 19.5) cm

YOKE CHART

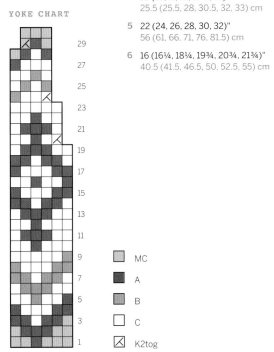

MC	
A	
B	
C	
K2tog	

└─ 6-st repeat ─┘

Clearsight Pullover

We often think of intricately patterned sweaters when we think of yoked garments, but they work just as well when completely unadorned. This gloriously plain "blank slate" sweater will help you get comfortable with yoke techniques without worrying about stitch patterning, and provides a lovely canvas onto which you can insert your own stitch patterns should you so choose. I've worked this sweater in a soft, easygoing superwash wool that is economical and comes in a variety of colors, and kept the stitch counts easy to improvise on.

FINISHED MEASUREMENTS

34¼ (36, 38¼, 40, 42¼, 44, 46¼, 48, 50¼, 52, 54¼, 58¼)" [87 (91.5, 97, 101.5, 107.5, 112, 117.5, 122, 127.5, 132, 138, 148) cm] bust

NOTE: Pullover is intended to be worn with 2–4" (5–10 cm) positive ease in the bust.

YARN

Valley Yarns Valley Superwash DK [100% extra fine merino wool; 137 yards (125 meters)/ 50 grams]: 8 (8, 9, 9, 10, 11, 11, 12, 13, 14, 14, 16) balls #06 Burgundy

NEEDLES

One 24–36" (60–90 cm) long (depending on bust size) circular needle size US 5 (3.75 mm)

One 40" (100 cm) long circular needle size US 5 (3.75 mm), for Yoke

One set of five double-pointed needles (dpns) size US 5 (3.75 mm)

Change needle size if necessary to obtain correct gauge.

NOTIONS

Stitch markers; stitch holders or waste yarn

GAUGE

22 sts and 32 rnds = 4" (10 cm) in St st

STITCH PATTERN

TWISTED RIB
(even number of sts; 1-rnd repeat)
ALL RNDS: *K1-tbl, p1; repeat from * to end.

NOTES

The Body of this pullover is worked in the round from the bottom to the underarm, then set aside while the Sleeves are worked in the round from the bottom to the underarm. The Body and Sleeves are then joined and the Yoke is worked to the neck, with circular Yoke shaping; the Back neck is shaped using short rows.

BODY

Using shorter circular needle, CO 188 (198, 210, 220, 232, 242, 254, 264, 276, 286, 298, 320) sts. Join for working in the rnd, being careful not to twist sts; pm for beginning of rnd and after 94 (99, 105, 110, 116, 121, 127, 132, 138, 143, 149, 160) sts for side. Begin Twisted Rib; work even for 1½" (4 cm).

Change to St st; knit 2 rnds.

NEXT RND: K31 (33, 35, 36, 38, 40, 42, 44, 46, 47, 49, 53), pm for waist shaping, k32 (33, 35, 38, 40, 41, 43, 44, 46, 49, 51, 54), pm for waist shaping, knit to side marker, sm, k23 (24, 26, 27, 29, 30, 31, 33, 34, 35, 37, 40), pm for waist shaping, k48 (51, 53, 56, 58, 61, 65, 66, 70, 73, 75, 80), pm for waist shaping, knit to end.

SHAPE WAIST

DECREASE RND: Decrease 4 sts this rnd, then every 10 rnds 4 times, as follows: [Knit to 2 sts before shaping marker, ssk, sm, knit to next shaping marker, sm, k2tog] twice, knit to end—168 (178, 190, 200, 212, 222, 234, 244, 256, 266, 278, 300) sts remain. Work even until piece measures 8" (20.5 cm) from the beginning.

SHAPE BUST

INCREASE RND: Increase 4 sts this rnd, then every 8 rnds 4 times, as follows: [Knit to shaping marker, M1R, sm, knit to next shaping marker, sm, M1L] twice, knit to end—188 (198,

Crew neckline
and elbow sleeves
make great
layering piece

Trim waist
shaping
flatters the
figure

210, 220, 232, 242, 254, 264, 276, 286, 298, 320) sts. Work even, removing waist shaping markers on first rnd (leaving beginning-of-rnd and side markers in place), until piece measures 14 (14, 14½, 14½, 14½, 15, 15, 15, 15½, 15½, 15½, 16)" [35.5 (35.5, 37, 37, 37, 38, 38, 38, 39.5, 39.5, 39.5, 40.5) cm] from the beginning.

NEXT RND: [Knit to 6 (6, 6, 6, 6, 7, 7, 7, 7, 7, 9, 9) sts before marker, BO 12 (12, 12, 12, 12, 14, 14, 14, 14, 14, 18, 18) sts (removing marker)] twice—82 (87, 93, 98, 104, 107, 113, 118, 124, 129, 131, 142) sts remain each for Front and Back. Place sts on holder or waste yarn and set aside; do not cut yarn.

SLEEVES

Using dpns, CO 58 (62, 64, 66, 70, 72, 80, 84, 88, 94, 98, 106) sts. Join for working in the rnd, being careful not to twist sts;

pm for beginning of rnd. Begin Twisted Rib; work even for 1" (2.5 cm).

Change to St st; knit 2 rnds.

SHAPE SLEEVE

INCREASE RND: Increase 2 sts this rnd, then every 8 (14, 10, 10, 6, 4, 8, 6, 4, 4, 4, 4) rnds 2 (1, 2, 2, 2, 3, 3, 4, 3, 1, 1, 5) time(s), then every 0 (0, 0, 0, 8, 6, 0, 0, 6, 6, 6, 6) rnds 0 (0, 0, 0, 1, 2, 0, 0, 2, 4, 4, 2) time(s), as follows: K2, M1R, knit to last 2 sts, M1L, knit to end—64 (66, 70, 72, 78, 84, 88, 94, 100, 106, 110, 122) sts. Work even until piece measures 5 (5, 5½, 5½, 5½, 6, 6, 6, 6, 6½, 6½, 7)" [12.5 (12.5, 14, 14, 14, 15, 15, 15, 15, 16.5, 16.5, 18) cm] from the beginning, ending last rnd 6 (6, 6, 6, 6, 7, 7, 7, 7, 7, 9, 9) sts before beginning-of-rnd marker.

NEXT RND: BO 12 (12, 12, 12, 12, 14, 14, 14, 14, 14, 18, 18) sts (removing marker), knit to end—52 (54, 58, 60, 66, 70, 74, 80, 86, 92, 92, 104) sts remain. Place sts on holder or waste yarn for first Sleeve and set aside; leave sts on needles for second Sleeve.

YOKE

JOINING RND: With RS facing, using longer circular needle and yarn attached to Back, k41 (43, 46, 49, 52, 53, 56, 59, 62, 64, 65, 71) Back sts, pm for beginning-of-rnd, knit to end of Back, knit across Left Sleeve, pm, knit across Front, pm, knit across Right Sleeve, knit to beginning-of-rnd marker—268 (282, 302, 316, 340, 354, 374, 396, 420, 442, 446, 492) sts.

SHAPE YOKE

Note: Change to shorter circular needle when necessary for number of sts on needle.

SIZES 34¼, 44, AND 46¼" (87, 112, AND 117.5 CM) ONLY
INCREASE RND: Working increase(s) as M1L, increase 2 (-, -, -, -, 1, 1, -, -, -, -, -) st(s) evenly spaced across Back—270 (-, -, -, -, 355, 375, -, -, -, -, -) sts.

SIZES 36, 38¼, 40, 48, 52, 54¼, AND 58¼" (91.5, 97, 101.5, 122, 132, 138, AND 148 CM) ONLY
DECREASE RND: Working decrease(s) as k2tog, decrease - (2, 2, 1, -, -, -, 1, -, 2, 1, 2) st(s) evenly across Back— - (280, 300, 315, -, -, -, 395, -, 440, 445, 490) sts remain.

ALL SIZES
Knit 41 (44, 46, 37, 39, 40, 41, 43, 44, 46, 47, 48) rnds, removing markers between Back and Sleeves (leaving beginning-of-rnd and Front markers in place) on first rnd; Yoke should measure approximately 5½ (5¾, 6, 5, 5, 5¼, 5½, 5¾, 5¾, 6, 6¼, 6¼)" [14 (14.5, 15, 12.5, 12.5, 13.5, 14, 14.5, 14.5, 15, 16, 16) cm].

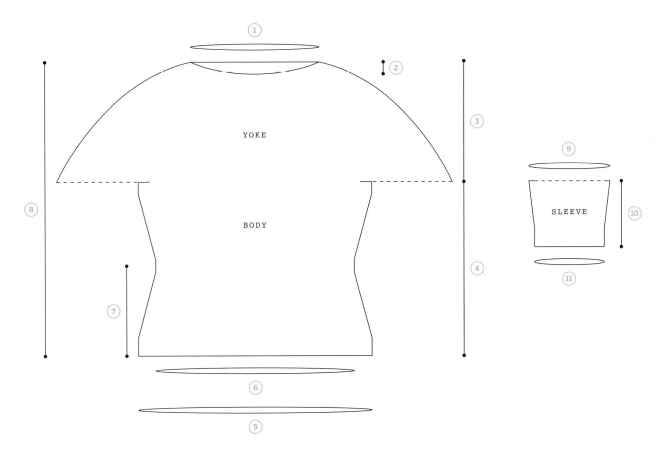

YOKE AND BODY

1 19¾ (20¼, 21¾, 22¼, 22½, 22½, 23¼, 23¼, 23¾, 23¾, 24, 24¾)"
   50 (51.5, 55, 56.5, 57, 57, 59, 59, 60.5, 60.5, 61, 63) cm

2 ¾"/2 cm

3 9¾ (10¼, 10¾, 10¾, 11, 11¼, 11½, 12, 12¼, 12¾, 13, 13¼)"
   25 (26, 27.5, 27.5, 28, 28.5, 29, 30.5, 31, 32.5, 33, 33.5) cm

4 14 (14, 14½, 14½, 14½, 15, 15, 15, 15½, 15½, 15½, 16)"
   35.5 (35.5, 37, 37, 37, 38, 38, 38, 39.5, 39.5, 39.5, 40.5) cm

5 34¼ (36, 38¼, 40, 42¼, 44, 46¼, 48, 50¼, 52, 54¼, 58¼)" hip and bust
   87 (91.5, 97, 101.5, 107.5, 112, 117.5, 122, 127.5, 132, 138, 148) cm

6 30½ (32¼, 34½, 36¼, 38½, 40¼, 42½, 44¼, 46½, 48¼, 50½, 54½)" waist
   77.5 (82, 87.5, 92, 98, 102, 108, 112.5, 118, 122.5, 128.5, 138.5) cm

7 7½"/19 cm

8 23¾ (24¼, 25¼, 25¼, 25½, 26¼, 26½, 27, 27¾, 28¼, 28½, 29¼)"
   60.5 (61.5, 64, 64, 65, 66.5, 67.5, 68.5, 70.5, 72, 72.5, 74.5) cm

SLEEVE

9 11¾ (12, 12¾, 13, 14¼, 15¼, 16, 17, 18¼, 19¼, 20, 22¼)"
   30 (30.5, 32.5, 33, 36, 38.5, 40.5, 43, 46.5, 49, 51, 56.5) cm

10 5 (5, 5½, 5½, 5½, 6, 6, 6, 6, 6½, 6½, 7)"
    12.5 (12.5, 14, 14, 14, 15, 15, 15, 15, 16.5, 16.5, 18) cm

11 10½ (11¼, 11¾, 12, 12¾, 13, 14½, 15¼, 16, 17, 17¾, 19¼)"
    26.5 (28.5, 30, 30.5, 32.5, 33, 37, 38.5, 40.5, 43, 45, 49) cm

DECREASE RND 1: *K3, k2tog; repeat from * to end—216 (224, 240, 252, 272, 284, 300, 316, 336, 352, 356, 392) sts remain. Knit 11 (12, 13, 12, 13, 13, 14, 14, 15, 15, 16, 16) rnds; Yoke should measure approximately 7 (7½, 7¾, 6½, 6¾, 7, 7¼, 7½, 7¾, 8, 8¼, 8½)" [18 (19, 19.5, 16.5, 17, 18, 18.5, 19, 19.5, 20.5, 21, 21.5) cm].

DECREASE RND 2: *K2, k2tog; repeat from * to end—162 (168, 180, 189, 204, 213, 225, 237, 252, 264, 267, 294) sts remain. Knit 5 (5, 6, 12, 12, 13, 13, 14, 14, 15, 15, 15) rnds; Yoke should measure approximately 7¾ (8¼, 8¾, 8¼, 8½, 8¾, 9, 9½, 9½, 10, 10¼, 10½)" [19.5 (21, 22, 20.5, 21.5, 22, 23, 23.5, 24, 25.5, 26, 26.5) cm].

DECREASE RND 3: *K1, k2tog; repeat from * to end—108 (112, 120, 126, 136, 142, 150, 158, 168, 176, 178, 196) sts remain. Knit 1 rnd.

SHAPE BACK NECK

Note: Back neck is shaped using short rows (see Special Techniques, page 174).

SHORT ROW 1 (RS): Knit to 1 st before first marker, w&t.

SHORT ROW 2 (WS): Purl to 1 st before second marker, w&t.

SHORT ROW 3: Knit to 6 sts before wrapped st from previous RS row, w&t.

SHORT ROW 4: Purl to 6 sts before wrapped st from previous WS row, w&t.

SHORT ROWS 5 AND 6: Repeat Short Rows 3 and 4.

SHORT ROW 7: Knit to end.

Knit 0 (0, 0, 3, 2, 2, 2, 3, 4, 4, 4, 4) rnds, knitting wraps together with wrapped sts as you come to them.

SIZE 40" (101.5 CM) ONLY

DECREASE RND 4: [K29, k2tog, k30, k2tog] twice—122 sts remain.

SIZE 42¼" (107.5 CM) ONLY

DECREASE RND 4: *K9, k2tog, [k10, k2tog] twice; repeat from * to end—124 sts remain.

SIZE 44" (112 CM) ONLY

DECREASE RND 4: K5, k2tog, [k6, k2tog] 16 times, k5, k2tog—124 sts remain.

SIZE 46¼" (117.5 CM) ONLY

DECREASE RND 4: [K4, k2tog] twice, [k5, k2tog] 18 times, [k4, k2tog] twice—128 sts remain.

SIZE 48" (122 CM) ONLY

DECREASE RND 4: [(K3, k2tog) 3 times, k4, k2tog] 7 times, k3, k2tog, k4, k2tog—128 sts remain.

SIZE 50¼" (127.5 CM) ONLY

DECREASE RND 4: [K2, k2tog] 3 times, [k3, k2tog, k2, k2tog] 16 times, [k2, k2tog] 3 times—130 sts remain.

SIZE 52" (132 CM) ONLY

DECREASE RND 4: [K2, k2tog] 3 times, [k1, k2tog, (k2, k2tog) 4 times] 8 times, [k2, k2tog] 3 times—130 sts remain.

SIZE 54¼" (138 CM) ONLY

DECREASE RND 4: [K1, k2tog] 3 times, [k2, k2tog] 40 times, [k1, k2tog] 3 times—132 sts remain.

SIZE 58¼" (148 CM) ONLY

DECREASE RND 4: [K1, k2tog] 6 times, [k2, k2tog, (k1, k2tog) twice] 16 times, [k1, k2tog] 6 times—136 sts remain.

ALL SIZES

Work even if necessary until Yoke measures 8¾ (9¼, 9¾, 9¾, 10, 10¼, 10½, 11, 11¼, 11¾, 12, 12¼)" [22 (23.5, 25, 25, 25.5, 26, 26.5, 28, 28.5, 30, 30.5, 31) cm] at center Back neck.

Change to Twisted Rib; work even for 1" (2.5 cm).
BO all sts in pattern.

FINISHING

Block piece as desired. Sew underarm seams.

Maypole

Colorwork may be the most common addition to a yoke sweater pattern, but I've always been intrigued by using diminishing cables with these sweaters. In this yoked pullover, worked in a fuzzy, cozy wool-alpaca blend, cables are adorned with eyelets and get smaller and smaller the closer you get to the neckline. The depth on this yoke is shorter than in traditional colorwork garments, allowing for you to choose a snugger fit—without losing freedom of movement—if you prefer.

FINISHED MEASUREMENTS

34 (36, 38, 40, 42, 44, 46, 48, 50, 52, 54, 58)" [86.5 (91.5, 96.5, 101.5, 106.5, 112, 117, 122, 127, 132, 137, 147.5) cm] bust

NOTE: Pullover is intended to be worn with 2–4" (5–10 cm) positive ease.

YARN

Berroco Ultra Alpaca [50% alpaca/50% wool; 215 yards (198 meters)/100 grams]: 5 (5, 5, 6, 6, 7, 7, 7, 8, 8, 9, 10) hanks #6214 Steel Cut Oats

NEEDLES

One 24–36" (60–90 cm) long (depending on bust size) circular needle size US 7 (4.5 mm)

One 40" (100 cm) long circular needle size US 7 (4.5 mm), for Yoke

One set of five double-pointed needles (dpns) size US 7 (4.5 mm)

Change needle size if necessary to obtain correct gauge.

NOTIONS

Stitch markers; stitch holders or waste yarn; cable needle

GAUGE

20 sts and 30 rnds = 4" (10 cm) in St st

STITCH PATTERN

1X1 RIB
(even number of sts; 1-rnd repeat)
ALL RNDS: *K1, p1; repeat from * to end.

NOTES

The Body of this pullover is worked in the round from the bottom to the underarm, then set aside while the Sleeves are worked in the round from the bottom to the underarm. The Body and Sleeves are then joined and the Yoke is worked to the neck, with circular Yoke shaping; the Back neck is shaped using short rows.

BODY

Using shorter circular needle, CO 170 (180, 190, 200, 210, 220, 230, 240, 250, 260, 270, 290) sts. Join for working in the rnd, being careful not to twist sts; pm for beginning of rnd and after 85 (90, 95, 100, 105, 110, 115, 120, 125, 130, 135, 145) sts for side. Begin 1x1 Rib; work even for 1½" (4 cm).

Change to St st; knit 4 rnds.

NEXT RND: K28 (30, 31, 33, 35, 36, 38, 40, 41, 43, 45, 48), pm for waist shaping, k29 (30, 33, 34, 35, 38, 39, 40, 43, 44, 45, 49), pm for waist shaping, knit to end.

SHAPE WAIST

DECREASE RND: Decrease 2 sts this rnd, then every 10 rnds 3 times, as follows: Knit to 2 sts before first shaping marker, ssk, sm, knit to next shaping marker, sm, k2tog, knit to end—162 (172, 182, 192, 202, 212, 222, 232, 242, 252, 262, 282) sts remain. Work even until piece measures 7½" (19 cm) from the beginning.

SHAPE BUST

INCREASE RND: Increase 2 sts this rnd, then every 8 rnds 3 times, as follows: Knit to first shaping marker, M1R, sm, knit to next shaping marker, sm, M1L, knit to end—170 (180, 190, 200, 210, 220, 230, 240, 250, 260, 270, 290) sts. Work even, removing waist shaping markers on first rnd (leaving beginning-of-rnd and side markers in place), until piece measures 13½ (13½, 14, 14, 14, 14½, 14½, 14½, 15, 15, 15, 15½)"

DIFFICULTY LEVEL:

YOKES

MAYPOLE

Diminishing cables form the yoke shaping

Sporty ¾ sleeves

[34.5 (34.5, 35.5, 35.5, 35.5, 37, 37, 37, 38, 38, 38, 39.5) cm] from the beginning.

NEXT RND: [Knit to 5 (5, 5, 5, 5, 7, 7, 7, 7, 7, 8, 8) sts before marker, BO 10 (10, 10, 10, 10, 14, 14, 14, 14, 14, 16, 16) sts (removing marker)] twice—75 (80, 85, 90, 95, 96, 101, 106, 111, 116, 119, 129) sts remain each for Front and Back. Place sts on holder or waste yarn and set aside; do not cut yarn.

SLEEVES

Using dpns, CO 46 (48, 48, 50, 56, 60, 66, 70, 76, 76, 80, 90) sts. Join for working in the rnd, being careful not to twist sts; pm for beginning of rnd. Begin 1x1 Rib; work even for 1½" (4 cm).

Change to St st; knit 2 rnds.

SHAPE SLEEVE

INCREASE RND: Increase 2 sts this rnd, then every 13 (13, 10, 10, 12, 10, 12, 11, 12, 7, 7, 9) rnds 5 (3, 7, 5, 5, 5, 5, 7, 3, 2, 2, 9) times, then every 0 (15, 0, 12, 14, 12, 14, 0, 14, 9, 9, 0) rnds 0 (2, 0, 2, 1, 2, 1, 0, 3, 7, 7, 0) time(s), as follows: K2, M1R, knit to last 2 sts, M1L, knit to end—58 (60, 64, 66, 70, 76, 80, 86, 90, 96, 100, 110) sts. Work even until piece measures 12 (12½, 12½, 13, 13, 13, 13, 13½, 13½, 13½, 13½, 14)" [30.5 (32, 32, 33, 33, 33, 33, 34.5, 34.5, 34.5, 34.5, 35.5) cm] from the beginning, ending last rnd 5 (5, 5, 5, 5, 7, 7, 7, 7, 7, 8, 8) sts before beginning-of-rnd marker.

NEXT RND: BO 10 (10, 10, 10, 10, 14, 14, 14, 14, 14, 16, 16) sts (removing marker), knit to end—48 (50, 54, 56, 60, 62, 66, 72, 76, 82, 84, 94) sts remain. Place sts on holder or waste yarn for first Sleeve and set aside; leave sts on needles for second Sleeve.

YOKE

With RS facing, using longer circular needle and yarn attached to Back, k37 (40, 42, 45, 47, 48, 50, 53, 55, 58, 59, 64) Back sts, pm for beginning of rnd, knit to end of Back, knit across Left Sleeve sts, pm, knit across Front sts, pm, knit across Right Sleeve sts, knit to beginning of rnd—246 (260, 278, 292, 310, 316, 334, 356, 374, 396, 406, 446) sts.

SHAPE YOKE

Note: Change to shorter circular needle when necessary for number of sts on needle.

SIZES 34, 38, 44, 48, 52, 54, AND 58" (86.5, 96.5, 112, 122, 132, 137, AND 147.5 CM) ONLY

INCREASE RND: Working increases as M1L, increase 4 (-, 2, -, -, 4, -, 4, -, -, 4, 4, 4) sts evenly across Back—250 (-, 280, -, -, 320, -, 360, -, 400, 410, 450) sts.

SIZES 40, 46, AND 50" (101.5, 117, AND 127 CM) ONLY

DECREASE RND: Working decreases as k2tog, decrease - (-, -, 2, -, -, 4, -, 4, -, -, -) sts evenly across Back— - (-, -, 290, -, -, 330, -, 370, -, -, -) sts remain.

ALL SIZES

Knit 0 (1, 5, 7, 9, 11, 12, 16, 16, 20, 22, 24) rnd(s), removing all markers except beginning-of-rnd marker and placing 2 new markers, each 63 (65, 70, 73, 78, 80, 83, 90, 93, 100, 103, 113) sts to either side of beginning-of-rnd marker (at center point of Sleeves).

SHAPE BACK NECK

Note: Back neck is shaped using short rows (see Special Techniques, page 174).

SHORT ROW 1 (RS): Knit to 1 st before first marker, w&t.
SHORT ROW 2 (WS): Purl to 1 st before second marker, w&t.
SHORT ROW 3: Knit to 4 sts before wrapped st from previous RS row, w&t.
SHORT ROW 4: Purl to 4 sts before wrapped st from previous WS row, w&t.
SHORT ROWS 5 AND 6: Repeat Short Rows 3 and 4.
SHORT ROW 7: Knit to end.

Knit 2 (2, 3, 6, 5, 6, 5, 5, 5, 4, 4, 4) rnds, knitting wraps together with wrapped sts as you come to them, and removing all markers except beginning-of-rnd marker.

Work Rnds 1–58 of Yoke Chart (see page 140), working decreases as indicated in Chart—125 (130, 140, 145, 155, 160, 165, 180, 185, 200, 205, 225) sts remain when Chart is complete. Yoke should measure approximately 9¼ (9¼, 10, 10¾, 10¾, 11¼, 11¼, 11¾, 11¾, 12¼, 12½, 12¾)" [23.5 (23.5, 25.5, 27.5, 27.5, 28.5, 28.5, 30, 30, 31, 32, 32.5) cm] at center Back neck.

SIZE 34" (86.5 CM) ONLY

DECREASE RND 1: *P1, k2tog, p1, k1, [p1, k2, p1, k1] twice, p1, k2tog, p1, k1, p1, k2, p1, k1; repeat from * to end—115 sts remain.

SIZE 36" (91.5 CM) ONLY

DECREASE RND 1: *[P1, k2tog, p1, k1] twice, p1, k2, p1, k1, p1, k2tog, p1, k1, p1, k2, p1, k1; repeat from * to last 5 sts, p1, k2, p1, k1—115 sts remain.

SIZE 38" (96.5 CM) ONLY

DECREASE RND 1: *P1, k2, p1, k1, [p1, k2tog, p1, k1] 8 times; repeat from * to last 5 sts, p1, k2tog, p1, k1—115 sts remain.

STITCH PATTERNING ON YOKES

THESE YOKE SWEATERS all provide you with a great jumping-off point for adding your own personal touches by swapping out stitch patterning.

Stitches are removed from the yokes in two different ways, and that method dictates which stitch pattern substitution you can do.

1. FEWER, DISTINCT SHAPING ROWS The plain Clearsight Yoke decreases stitches in just a handful of decrease rnds. Feel free to substitute in bands of stitch patterning around those decrease rnds: stripes, bands of textured patterns, short lace motifs—you name it. As long as they don't disturb the decrease rnds, you're good to go!

2. GRADUAL SHAPING The Maypole and Snowdrift Pullovers work on a different principle: Over the course of the yoke, each sweater "shrinks" its stitch patterning gradually from a 14- or 16-stitch repeat to a 5- or 8-stitch repeat (respectively). So as long as you have a stitch pattern that meets the same "shrinking" criteria as the one pictured, you can switch the stitch patterning I used for one of your own invention. (Hint: This is a great place to get out a piece of knitter's graph paper and play around!)

SIZE 40" (101.5 CM) ONLY

DECREASE RND 1: *P1, k2, p1, k1, [p1, k2tog, p1, k1] 6 times; repeat from * to last 5 sts, p1, k2tog, p1, k1—120 sts remain.

SIZE 42" (106.5 CM) ONLY

DECREASE RND 1: *P1, k2tog, p1, k1; repeat from * to end—124 sts remain.

Work even for 2 rnds.

DECREASE RND 2: *[P1, k1] 14 times, p2tog, p1, [k1, p1] 14 times, p1, p2tog; repeat from * to end—120 sts remain.

SIZE 44" (112 CM) ONLY

DECREASE RND 1: *P1, k2tog, p1, k1; repeat from * to end—128 sts remain.

Work even for 2 rnds.

DECREASE RND 2: *[P1, k1] 7 times, k2tog; repeat from * to end—120 sts remain.

SIZE 46" (117 CM) ONLY

DECREASE RND 1: *P1, k2tog, p1, k1; repeat from * to end—132 sts remain.

Work even for 2 rnds.

DECREASE RND 2: *[P1, k1] 4 times, p2tog, p1, [k1, p1] 4 times, p1, p2tog; repeat from * to end—120 sts remain.

SIZE 48" (122 CM) ONLY

DECREASE RND 1: *P1, k2tog, p1, k1; repeat from * to end—144 sts remain.

Work even for 2 rnds.

DECREASE RND 2: *[P1, k1] twice, k2tog; repeat from * to end—120 sts remain.

SIZE 50" (127 CM) ONLY

DECREASE RND 1: *P1, k2tog, p1, k1; repeat from * to end—148 sts remain.

Work even for 2 rnds.

DECREASE RND 2: [P1, k1] twice, k2tog, p1, *k1, p1, p2tog, [k1, p1] twice, k1, k2tog, p1; repeat from * to last 9 sts, [k1, p1] 4 times, k1—125 sts remain.

SIZE 52" (132 CM) ONLY

DECREASE RND 1: *P1, k2tog, p1, k1; repeat from * to end—160 sts remain.

Work even for 2 rnds.

DECREASE RND 2: *[P1, k1, k2tog] 7 times, [p1, k1] twice; repeat from * to end—125 sts remain.

SIZE 54" (137 CM) ONLY

DECREASE RND 1: *P1, k2tog, p1, k1; repeat from * to end—164 sts remain.

Work even for 2 rnds.

DECREASE RND 2: [P1, k1] twice, *p1, k1, k2tog; repeat from * to last 4 sts, [p1, k1] twice—125 sts remain.

SIZE 58" (147.5 CM) ONLY
DECREASE RND 1: *P1, k2tog, p1, k1; repeat from * to end—180 sts remain.
Work even for 2 rnds.
DECREASE RND 2: *P1, k1, k2tog; repeat from * to end—135 sts remain.

ALL SIZES
BO all sts in pattern.

FINISHING

Block piece as desired. Sew underarm seams.

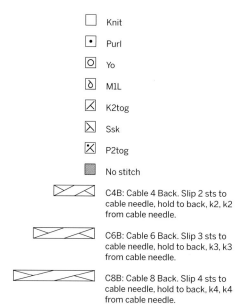

☐	Knit
•	Purl
Ⓞ	Yo
ᕲ	M1L
⧄	K2tog
⧅	Ssk
⧄	P2tog
▨	No stitch

C4B: Cable 4 Back. Slip 2 sts to cable needle, hold to back, k2, k2 from cable needle.

C6B: Cable 6 Back. Slip 3 sts to cable needle, hold to back, k3, k3 from cable needle.

C8B: Cable 8 Back. Slip 4 sts to cable needle, hold to back, k4, k4 from cable needle.

YOKE CHART

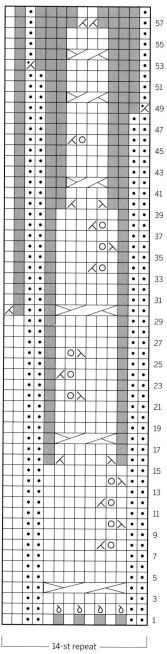

← 14-st repeat →

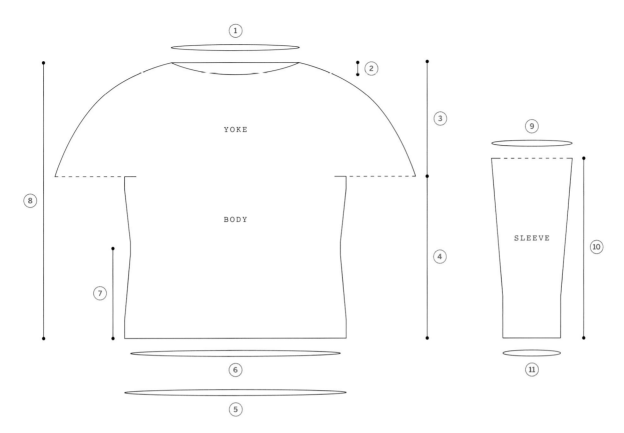

YOKE AND BODY

1 23 (23, 23, 24, 24, 24, 24, 24, 25, 25, 25, 27)"
58.5 (58.5, 58.5, 61, 61, 61, 61, 61, 63.5, 63.5, 63.5, 68.5) cm

2 1"/2.5 cm

3 10¼ (10¼, 11, 11¾, 12, 12½, 12½, 13, 13, 13½, 13¾, 14)"
26 (26, 28, 30, 30.5, 32, 32, 33, 33, 34.5, 35, 35.5) cm

4 13½ (13½, 14, 14, 14, 14½, 14½, 14½, 15, 15, 15, 15½)"
34.5 (34.5, 35.5, 35.5, 35.5, 37, 37, 37, 38, 38, 38, 39.5) cm

5 34 (36, 38, 40, 42, 44, 46, 48, 50, 52, 54, 58)" hip and bust
86.5 (91.5, 96.5, 101.5, 106.5, 112, 117, 122, 127, 132, 137, 147.5) cm

6 32½ (34½, 36½, 38½, 40½, 42½, 44½, 46½, 48½, 50½, 52½, 56½)" waist
82.5 (87.5, 92.5, 98, 103, 108, 113, 118, 123, 128.5, 133.5, 143.5) cm

7 7"/18 cm

8 23¾ (23¾, 25, 25¾, 26, 27, 27, 27½, 28, 28½, 28¾, 29½)"
60.5 (60.5, 63.5, 65.5, 66, 68.5, 68.5, 70, 71, 72.5, 73, 75) cm

SLEEVE

9 11½ (12, 12¾, 13¼, 14, 15¼, 16, 17¼, 18, 19¼, 20, 22)"
29 (30.5, 32.5, 33.5, 35.5, 38.5, 40.5, 44, 45.5, 49, 51, 56) cm

10 12 (12½, 12½, 13, 13, 13, 13, 13½, 13½, 13½, 13½, 14)"
30.5 (32, 32, 33, 33, 33, 33, 34.5, 34.5, 34.5, 34.5, 35.5) cm

11 9¼ (9½, 9½, 10, 11¼, 12, 13¼, 14, 15¼, 15¼, 16, 18)"
23.5 (24, 24, 25.5, 28.5, 30.5, 33.5, 35.5, 38.5, 38.5, 40.5, 45.5) cm

Snowdrift Pullover

I couldn't let this chapter end without including at least one sweater that evokes my childhood in Maine. When the temperatures drop, the double- and triple-thick fabrics of Fair Isle yoke sweaters keep you toasty warm—and offer a lovely chance to play with color. A turtleneck tops things off and promises protection from impromptu snowball fights. This snowflake pattern is relatively simple to work, and I've chosen a soft, warm yarn with an extensive color palette for the garment. The depth on this yoke is somewhat generous to allow for the beautiful snowflakes, so please be sure to choose a size with some positive ease in the bust.

FINISHED MEASUREMENTS

33¾ (36¼, 38¼, 40, 41¾, 44¼, 46¼, 48, 49¾, 52¼, 54¼, 57¾)" [85.5 (92, 97, 101.5, 106, 112.5, 117.5, 122, 126.5, 132.5, 138, 146.5) cm bust

NOTE: Pullover is intended to be worn with 2–4" (5–10 cm) positive ease in the bust.

YARN

Classic Elite Yarns Fresco [60% wool/30% baby alpaca/10% angora; 164 yards (150 meters)/50 grams]: 11 (11, 12, 13, 14, 15, 16, 16, 17, 18, 18, 20) skeins #5397 Fern **(MC)**; 2 (2, 2, 3, 3, 3, 4, 4, 4, 5, 5, 5) skeins #5301 Parchment **(A)**; 1 (1, 1, 2, 2, 2, 2, 2, 2, 2, 2, 3) skein(s) each #5349 Blue Teal **(B)** and #5336 Oatmeal **(C)**; 1 skein #5381 Dark Mustard **(D)**

NEEDLES

One 24–36" (60–90 cm) long (depending on bust size) circular needle size US 4 (3.5 mm)

One 40" (100 cm) long circular needle size US 4 (3.5 mm), for Yoke

One set of five double-pointed needles (dpns) size US 4 (3.5 mm)

One 16" (40 cm) long circular needle size US 5 (3.75 mm), for Collar

Change needle size if necessary to obtain correct gauge.

NOTIONS

Stitch markers; stitch holders or waste yarn

GAUGE

26 sts and 35 rnds = 4" (10 cm) in St st

NOTE: Be sure to swatch the Fair Isle pattern; you may need to change the needle size for the Fair Isle sections.

STITCH PATTERN

2X2 RIB

(multiple of 4 sts; 1-rnd repeat)

ALL RNDS: *K2, p2; repeat from * to end.

NOTES

The Body of this pullover is worked in the round from the bottom to the underarm, then set aside while the Sleeves are worked in the round from the bottom to the underarm. The Body and Sleeves are then joined and the Yoke is worked to the neck, with circular Yoke shaping; the Back neck is shaped using short rows.

BODY

Using longer size US 4 (3.5 mm) circular needle and MC, CO 220 (236, 248, 260, 272, 288, 300, 312, 324, 340, 352, 376) sts. Join for working in the rnd, being careful not to twist sts; pm for beginning of rnd and after 110 (118, 124, 130, 136, 144, 150, 156, 162, 170, 176, 188) sts for side. Begin 2x2 Rib; work even for 2¼" (5.5 cm).

Change to St st; knit 2 rnds.

NEXT RND: K36 (39, 41, 43, 45, 48, 50, 52, 54, 56, 58, 62), pm for waist shaping, k38 (40, 42, 44, 46, 48, 50, 52, 54, 58, 60, 64) sts, pm for waist shaping, knit to side marker, sm, knit to end.

Sport-weight
stranded colorwork
in lusciously
soft yarn

Dart-style
waist shaping on
the back only

SHAPE WAIST

DECREASE RND: Decrease 2 sts this rnd, then every 10 rnds 4 times, as follows: Knit to 2 sts before first shaping marker, ssk, sm, knit to next shaping marker, sm, k2tog, knit to end—210 (226, 238, 250, 262, 278, 290, 302, 314, 330, 342, 366) sts remain. Work even until piece measures 8½" (21.5 cm) from the beginning.

SHAPE BUST

INCREASE RND: Increase 2 sts this rnd, then every 10 rnds 4 times, as follows: Knit to first shaping marker, M1R, sm, knit to next shaping marker, sm, M1L, knit to end—220 (236, 248, 260, 272, 288, 300, 312, 324, 340, 352, 376) sts. Work even, removing waist shaping markers on first rnd (leaving beginning-of-rnd and side markers in place), until piece measures 14½ (14½, 15, 15, 15, 15½, 15½, 15½, 16, 16, 16, 16½)" [37 (37, 38, 38, 38, 39.5, 39.5, 39.5, 40.5, 40.5, 40.5, 42) cm] from the beginning.

NEXT RND: [Knit to 7 (7, 7, 7, 7, 9, 9, 9, 9, 9, 10, 10) sts before marker, BO 14 (14, 14, 14, 14, 18, 18, 18, 18, 18, 20, 20) sts (removing marker)] twice, knit to end—96 (104, 110, 116, 122, 126, 132, 138, 144, 152, 156, 168) sts remain each for Front and Back. Place all sts on holder or waste yarn and set aside; do not cut yarn.

SLEEVES

Using dpns and MC, CO 56 (56, 56, 60, 60, 60, 60, 60, 60, 60, 64, 64) sts. Join for working in the rnd, being careful not to twist sts; pm for beginning of rnd. Begin 2x2 Rib; work even for 3½" (9 cm).

Change to St st; knit 2 rnds.

SHAPE SLEEVE

INCREASE RND: Increase 2 sts this rnd, then every 12 (11, 9, 9, 7, 6, 5, 4, 4, 3, 2, 2) rnds 8 (10, 11, 9, 10, 13, 14, 16, 27, 20, 9, 23) times, then every 14 (0, 11, 11, 9, 8, 7, 6, 6, 5, 4, 4) rnds 1 (0, 1, 3, 5, 5, 7, 9, 1, 11, 23, 16) time(s), as follows: K2, M1R, knit to last 2 sts, M1L, knit to end—76 (78, 82, 86, 92, 98, 104, 112, 118, 124, 130, 144) sts. Work even until piece measures 18 (18, 18, 18½, 18½, 19, 19, 19, 18½, 18½, 18, 18)" [45.5 (45.5, 45.5, 47, 47, 48.5, 48.5, 48.5, 47, 47, 45.5, 45.5) cm] from the beginning, ending last rnd 7 (7, 7, 7, 9, 9, 9, 9, 9, 10, 10) sts before beginning-of-rnd marker.

NEXT RND: BO 14 (14, 14, 14, 14, 18, 18, 18, 18, 18, 20, 20) sts (removing marker), knit to end—62 (64, 68, 72, 78, 80, 86, 94, 100, 106, 110, 124) sts remain. Place sts on holder or waste yarn for first Sleeve and set aside; leave sts on needles for second Sleeve.

YOKE

With RS facing, using longer size US 4 (3.5 mm) circular needle and yarn attached to Back, k48 (52, 55, 58, 61, 63, 66, 69, 72, 76, 78, 84) Back sts, pm for beginning of rnd, knit to end of Back, knit across Left Sleeve sts, pm, knit across Front sts, pm, knit across Right Sleeve sts, knit to beginning of rnd—316 (336, 356, 376, 400, 412, 436, 464, 488, 516, 532, 584) sts.

SHAPE YOKE

Note: Change to shorter size US 4 (3.5 mm) circular needle when necessary for number of sts on needle.

SIZES 33¾, 40, 44¼, 49¾, AND 57¾" (85.5, 101.5, 112.5, 126.5, AND 146.5) CM ONLY

INCREASE RND: Working increases as M1L, increase 4 (-, -, 8, -, 4, -, -, 8, -, -, 8) sts evenly across Back—320 (-, -, 384, -, 416, -, -, 496, -, -, 592) sts.

SIZES 38¼, 46¼, 52¼, AND 54¼" (97, 117.5, 132.5, AND 138 CM) ONLY

DECREASE RND: Working decreases as k2tog, decrease - (-, 4, -, -, -, 4, -, -, 4, 4, -) sts evenly across Back— - (-, 352, -, -, -, 432, -, -, 512, 528, -) sts remain.

ALL SIZES

Knit 2 (2, 5, 7, 12, 14, 16, 21, 23, 27, 29, 32) rnds, removing all markers except beginning-of-rnd marker on first rnd.

Work Rnds 1–52 of Yoke Chart (see page 146), working decreases as indicated in Chart—160 (168, 176, 192, 200, 208, 216, 232, 248, 256, 264, 296) sts remain when Chart is complete. Yoke should measure approximately 6½ (6¼, 6¾, 7, 7½, 7¾, 8, 8½, 8¾, 9¼, 9½, 9¾)" [16.5 (16, 17, 18, 19, 19.5, 20.5, 21.5, 22, 23.5, 24, 25) cm] at center Back neck.

Knit 1 rnd, placing markers 32 (34, 36, 38, 40, 40, 42, 44, 44, 46, 48, 50) sts to either side of center Front.

SHAPE BACK NECK

Note: Back neck is shaped using short rows (see Special Techniques, page 174).

SHORT ROW 1 (RS): Knit to 1 st before first marker, w&t.

SHORT ROW 2 (WS): Purl to 1 st before second marker, w&t.

SHORT ROW 3: Knit to 6 sts before wrapped st from previous RS row, w&t.

SHORT ROW 4: Purl to 6 sts before wrapped st from previous WS row, w&t.

SHORT ROWS 5–8: Repeat Short Rows 3 and 4.

SHORT ROW 9: Knit to end.

Knit 2 (2, 2, 5, 5, 5, 5, 4, 4, 4, 4, 4) rnds, knitting wraps together with wrapped sts as you come to them.

SIZE 33¾" (85.5 CM) ONLY

DECREASE RND 1: *[K5, k2tog] twice, k4, k2tog; repeat from * to end—136 sts remain.

SIZE 36¼" (92 CM) ONLY

DECREASE RND 1: *[K3, k2tog] 3 times, k4, k2tog; repeat from * to end—136 sts remain.

SIZE 38¼" (97 CM) ONLY

DECREASE RND 1: *[K3, k2tog] 8 times, k2, k2tog; repeat from * to end—140 sts remain.

SIZE 40" (101.5 CM) ONLY

DECREASE RND 1: *K6, k2tog; repeat from * to end—168 sts remain.

Knit 4 rnds.

DECREASE RND 2: *K5, k2tog; repeat from * to end—144 sts remain.

Knit 4 rnds.

DECREASE RND 3: *K2tog, k34; repeat from * to end—140 sts remain.

SIZE 41¾" (106 CM) ONLY

DECREASE RND 1: *K6, k2tog; repeat from * to end—175 sts remain.

Knit 4 rnds.

DECREASE RND 2: *K5, k2tog; repeat from * to end—150 sts remain.

Knit 4 rnds.

DECREASE RND 3: *K2tog, k13; repeat from * to end—140 sts remain.

SIZE 44¼" (112.5 CM) ONLY

DECREASE RND 1: *K6, k2tog; repeat from * to end—182 sts remain.

Knit 4 rnds.

DECREASE RND 2: *K5, k2tog; repeat from * to end—156 sts remain.

Knit 4 rnds.

DECREASE RND 3: *K2tog, k7, [k2tog, k8] 3 times; repeat from * to end—140 sts remain.

SIZE 46¼" (117.5 CM) ONLY

DECREASE RND 1: *K6, k2tog; repeat from * to end—189 sts remain.

Knit 4 rnds.

DECREASE RND 2: *K5, k2tog; repeat from * to end—162 sts remain.

Knit 4 rnds.

DECREASE RND 3: *K2tog, k7; repeat from * to end—144 sts remain.

SIZE 48" (122 CM) ONLY

DECREASE RND 1: *K6, k2tog; repeat from * to end—203 sts remain.

Knit 3 rnds.

DECREASE RND 2: *K5, k2tog; repeat from * to end—174 sts remain.

Knit 3 rnds.

DECREASE RND 3: *K4, k2tog; repeat from * to end—145 sts remain.

Knit 3 rnds.

DECREASE RND 4: K2tog, knit to end—144 sts remain.

SIZE 49¾" (126.5 CM) ONLY

DECREASE RND 1: *K6, k2tog; repeat from * to end—217 sts remain.

Knit 3 rnds.

DECREASE RND 2: *K5, k2tog; repeat from * to end—186 sts remain.

Knit 3 rnds.

DECREASE RND 3: *K4, k2tog; repeat from * to end—155 sts remain.

Knit 3 rnds.

DECREASE RND 4: [K2tog, k12] 10 times, k2tog, k13—144 sts remain.

SIZE 52¼" (132.5 CM) ONLY

DECREASE RND 1: *K6, k2tog; repeat from * to end—224 sts remain.

Knit 3 rnds.

DECREASE RND 2: *K5, k2tog; repeat from * to end—192 sts remain.

Knit 3 rnds.

DECREASE RND 3: *K4, k2tog; repeat from * to end—160 sts remain.

Knit 3 rnds.

DECREASE RND 4: *K2tog, k8; repeat from * to end—144 sts remain.

SIZE 54¼" (138 CM) ONLY

DECREASE RND 1: *K6, k2tog; repeat from * to end—231 sts remain.

Knit 3 rnds.

DECREASE RND 2: *K5, k2tog; repeat from * to end—198 sts remain.

Knit 3 rnds.

DECREASE RND 3: *K4, k2tog; repeat from * to end—165 sts remain.

Knit 3 rnds.

DECREASE RND 4: K2tog, k7, [k2tog, k8] 3 times, k2tog, k7, [k2tog, k8] twice, k2tog, k7, [k2tog, k8] 3 times, k2tog, k7, [k2tog, k8] twice, k2tog, k7, [k2tog, k8] twice—148 sts remain.

SIZE 57¾" (146.5 CM) ONLY

DECREASE RND 1: *K6, k2tog; repeat from * to end—259 sts remain.

Knit 3 rnds.

DECREASE RND 2: *K5, k2tog; repeat from * to end—222 sts remain.

Knit 3 rnds.

DECREASE RND 3: *K4, k2tog; repeat from * to end—185 sts remain.

Knit 3 rnds.

DECREASE RND 4: *K3, k2tog; repeat from * to end—148 sts remain.

ALL SIZES

Work even if necessary until Yoke measures 7¾ (7¾, 8, 10¼, 10¾, 11, 11¼, 11½, 11¾, 12¼, 12½, 12¾)" [19.5 (19.5, 20.5, 26, 27.5, 28, 28.5, 29, 30, 31, 32, 32.5) cm], measured at center Back neck.

COLLAR

Change to 2x2 Rib; work even for 4" (10 cm).

Change to larger circular needle; work even until Collar measures 9" (23 cm).
BO all sts in pattern.

FINISHING

Block piece as desired. Sew underarm seams.

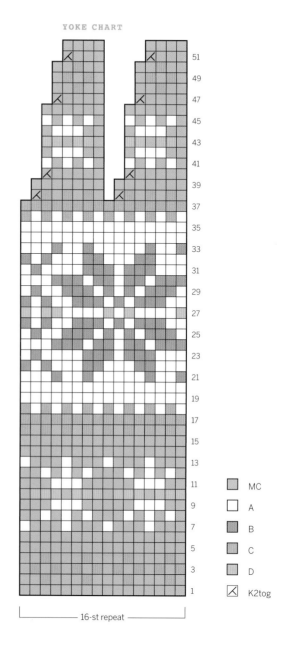

YOKE CHART

16-st repeat

MC
A
B
C
D
K2tog

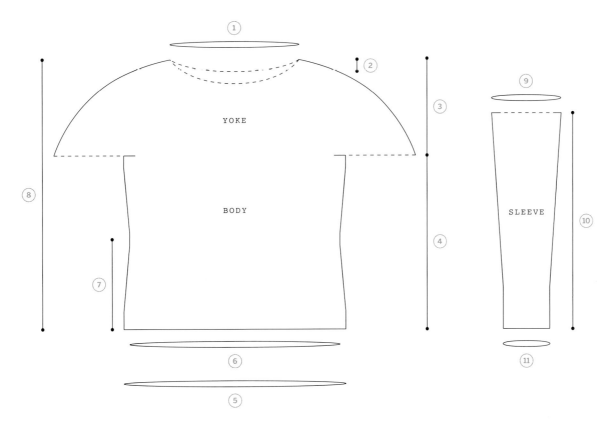

YOKE AND BODY

1   21 (21, 21½, 21½, 21½, 21½, 22¼, 22¼, 22¼, 22¼, 22¾, 22¾)"
    53.5 (53.5, 54.5, 54.5, 54.5, 54.5, 56.5, 56.5, 56.5, 56.5, 58, 58) cm

2   1"/2.5 cm

3   7¾ (7¾, 8, 10¼, 10¾, 11, 11¼, 11½, 11¾, 12¼, 12½, 12¾)"
    19.5 (19.5, 20.5, 26, 27.5, 28, 28.5, 29, 30, 31, 32, 32.5) cm

4   14½ (14½, 15, 15, 15, 15½, 15½, 15½, 16, 16, 16, 16½)"
    37 (37, 38, 38, 38, 39.5, 39.5, 39.5, 40.5, 40.5, 40.5, 42) cm

5   33¾ (36¼, 38¼, 40, 41¾, 44¼, 46¼, 48, 49¾, 52¼, 54¼, 57¾)" hip and bust
    85.5 (92, 97, 101.5, 106, 112.5, 117.5, 122, 126.5, 132.5, 138, 146.5) cm

6   32¼ (34¾, 36½, 38½, 40¼, 42¾, 44½, 46½, 48¼, 50¾, 52½, 56¼)" waist
    82 (88.5, 92.5, 98, 102, 108.5, 113, 118, 122.5, 129, 133.5, 143) cm

7   8"/20.5 cm

8   22¼ (22¼, 23, 25¼, 25¾, 26½, 26¾, 27, 27¾, 28¼, 28½, 29¼)"
    56.5 (56.5, 58.5, 64, 65.5, 67.5, 68, 68.5, 70.5, 72, 72.5, 74.5) cm

SLEEVE

9   11¾ (12, 12½, 13¼, 14¼, 15, 16, 17¼, 18¼, 19, 20, 22¼)"
    30 (30.5, 32, 33.5, 36, 38, 40.5, 44, 46.5, 48.5, 51, 56.5) cm

10 18 (18, 18, 18½, 18½, 19, 19, 19, 18½, 18½, 18, 18)"
    45.5 (45.5, 45.5, 47, 47, 48.5, 48.5, 48.5, 47, 47, 45.5, 45.5) cm

11 8½ (8½, 8½, 9¼, 9¼, 9¼, 9¼, 9¼, 9¼, 9¼, 9¾, 9¾)"
    21.5 (21.5, 21.5, 23.5, 23.5, 23.5, 23.5, 23.5, 23.5, 23.5, 25, 25) cm

SET-IN SLEEVES

The set-in sleeve is the construction of sweater you're probably used to wearing—most commercial clothing is made this way. These sweaters have a reputation for being scary, but honestly nothing could be further from the truth! Since they're worked in pieces, you can tackle your sweater one bite-sized chunk at a time.

Set-in-sleeve sweaters have a more precise fit than the other sweaters in this book, and are designed to allow your body easy and free range of movement. They'll work best with eases anywhere in the 0–4" (0–10 cm) range, and you can adjust the ease of the body of your sweater separately from the fit in your shoulders, too! (For a detailed look at that, see either of my first two books, *Knit to Flatter* or *Knit Wear Love*.)

I've given you a few quintessential looks here. I highly encourage you to start small, with my Birdie Cardi Mini (page 151), especially if this is your first set-in-sleeve garment—it'll give you great practice with seaming and the overall construction of these sweaters.

Once you're feeling confident, you've got a few places to go from there. The Downy Cardigan (page 154) is everything a cardigan should be: cozy, warm, and snuggly. Wear the versatile collar in several different ways: buttoned up or unbuttoned, folded over or scrunched into a cowl. The Horseshoe Pullover (page 160) is worked in a great staple sweater yarn, and offers you a bit of cable excitement (but just on the front, to keep things simple)! And the Collegiate Cardi (page 165), with its pockets, stripes, and stitch patterning, makes a lovely capstone for your sweater journey through this book.

Small stitch
pattern repeat
makes for
easier shaping

DIFFICULTY LEVEL:

SET-IN
SLEEVES

BIRDIE CARDI MINI

Simple 1x1
ribbed trim

Birdie Cardi Mini

The set-in-sleeve garment is the construction most likely to cause hesitation on the part of the knitter, perhaps because of the seams involved in putting it together. Well, hesitate no more: This mini cardigan is adorable, shows off how polished set-in-sleeve garments look, and provides you with a quick and easy way to get your mattress stitch skills up to snuff. A simple stitch pattern is emphasized by the easy-care yarn to make a garment any young gift recipient will love to wear.

SIZES
To fit children 1 (2, 3/4, 5/6, 7/8, 9/10) year(s)

FINISHED MEASUREMENTS
21 (24, 26¾, 28½, 30¾, 31½)" [53.5 (61, 68, 72.5, 78, 80) cm] chest, buttoned

NOTE: Cardigan is intended to be worn with 2–4" [5–10 cm] ease in the chest.

YARN
Berroco Vintage [52% acrylic/40% wool/8% nylon; 217 yards (198 meters)/100 grams]: 2 (3, 3, 4, 4, 5) hanks #5157 Paprika

NEEDLES
One pair straight needles, size US 7 (4.5 mm)

One 24" (60 cm) long circular needle size US 7 (4.5 mm), for Front Bands/Neckband

Change needle size if necessary to obtain correct gauge.

NOTIONS
Stitch markers; cable needle; five ¾" [19 mm] buttons

GAUGE
20 sts and 28 rows = 4" (10 cm) in St st

20 sts and 28 rows = 4" (10 cm) in Dot Texture

SPECIAL ABBREVIATIONS
LT (LEFT TWIST): Slip 1 st to cable needle and hold to front, k1, k1 from cn. To work without a cable needle, insert needle from back to front between first and second sts and knit second st, then knit first st and slip both sts from left needle together.

RT (RIGHT TWIST): Slip 1 st to cable needle and hold to back, k1, k1 from cn. To work without a cable needle, skip first st and knit into front of second st, then knit first st and slip both sts from left needle together.

STITCH PATTERNS
1X1 RIB
(even number of sts; 1-row repeat)
ALL ROWS: *K1, p1; repeat from * to end.

NOTES
Armhole and Sleeve cap decreases should be worked to match the slant of the edge being shaped (when seen from the RS), as follows:

FOR LEFT-SLANTING EDGES:
On RS rows, k1, ssk, work to end; on WS rows, work to last 3 sts, ssp, p1.

FOR RIGHT-SLANTING EDGES:
On RS rows, work to last 3 sts, k2tog, k1; on WS rows, p1, p2tog, work to end.

Back and Front neck decreases should be worked to match the slant of the edge being shaped, as follows: For left-slanting edges, ssk, work to end. For right-slanting edges, work to last 2 sts, k2tog.

You may work Dot Texture from text or Chart.

BACK
CO 52 (60, 64, 72, 76, 80) sts. Begin 1x1 Rib; work even for 1" (2.5 cm), ending with a WS row.

NEXT ROW (RS): Change to St st; work even until piece measures 10 (11, 11¼, 12, 13½, 14)" [25.5 (28, 28.5, 30.5, 34.5, 35.5) cm] from the beginning, ending with a WS row.

SHAPE ARMHOLES

BO 4 (3, 4, 5, 6, 6) sts at beginning of next 2 rows, then decrease 1 st each side every RS row 3 (3, 3, 4, 4, 5) times—38 (48, 50, 54, 56, 58) sts remain. Work even until armhole measures 3 (3½, 4¼, 5, 5½, 6)" [7.5 (9, 11, 12.5, 14, 15) cm], ending with a WS row.

SHAPE NECK

NEXT ROW (RS): K10 (12, 13, 14, 15, 15), join a second ball of yarn, BO center 18 (24, 24, 26, 26, 28) sts, knit to end. Working both sides at the same time, decrease 1 st at each neck edge every RS row once—9 (11, 12, 13, 14, 14) sts rem each shoulder. Work even until armhole measures 4 (4½, 5¼, 6, 6½, 7)" [10 (11.5, 13.5, 15, 16.5, 18) cm], ending with a WS row.

SHAPE SHOULDERS

BO 5 (6, 6, 7, 7, 7) sts at each armhole edge once, then 4 (5, 6, 6, 7, 7) sts once.

RIGHT FRONT

CO 24 (28, 32, 32, 36, 36) sts. Begin 1x1 Rib; work even for 1" (2.5 cm), ending with a WS row.

NEXT ROW (RS): Change to Dot Texture—Right Front (see opposite); work even until piece measures 9½ (10½, 10¾, 11½, 13, 13½)" [24 (26.5, 27.5, 29, 33, 34.5) cm] from the beginning, ending with a WS row.

SHAPE NECK AND ARMHOLE

Note: Neck and armhole shaping will be worked at the same time; please read entire section through before beginning.

NECK DECREASE ROW (RS): Decrease 1 st at neck edge this row, then every 2 (2, 2, 4, 2, 4) rows 1 (6, 7, 7, 1, 7) time(s), then every 4 (4, 4, 6, 4, 6) rows 6 (4, 5, 2, 10, 3) times. AT THE SAME TIME, when armhole measures 10 (11, 11¼, 12, 13½, 14)" [25.5 (28, 28.5, 30.5, 34.5, 35.5) cm], ending with a RS row, shape armhole as follows:
Continuing to work neck shaping, BO 4 (3, 4, 5, 6, 6) sts at armhole edge once, then decrease 1 st at armhole edge every RS row 3 (3, 3, 4, 4, 5) times—9 (11, 12, 13, 14, 14) sts remain. Work even until armhole measures 4 (4½, 5¼, 6, 6½, 7)" [10 (11.5, 13.5, 15, 16.5, 18) cm], ending with a RS row.

SHAPE SHOULDER

BO 5 (6, 6, 7, 7, 7) sts at armhole edge once, then 4 (5, 6, 6, 7, 7) sts once.

LEFT FRONT

CO 24 (28, 32, 32, 36, 36) sts. Begin 1x1 Rib; work even for 1" (2.5 cm), ending with a WS row.

NEXT ROW (RS): Change to Dot Texture—Left Front (see opposite); work even until piece measures 9½ (10½, 10¾, 11½, 13, 13½)" [24 (26.5, 27.5, 29, 33, 34.5) cm], ending with a WS row.

SHAPE NECK AND ARMHOLE

Note: Neck and armhole shaping will be worked at the same time; please read entire section through before beginning.

NECK DECREASE ROW (RS): Decrease 1 st at neck edge this row, then every 2 (2, 2, 4, 2, 4) rows 1 (6, 7, 7, 1, 7) time(s), then every 4 (4, 4, 6, 4, 6) rows 6 (4, 5, 2, 10, 3) times. AT THE SAME TIME, when armhole measures 10 (11, 11¼, 12, 13½, 14)" [25.5 (28, 28.5, 30.5, 34.5, 35.5) cm], ending with a WS row, shape armhole as follows:
Continuing to work neck shaping, BO 4 (3, 4, 5, 6, 6) sts at armhole edge once, then decrease 1 st at armhole edge every RS row 3 (3, 3, 4, 4, 5) times—9 (11, 12, 13, 14, 14) sts remain. Work even until armhole measures 4 (4½, 5¼, 6, 6½, 7)" [10 (11.5, 13.5, 15, 16.5, 18) cm], ending with a WS row.

SHAPE SHOULDER

BO 5 (6, 6, 7, 7, 7) sts at armhole edge once, then 4 (5, 6, 6, 7, 7) sts once.

SLEEVES

CO 20 (20, 26, 30, 36, 40) sts. Begin 1x1 Rib; work even for 1" (2.5 cm), ending with a WS row.

NEXT ROW (RS): Change to St st; work even for 2 rows.

SHAPE SLEEVE

INCREASE ROW (RS): Increase 1 st each side this row, then every 6 (6, 6, 8, 8, 10) rows 6 (9, 6, 9, 2, 8) times, then every 8 (0, 8, 0, 10, 12) rows 1 (0, 3, 0, 7, 1) time(s), as follows: K1, M1R, knit to last st, M1L, k1—36 (40, 46, 50, 56, 60) sts. Work even until piece measures 9 (10½, 11¼, 13, 15, 16)" [23 (26.5, 28.5, 33, 38, 40.5) cm] from the beginning, ending with a WS row.

SHAPE CAP

BO 4 (3, 4, 5, 6, 6) sts at beginning of next 2 rows—28 (34, 38, 40, 44, 48) sts remain. Work even for 2 (0, 0, 2, 2, 2) rows.

NEXT ROW (RS): Decrease 1 st each side this row, then every 4 rows 0 (0, 0, 1, 1, 0) time(s), then every RS row 7 (6, 9, 10, 11, 14) times, then every row 0 (4, 2, 0, 0, 0) times, as follows: On RS rows, k1, ssk, knit to last 3 sts, k2tog, k1; on WS rows, p1, p2tog, purl to last 3 sts, ssp, p1. BO remaining 12 (12, 14, 16, 18, 18) sts.

FINISHING

Sew shoulder seams. Set in Sleeves. Sew side and Sleeve seams. Block as desired.

FRONT BANDS/NECKBAND

With RS facing, beginning at lower Right Front edge, pick up and knit sts along Front edges and Back neck edge, picking up 1 st for every BO st, 3 sts for every 4 rows along vertical edges, and 4 sts for every 5 rows along diagonal edges. Place 5 markers along Right Front for buttonholes, the first 1" (2.5 cm) up from bottom edge, the last at beginning of neck shaping, and the remaining 3 evenly spaced between. Begin 1x1 Rib; work even for ½" (1.5 cm).

BUTTONHOLE ROW (RS): [Work to marker, remove marker, BO 2 sts] 5 times, work to end.

Work even until band measures 1" (2.5 cm), CO 2 sts over BO sts on first row. BO all sts in pattern.

Sew buttons opposite buttonholes.

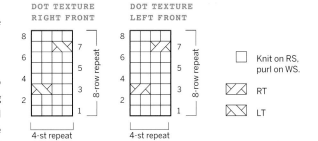

DOT TEXTURE—RIGHT FRONT
(multiple of 4 sts; 8-row repeat)

ROW 1 (RS): Knit.
ROW 2 AND ALL WS ROWS: Purl.
ROW 3: *K2, LT; repeat from * to end.
ROW 5: Knit.
ROW 7: *LT, k2; repeat from * to end.
ROW 8: Purl.
Repeat Rows 1–8 for Dot Texture—Right Front.

DOT TEXTURE—LEFT FRONT
(multiple of 4 sts; 8-row repeat)

ROW 1 (RS): Knit.
ROW 2 AND ALL WS ROWS: Purl.
ROW 3: *K2, RT; repeat from * to end.
ROW 5: Knit.
ROW 7: *RT, k2; repeat from * to end.
ROW 8: Purl.
Repeat Rows 1–8 for Dot Texture—Left Front.

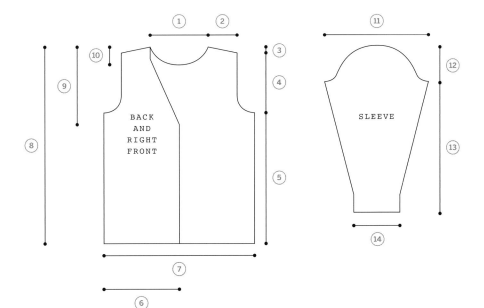

BACK AND RIGHT FRONT

1. 4 (5¼, 5¼, 5½, 5½, 6)"
   10 (13.5, 13.5, 14, 14, 15) cm
2. 1¾ (2¼, 2½, 2½, 2¾, 2¾)"
   4.5 (5.5, 6.5, 6.5, 7, 7) cm
3. ½"/1.5 cm
4. 4 (4½, 5¼, 6, 6½, 7)"
   10 (11.5, 13.5, 15, 16.5, 18) cm
5. 10 (11, 11¼, 12, 13½, 14)"
   25.5 (28, 28.5, 30.5, 34.5, 35.5) cm
6. 4¾ (5½, 6½, 6½, 7¼, 7¼)"
   12 (14, 16.5, 16.5, 18.5, 18.5) cm
7. 10½ (12, 12¾, 14½, 15¼, 16)"
   26.5 (30.5, 32.5, 37, 38.5, 40.5) cm
8. 14½ (16, 17, 18½, 20½, 21½)"
   37 (40.5, 43, 47, 52, 54.5) cm
9. 5 (5½, 6¼, 7, 7½, 8)"
   12.5 (14, 16, 18, 19, 20.5) cm
10. 1½"/4 cm

SLEEVE

11. 7¼ (8, 9¼, 10, 11¼, 12)"
    18.5 (20.5, 23.5, 25.5, 28.5, 30.5) cm
12. 2¾ (2¾, 3¼, 4¼, 4½, 4¾)"
    7 (7, 8.5, 11, 11.5, 12) cm
13. 9 (10½, 11¼, 13, 15, 16)"
    23 (26.5, 28.5, 33, 38, 40.5) cm
14. 4 (4, 5¼, 6, 7¼, 8)"
    10 (10, 13.5, 15, 18.5, 20.5) cm

Downy Cardigan

Sometimes you just need your sweater to be snuggly, cozy around your neck, and have thumbholes. For those times, this cardigan has you covered. It features extra-long sleeves that can be worn as shown or cuffed, a cowl neck that can be worn as shown or unbuttoned into a generous collar, and waist shaping located on the back only for a forgiving fit. The lofty, light-as-air yarn is strong thanks to a tube construction, and ever-so-soft thanks to superfine alpaca. It will keep you warm and invite hugs wherever you go.

FINISHED MEASUREMENTS
33½ (34½, 38, 39¼, 40¼, 43½, 46½, 47, 50¾, 51¾, 53, 56½)" [85 (87.5, 96.5, 99.5, 102, 110.5, 118, 119.5, 129, 131.5, 134.5, 143.5) cm] bust, buttoned

NOTE: Cardigan is intended to be worn with 3–4" (7.5–10 cm) ease in the bust, buttoned

YARN
Blue Sky Alpacas Techno [68% baby alpaca/22% silk/10% extra fine merino; 120 yards (109 meters)/50 grams]: 8 (8, 9, 9, 9, 10, 11, 11, 12, 13, 13, 14) hanks #1971 Metro Silver

NEEDLES
One pair straight needles size US 9 (5.5 mm)

One 24" (60 cm) long circular needle size US 9 (5.5 mm), for Collar and Front Bands

Set of five double-pointed needles (dpns) size US 9 (5.5 mm), for Thumbhole Edging

Change needle size if necessary to obtain correct gauge.

NOTIONS
Stitch markers; 12 (12, 12, 13, 13, 13, 13, 14, 14, 14, 14, 14) ¾" (19 mm) buttons

GAUGE
14½ sts and 22 rows = 4" (10 cm) in St st

STITCH PATTERN
BROKEN RIB
(mulitple of 4 sts plus 2; 2-row repeat)
ROW 1 (RS): K2, *p2, k2; repeat from * to end.
ROW 2: Purl.
Repeat Rows 1 and 2 for Broken Rib.

NOTES
Armhole, neck, and Sleeve cap decreases should be worked to match the slant of the edge being shaped, as follows:
FOR LEFT-SLANTING EDGES:
On RS rows, k1, ssk, work to end; on WS rows, work to last 3 sts, ssp, p1.
FOR RIGHT-SLANTING EDGES:
On RS rows, work to last 3 sts, k2tog, k1; on WS rows, p1, p2tog, work to end.

BACK
CO 58 (62, 66, 70, 74, 78, 82, 86, 90, 94, 98, 102) sts. Begin Broken Rib; work even for 1¾" (4.5 cm), ending with a WS row.

Change to St st; work even until piece measures 2½ (2½, 2½, 2½, 2½, 2½, 2¾, 2¾, 2¾, 2¾, 2¾, 2½)" [6.5 (6.5, 6.5, 6.5, 6.5, 6.5, 7, 7, 7, 7, 7, 6.5) cm] from the beginning, ending with a RS row.

NEXT ROW (WS): P19 (21, 22, 23, 25, 26, 27, 29, 30, 31, 33, 34) sts, pm, p20 (20, 22, 24, 24, 26, 28, 28, 30, 32, 32, 34) sts, pm, purl to end.

SHAPE WAIST
DECREASE ROW (RS): Decrease 2 sts this row, then every 8 rows 4 times, as follows: Knit to 2 sts before first marker, ssk, sm, knit to next marker, sm, k2tog, knit to end—48 (52, 56, 60, 64, 68, 72, 76, 80, 84, 88, 92) sts remain. Work even until piece measures 9½" (24 cm) from the beginning, ending with a WS row.

SHAPE BUST
INCREASE ROW (RS): Increase 2 sts this row, then every 10 rows 2 (2, 2, 2, 2, 2, 2, 1, 1, 1, 1, 2) time(s), as follows: Knit to first marker, M1R, sm, knit to next marker, sm, M1L, knit to end—54 (58, 62, 66, 70, 74, 78, 80, 84, 88, 92, 98) sts. Work even, removing markers on first row, until piece measures 16 (16¼, 16½, 16¾, 17, 17¼, 17½, 17½, 18, 18, 18, 18)" [40.5 (41.5, 42, 42.5, 43, 44, 44.5, 44.5, 45.5, 45.5, 45.5, 45.5) cm] from the beginning, ending with a WS row.

DIFFICULTY LEVEL:

SET-IN
SLEEVES

DOWNY CARDIGAN

Cozy yarn +
thumbholes = happy
sweater face

Broken rib and
garter trims

SHAPE ARMHOLES

BO 4 (4, 4, 4, 4, 4, 6, 6, 6, 8, 8, 8) sts at beginning of next 2 rows, then 0 (0, 2, 2, 2, 2, 2, 2, 4, 4, 6, 6) sts at beginning of next 2 rows, then decrease 1 st each side every RS row 2 (3, 2, 3, 3, 4, 3, 4, 3, 3, 3, 4) times—42 (44, 46, 48, 52, 54, 56, 56, 58, 58, 58, 62) sts remain. Work even until armhole measures 5½ (6, 6¼, 6½, 7, 7¼, 7½, 8, 8¼, 8¾, 9, 9½)" [14 (15, 16, 16.5, 18, 18.5, 19, 20.5, 21, 22, 23, 24) cm], ending with a WS row.

SHAPE NECK

NEXT ROW (RS): K14 (15, 15, 16, 17, 17, 18, 18, 18, 18, 18, 20), join a second ball of yarn, BO center 14 (14, 16, 16, 18, 20, 20, 20, 22, 22, 22, 22) sts, work to end. Working both sides at the same time, decrease 1 st at each neck edge every RS row twice—12 (13, 13, 14, 15, 15, 16, 16, 16, 16, 16, 18) sts remain each shoulder. Work even until armhole measures 6½ (7, 7¼, 7½, 8, 8¼, 8½, 9, 9¼, 9¾, 10, 10½)" [16.5 (18, 18.5, 19, 20.5, 21, 21.5, 23, 23.5, 25, 25.5, 26.5) cm], ending with a WS row.

SHAPE SHOULDERS

BO 6 (7, 7, 7, 8, 8, 8, 8, 8, 8, 9) sts at each armhole edge once, then 6 (6, 6, 7, 7, 7, 8, 8, 8, 8, 9) sts once.

RIGHT FRONT

CO 31 (31, 35, 35, 35, 39, 43, 43, 47, 47, 47, 51) sts.

ROW 1 (RS): K3, *p2, k2; repeat from * to end.

ROW 2: Purl.

Repeat Rows 1 and 2 until piece measures 1¾" (4.5 cm), ending with a WS row.

Change to St st; work even until piece measures 16 (16¼, 16½, 16¾, 17, 17¼, 17½, 17½, 18, 18, 18, 18)" [40.5 (41.5, 42, 42.5, 43, 44, 44.5, 44.5, 45.5, 45.5, 45.5, 45.5) cm] from the beginning, ending with a RS row.

SHAPE ARMHOLE

BO 4 (4, 4, 4, 4, 4, 6, 6, 6, 8, 8, 8) sts at armhole edge once, then 0 (0, 2, 2, 2, 2, 2, 2, 4, 4, 6, 6) sts once, then decrease 1 st at armhole edge every RS row 2 (3, 2, 3, 3, 4, 3, 4, 3, 3, 3, 4) times—25 (24, 27, 26, 26, 29, 32, 31, 34, 32, 30, 33) sts remain. Work even until armhole measures 2½ (3, 3¼, 3½, 4, 4¼, 4½, 5, 5¼, 5¾, 6, 6½)" [6.5 (7.5, 8.5, 9, 10, 11, 11.5, 12.5, 13.5, 14.5, 15, 16.5) cm], ending with a WS row.

SHAPE NECK

BO 7 (6, 7, 6, 6, 7, 8, 8, 9, 8, 7, 9) sts at neck edge once, then decrease 1 st at neck edge every row 3 (2, 3, 3, 2, 3, 5, 3, 7, 5, 3, 3) times, then every RS row 3 (3, 4, 3, 3, 4, 3, 4, 2, 3, 4, 3) times—12 (13, 13, 14, 15, 15, 16, 16, 16, 16, 16, 18) sts remain. Work even until armhole measures 6½ (7, 7¼, 7½, 8, 8¼, 8½, 9, 9¼, 9¾, 10, 10½)" [16.5 (18, 18.5, 19, 20.5, 21, 21.5, 23, 23.5, 25, 25.5, 26.5) cm], ending with a RS row.

SHAPE SHOULDER

BO 6 (7, 7, 7, 8, 8, 8, 8, 8, 8, 9) sts at armhole edge once, then 6 (6, 6, 7, 7, 7, 8, 8, 8, 8, 9) sts once.

LEFT FRONT

CO 31 (31, 35, 35, 35, 39, 43, 43, 47, 47, 47, 51) sts.

ROW 1 (RS): *K2, p2; repeat from * to last 3 sts, k3.

ROW 2: Purl.

Repeat Rows 1 and 2 until piece measures 1¾" (4.5 cm), ending with a WS row.

Change to St st; work even until piece measures 16 (16¼, 16½, 16¾, 17, 17¼, 17½, 17½, 18, 18, 18, 18)" [40.5 (41.5, 42, 42.5, 43, 44, 44.5, 44.5, 45.5, 45.5, 45.5, 45.5) cm] from the beginning, ending with a WS row.

SHAPE ARMHOLE

BO 4 (4, 4, 4, 4, 4, 6, 6, 6, 8, 8, 8) sts at armhole edge once, then 0 (0, 2, 2, 2, 2, 2, 2, 4, 4, 6, 6) sts once, then decrease 1 st at armhole edge every RS row 2 (3, 2, 3, 3, 4, 3, 4, 3, 3, 3,

CHANGING NECKLINES

Bonus Lesson

CHANGING OUT THE neckline in a set-in-sleeve sweater (and many other sweaters, for that matter) is actually a snap once you understand how the different neck shapes are formed. To start, you'll need to know the total number of stitches that must be removed in the neckline. Then, work shaping as follows:

SQUARE NECKS: Bind off all the stitches at once, at the desired depth.

BOAT NECKS: Bind off all but 4 or 6 stitches at once, approximately 2" (5 cm) from the shoulder. Work 2 or 3 decrease rows, and you're done!

V-NECKS: Decrease the stitches evenly along the entire neck depth. Take the number of rows in your neckline, and divide by the number of stitches you have to remove on each side of the neckline. Round down—this is how often you'll work your decreases. (Hint: Refresh your memory on the options on page 26 to figure out how you want your shaping to look!)

ROUND NECKS: Crew and scoop necklines use the same basic kind of shaping. The depth of the neckline and different rates of shaping differentiate crew necks from scoop necks. Bind off around half the stitches at the bottom of the neckline, then decrease the remaining stitches as indicated below.

Generally, crew necks are worked around 3" (7.5 cm) below the shoulder. After the initial bind-off, evenly split your decreases between every-row shaping and every-RS-row shaping.

Scoop necks are worked around 6" (15 cm) or more below the shoulder. After the initial bind-off, decrease stitches every RS row and then every fourth or sixth row.

Once you've got your basic neck shape down, you can then edge it in a bunch of ways—start by picking up stitches around your neckline and see where it takes you! (For more detail on necklines and how to adorn them, see my book *Knit Wear Love*.)

---

4) times—25 (24, 27, 26, 26, 29, 32, 31, 34, 32, 30, 33) sts remain. Work even until armhole measures 2½ (3, 3¼, 3½, 4, 4¼, 4½, 5, 5¼, 5¾, 6, 6½)" [6.5 (7.5, 8.5, 9, 10, 11, 11.5, 12.5, 13.5, 14.5, 15, 16.5) cm], ending with a RS row.

SHAPE NECK
BO 7 (6, 7, 6, 6, 7, 8, 8, 9, 8, 7, 9) sts at neck edge once, then decrease 1 st at neck edge every row 3 (2, 3, 3, 2, 3, 5, 3, 7, 5, 3, 3) times, then every RS row 3 (3, 4, 3, 3, 4, 3, 4, 2, 3, 4, 3) times—12 (13, 13, 14, 15, 15, 16, 16, 16, 16, 16, 18) sts remain. Work even until armhole measures 6½ (7, 7¼, 7½, 8, 8¼, 8½, 9, 9¼, 9¾, 10, 10½)" [16.5 (18, 18.5, 19, 20.5, 21, 21.5, 23, 23.5, 25, 25.5, 26.5) cm], ending with a WS row.

SHAPE SHOULDER
BO 6 (7, 7, 7, 8, 8, 8, 8, 8, 8, 8, 9) sts at armhole edge once, then 6 (6, 6, 7, 7, 7, 8, 8, 8, 8, 8, 9) sts once.

RIGHT SLEEVE
CO 28 (28, 32, 32, 32, 36, 36, 36, 36, 36, 36, 40) sts.
ROW 1 (RS): K3, *p2, k2; repeat from * to last st, k1.
ROW 2: Purl.
Repeat Rows 1 and 2 until piece measures 1" (2.5 cm) from the beginning, ending with a WS row.

SHAPE THUMBHOLE
NEXT ROW (RS): Work 7 (7, 8, 8, 8, 9, 9, 9, 9, 9, 9, 10) sts in pattern, join a second ball of yarn, BO 2 sts, work in pattern to end. Working both sides at the same time, work even until

thumbhole measures 1¾" (4.5 cm), ending with a WS row.

NEXT ROW (RS): Work to thumbhole, CO 2 sts, work to end with same ball of yarn. Cut second ball. Work even until piece measures 7" (18 cm) from the beginning, ending with a WS row.

Change to St st; work even for 2 rows.

SHAPE SLEEVE

INCREASE ROW (RS): Increase 1 st each side this row, then every 12 (10, 12, 10, 8, 10, 10, 8, 6, 6, 4, 4) rows 5 (6, 4, 4, 3, 4, 3, 7, 7, 12, 7, 7) times, then every 0 (0, 14, 12, 10, 12, 12, 10, 8, 0, 6, 6) rows 0 (0, 1, 2, 4, 2, 3, 1, 3, 0, 7, 7) time(s), as follows: K1, M1R, knit to last st, M1L, k1—40 (42, 44, 46, 48, 50, 50, 54, 58, 62, 66, 70) sts. Work even until piece measures 21½ (21½, 21½, 22, 22, 22, 22½, 22½, 22½, 23, 23, 23)" [54.5 (54.5, 54.5, 56, 56, 56, 57, 57, 57, 58.5, 58.5, 58.5) cm] from the beginning, ending with a WS row.

SHAPE CAP

BO 4 (4, 4, 4, 4, 4, 6, 6, 6, 8, 8, 8) sts at beginning of next 2 rows, then 0 (0, 2, 2, 2, 2, 2, 2, 4, 4, 5, 5) sts at beginning of next 2 rows—32 (34, 32, 34, 36, 38, 34, 38, 38, 38, 40, 44) sts remain.
Work even for 0 (0, 0, 0, 0, 0, 4, 4, 4, 4, 4, 4) rows.

DECREASE ROW (RS): Decrease 1 st each side this row, then every 6 rows 0 (0, 0, 0, 0, 0, 2, 2, 2, 3, 3, 3) times, then every 4 rows 0 (0, 0, 0, 0, 0, 1, 0, 1, 0, 0, 1) time(s), then every RS row 8 (9, 8, 9, 10, 11, 2, 5, 4, 4, 5, 2) times, then BO 1 (1, 1, 1, 1, 1, 2, 2, 2, 2, 2, 3) st(s) at beginning of next 4 rows. BO remaining 10 (10, 10, 10, 10, 10, 14, 14, 14, 14, 14, 18) sts.

LEFT SLEEVE

CO 28 (28, 32, 32, 32, 36, 36, 36, 36, 36, 36, 40) sts.
ROW 1 (RS): K3, *p2, k2; repeat from * to last st, k1.
ROW 2: Purl.
Repeat Rows 1 and 2 until piece measures 1" (2.5 cm) from the beginning, ending with a RS row.

SHAPE THUMBHOLE

NEXT ROW (WS): Work 7 (7, 8, 8, 8, 9, 9, 9, 9, 9, 9, 10) sts in pattern, join a second ball of yarn, BO 2 sts, work in pattern to end. Working both sides at the same time, work even until thumbhole measures 1¾" (4.5 cm), ending with a RS row.

NEXT ROW (WS): Work to thumbhole, CO 2 sts, work to end with same ball of yarn. Cut second ball. Work even until piece measures 7" (18 cm) from the beginning, ending with a WS row.

Complete as for Right Sleeve.

FINISHING

Block pieces as desired. Sew shoulder seams. Set in Sleeves; sew side and Sleeve seams.

COLLAR

With RS facing, using circular needle and beginning at Right Front neck edge, pick up and knit 6 (5, 6, 5, 5, 6, 7, 7, 8, 7, 6, 8) sts from Front neck BO sts, 16 (17, 17, 16, 17, 17, 18, 18, 18, 17, 16, 18) sts to shoulder, 5 sts to center Back neck BO sts, 14 (14, 16, 16, 18, 20, 20, 20, 22, 22, 22, 22) sts from Back neck BO sts, 5 sts to shoulder, 16 (17, 17, 16, 17, 17, 18, 18, 18, 17, 16, 18) sts to Left Front BO sts, then 6 (5, 6, 5, 5, 6, 7, 7, 8, 7, 6, 8) sts to Front neck edge—68 (68, 72, 68, 72, 76, 80, 80, 84, 80, 76, 84) sts. *Note: Exact st count is not essential, but be sure to end with a multiple of 4 sts.*

Begin St st; work even for 9" (23 cm), ending with a WS row.
ROW 1 (RS): K3, *p2, k2; repeat from * to last st, k1.
ROW 2: Purl.
Repeat Rows 1 and 2 for 1¼" (3 cm). BO all sts in pattern.

BUTTON BAND

With RS facing, using circular needle and beginning at top of Left Front Collar, pick up and knit approximately 2 sts for every 3 rows along Collar and Left Front edge, ending with approximately 104 (106, 108, 110, 113, 115, 116, 118, 121, 123, 124, 125) sts. *Note: Exact st count is not essential.*
Begin Garter st; work even for 9 rows. BO all sts knitwise.

BUTTONHOLE BAND

With RS facing, using circular needle and beginning at lower Right Front edge, pick up and knit approximately 2 sts for every 3 rows along Right Front edge and Collar, ending with approximately 104 (106, 108, 110, 113, 115, 116, 118, 121, 123, 124, 125) sts. *Note: Exact st count is not essential.*
Begin Garter st; work even for 4 rows.
BUTTONHOLE ROW (WS): K7 (8, 9, 6, 8, 9, 9, 6, 8, 9, 9, 10), [BO 2 sts, k6] 11 (11, 11, 12, 12, 12, 12, 13, 13, 13, 13, 13) times, BO 2 sts, knit to end. Work in Garter st for 4 rows, CO 2 sts over BO sts on first row. BO all sts knitwise.

THUMBHOLE EDGING

With RS facing, using dpns and beginning at base of Thumbhole, pick up and knit sts around thumbhole, picking up 1 st for every BO or CO st, and 2 sts for every 3 rows along vertical edges. Knit 1 row. BO all sts.

Sew buttons opposite buttonholes.

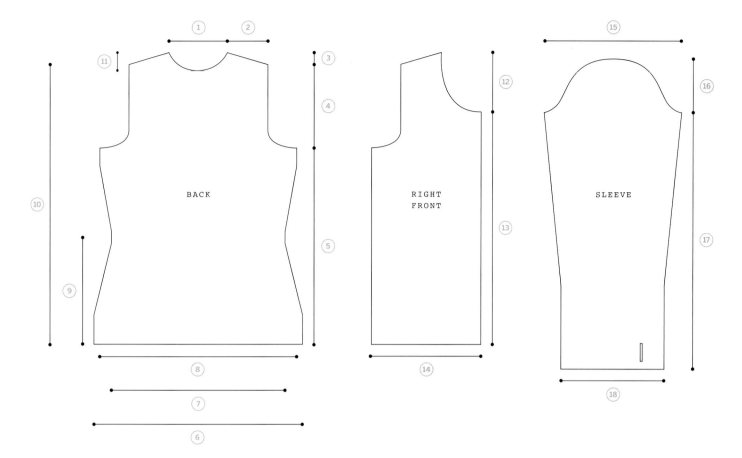

BACK

1 5 (5, 5½, 5½, 6, 6½, 6½, 6½, 7¼, 7¼, 7¼, 7¼)"
   12.5 (12.5, 14, 14, 15, 16.5, 16.5, 16.5, 18.5, 18.5, 18.5, 18.5) cm

2 3¼ (3½, 3½, 3¾, 4¼, 4¼, 4½, 4½, 4½, 4½, 4½, 5)"
   8.5 (9, 9, 9.5, 11, 11, 11.5, 11.5, 11.5, 11.5, 11.5, 12.5) cm

3 ¾"/2 cm

4 6½ (7, 7¼, 7½, 8, 8¼, 8½, 9, 9¼, 9¾, 10, 10½)"
   16.5 (18, 18.5, 19, 20.5, 21, 21.5, 23, 23.5, 25, 25.5, 26.5) cm

5 16 (16¼, 16½, 16¾, 17, 17¼, 17½, 17½, 18, 18, 18, 18)"
   40.5 (41.5, 42, 42.5, 43, 44, 44.5, 44.5, 45.5, 45.5, 45.5, 45.5) cm

6 16 (17, 18¼, 19¼, 20½, 21½, 22½, 23¾, 24¾, 26, 27, 28¼)" hip
   40.5 (43, 46.5, 49, 52, 54.5, 57, 60.5, 63, 66, 68.5, 72) cm

7 13¼ (14¼, 15½, 16½, 17¾, 18¾, 19¾, 21, 22, 23¼, 24¼, 25½)" waist
   33.5 (36, 39.5, 42, 45, 47.5, 50, 53.5, 56, 59, 61.5, 65) cm

8 15 (16, 17, 18¼, 19¼, 20½, 21½, 22, 23¼, 24¼, 25½, 27)" bust
   38 (40.5, 43, 46.5, 49, 52, 54.5, 56, 59, 61.5, 65, 68.5) cm

9 9"/23 cm

10 23¼ (24, 24½, 25, 25¾, 26¼, 26¾, 27¼, 28, 28½, 28¾, 29¼)"
    59 (61, 62, 63.5, 65.5, 66.5, 68, 69, 71, 72.5, 73, 74.5) cm

11 1¾"/4.5 cm

RIGHT FRONT

12 4¾"/12 cm

13 18½ (19¼, 19¾, 20¼, 21, 21½, 22, 22½, 23¼, 23¾, 24, 24½)"
    47 (49, 50, 51.5, 53.5, 54.5, 56, 57, 59, 60.5, 61, 62) cm

14 8½ (8½, 9¾, 9¾, 9¾, 10¾, 11¾, 11¾, 13, 13, 13, 14)"
    21.5 (21.5, 25, 25, 25, 27.5, 30, 30, 33, 33, 33, 35.5) cm

SLEEVE

15 11 (11½, 12¼, 12¾, 13¼, 13¾, 13¾, 15, 16, 17, 18¼, 19¼)"
    28 (29, 31, 32.5, 33.5, 35, 35, 38, 40.5, 43, 46.5, 49) cm

16 4¼ (4½, 4½, 5, 5¼, 5¾, 6, 6¼, 6¾, 7, 7½, 7)"
    11 (11.5, 11.5, 12.5, 13.5, 14.5, 15, 16, 17, 18, 19, 18) cm

17 21½ (21½, 21½, 22, 22, 22, 22½, 22½, 22½, 23, 23, 23)"
    54.5 (54.5, 54.5, 56, 56, 56, 57, 57, 57, 58.5, 58.5, 58.5) cm

18 7¾ (7¾, 8¾, 8¾, 8¾, 10, 10, 10, 10, 10, 10, 11)"
    19.5 (19.5, 22, 22, 22, 25.5, 25.5, 25.5, 25.5, 25.5, 25.5, 28) cm

Horseshoe Pullover

I challenge you to find a more classic pullover, or one you'll be prouder to wear out to lunch with a friend. A tailored fit, simple-to-work (but impressive to behold) cables, and elbow sleeves combine with a lustrous, hard-wearing yarn to make a garment you'll want to put on regularly for decades.

FINISHED MEASUREMENTS

29½ (31, 34½, 36, 37½, 39, 42½, 44, 45½, 47, 50½, 53½)" [75 (78.5, 87.5, 91.5, 95.5, 99, 108, 112, 115.5, 119.5, 128.5, 136) cm] bust

NOTE: Pullover is intended to be worn with 2" (5 cm) ease in the bust.

YARN

The Fibre Company Cumbria [90% wool/10% mohair; 238 yards (218 meters)/100 grams]: 3 (4, 4, 4, 5, 5, 5, 6, 6, 7, 7) hanks Eden Valley

NEEDLES

One pair straight needles size US 6 (4 mm)

One 24" (60 cm) long circular needle size US 6 (4 mm), for Neckband

Change needle size if necessary to obtain correct gauge.

NOTIONS

Stitch markers; stitch holder; cable needle

GAUGE

20 sts and 32 rows = 4" (10 cm) in St st

STITCH PATTERNS

2X2 RIB FLAT
(multiple of 4 sts + 2; 1-row repeat)

ROW 1 (RS): *K2, p2; repeat from * to last 2 sts, k2.

ROW 2: Knit the knit sts and purl the purl sts as they face you. Repeat Row 2 for 2x2 Rib Flat.

2X2 RIB IN THE RND
(multiple of 4 sts; 1-rnd repeat)

ALL RNDS: *K2, p2; repeat from * to end.

NOTES

Armhole, neck, and Sleeve cap decreases should be worked to match the slant of the edge being shaped, as follows:

FOR LEFT-SLANTING EDGES:
On RS rows, k1, ssk, work to end; on WS rows, work to last 3 sts, ssp, p1.

FOR RIGHT-SLANTING EDGES:
On RS rows, work to last 3 sts, k2tog, k1; on WS rows, p1, p2tog, work to end.

You make work Horseshoe Cable panel from text or chart.

BACK

CO 74 (78, 86, 90, 94, 98, 106, 110, 114, 118, 126, 134) sts. Begin 2x2 Rib Flat; work even for 2" (5 cm), ending with a WS row.
Change to St st; work even until piece measures 3" (7.5 cm) from the beginning, ending with a RS row.
NEXT ROW (WS): P25 (26, 29, 30, 31, 33, 35, 37, 38, 39, 42, 45), pm, p24 (26, 28, 30, 32, 32, 36, 36, 38, 40, 42, 44), pm, purl to end.

SHAPE WAIST

DECREASE ROW (RS): Decrease 2 sts this row, then every 12 rows 3 times, as follows: Knit to 2 sts before first marker, ssk, sm, knit to next marker, sm, k2tog, knit to end—66 (70, 78, 82, 86, 90, 98, 102, 106, 110, 118, 126) sts remain. Work even until piece measures 8½" (21.5 cm) from the beginning, ending with a WS row.

SHAPE BUST

INCREASE ROW (RS): Increase 2 sts this row, then every 12 rows 3 times, as follows: Knit to first marker, M1R, sm, knit to next marker, sm, M1L, knit to end—74 (78, 86, 90, 94, 98, 106, 110, 114, 118, 126, 134) sts. Work even, removing markers on first row, until piece measures 14½ (14¾, 15, 15¼, 15½, 15¾, 16, 16, 16½, 16½, 16½, 16½)" [37 (37.5, 38, 38.5, 39.5, 40, 40.5, 40.5, 42, 42, 42, 42) cm] from the beginning, ending with a WS row.

SHAPE ARMHOLES

BO 6 (6, 6, 6, 6, 6, 6, 8, 8, 10, 10) sts at beginning of next 2 rows, then 0 (0, 2, 2, 2, 2, 2, 4, 4, 4, 6, 8) sts at beginning of next 2 rows, then decrease 1 st each side every RS row 2 (3,

SET-IN SLEEVES

HORSESHOE PULLOVER

Cable panel shows off the yarn's stitch definition

Dart-style waist shaping on the back leaves cables undisturbed

3, 4, 4, 4, 7, 6, 6, 7, 7, 6) times—58 (60, 64, 66, 70, 74, 76, 78, 78, 80, 80, 86) sts remain. Work even until armhole measures 5½ (6, 6¼, 6½, 7, 7¼, 7½, 8, 8¼, 8¾, 9, 9½)" [14 (15, 16, 16.5, 18, 18.5, 19, 20.5, 21, 22, 23, 24) cm], ending with a WS row.

SHAPE NECK

NEXT ROW (RS): K18 (19, 20, 21, 22, 23, 23, 24, 24, 24, 24, 26), join a second ball of yarn, BO center 22 (22, 24, 24, 26, 28, 30, 30, 30, 32, 32, 34) sts, knit to end. Working both sides at the same time, decrease 1 st at each neck edge every RS row twice—16 (17, 18, 19, 20, 21, 21, 22, 22, 22, 22, 24) sts remain each shoulder. Work even until armhole measures 6½ (7, 7¼, 7½, 8, 8¼, 8½, 9, 9¼, 9¾, 10, 10½)" [16.5 (18, 18.5, 19, 20.5, 21, 21.5, 23, 23.5, 25, 25.5, 26.5) cm], ending with a WS row.

SHAPE SHOULDERS

BO 8 (9, 9, 10, 10, 11, 11, 11, 11, 11, 11, 12) sts at each armhole edge once, then 8 (8, 9, 9, 10, 10, 10, 11, 11, 11, 11, 12) sts once.

FRONT

CO 86 (90, 98, 102, 106, 110, 118, 122, 126, 130, 138, 146) sts. Pm on either side of center 40 sts.

NEXT ROW (RS): K1 (0, 0, 1, 0, 1, 1, 0, 1, 0, 0, 0), p2 (1, 1, 2, 1, 2, 2, 1, 2, 1, 1, 1), *k2, p2; repeat from * to first marker, sm, [k1-tbl, p2, k2, p1, k2, p1, k2, p2] 3 times, k1-tbl, sm, **p2, k2; repeat from ** to last 3 (1, 1, 3, 1, 3, 3, 1, 3, 1, 1, 1) st(s), p2 (1, 1, 2, 1, 2, 2, 1, 2, 1, 1, 1), k1 (0, 0, 1, 0, 1, 1, 0, 1, 0, 0, 0).

NEXT ROW (WS): P1 (0, 0, 1, 0, 1, 1, 0, 1, 0, 0, 0), k2 (1, 1, 2, 1, 2, 2, 1, 2, 1, 1, 1), *p2, k2; repeat from * to first marker, sm, [p1-tbl, k2, p2, k1, p2, k1, p2, k2] three times, p1-tbl, sm, **k2, p2; repeat from * to last 3 (1, 1, 3, 1, 3, 3, 1, 3, 1, 1, 1) st(s), k2 (1, 1, 2, 1, 2, 2, 1, 2, 1, 1, 1), p1 (0, 0, 1, 0, 1, 1, 0, 1, 0, 0, 0).

Work even until piece measures 2" (5 cm), ending with a WS row.

NEXT ROW (RS): Knit to first marker, sm, work Horseshoe Cable Panel (see page 164) to next marker, sm, knit to end.

NEXT ROW (WS): Purl to first marker, sm, work to next marker, sm, purl to end.

Work even until piece measures 14½ (14¾, 15, 15¼, 15½, 15¾, 16, 16, 16½, 16½, 16½, 16½)" [37 (37.5, 38, 38.5, 39.5, 40, 40.5, 40.5, 42, 42, 42, 42) cm] from the beginning, ending with a WS row. Pm on either side of center 20 (20, 20, 20, 22, 22, 24, 24, 24, 24, 26) neck sts.

SHAPE ARMHOLES

Note: Armhole and neck shaping are worked at the same time; please read entire section through before beginning.

BO 6 (6, 6, 6, 6, 6, 6, 8, 8, 10, 10) sts at beginning of next 2 rows, then 0 (0, 2, 2, 2, 2, 2, 4, 4, 4, 6, 8) sts at beginning of

next 2 rows, then decrease 1 st each side every RS row 2 (3, 3, 4, 4, 4, 7, 6, 6, 7, 7, 6) times. AT THE SAME TIME, when armhole measures ½" (1.5 cm), work neck shaping as follows:

NEXT ROW (RS): Continuing to work armhole shaping, work to first neck marker, join a second ball of yarn and BO 20 (20, 20, 20, 22, 22, 24, 24, 24, 24, 24, 26) sts, work to end. Working both sides at the same time, decrease 1 st at each neck edge every row 4 (4, 5, 5, 5, 5, 5, 5, 5, 6, 6, 6) times, then every RS row 5 (5, 5, 5, 6, 6, 6, 6, 6, 6, 6) times—16 (17, 18, 19, 20, 21, 21, 22, 22, 22, 22, 24) sts remain each shoulder when all shaping is complete. Work even until armhole measures 6½ (7, 7¼, 7½, 8, 8¼, 8½, 9, 9¼, 9¾, 10, 10½)" [16.5 (18, 18.5, 19, 20.5, 21, 21.5, 23, 23.5, 25, 25.5, 26.5) cm], ending with a WS row.

SHAPE SHOULDERS

BO 8 (9, 9, 10, 10, 11, 11, 11, 11, 11, 11, 12) sts at each armhole edge once, then 8 (8, 9, 9, 10, 10, 10, 11, 11, 11, 11, 12) sts once.

SLEEVES

CO 50 (54, 54, 58, 58, 58, 58, 62, 66, 74, 74, 78) sts. Begin 2x2 Rib Flat; work even for 2" (5 cm), ending with a WS row. Change to St st; work even for 2 rows, increasing 0 (0, 2, 0, 0,

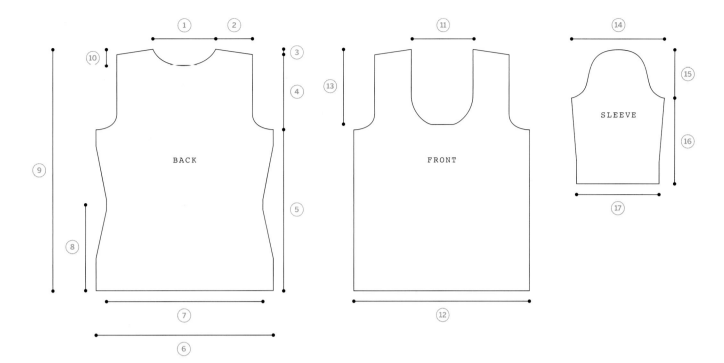

BACK

1 5¼ (5¼, 5½, 5½, 6, 6½, 6¾, 6¾, 6¾, 7¼, 7¼, 7½)"
13.5 (13.5, 14, 14, 15, 16.5, 17, 17, 17, 18.5, 18.5, 19) cm

2 3¼ (3½, 3½, 3¾, 4, 4¼, 4¼, 4½, 4½, 4½, 4½, 4¾)"
8.5 (9, 9, 9.5, 10, 11, 11, 11.5, 11.5, 11.5, 11.5, 12) cm

3 ½"/1.5 cm

4 6½ (7, 7¼, 7½, 8, 8¼, 8½, 9, 9¼, 9¾, 10, 10½)"
16.5 (18, 18.5, 19, 20.5, 21, 21.5, 23, 23.5, 25, 25.5, 26.5) cm

5 14½ (14¾, 15, 15¼, 15½, 15¾, 16, 16, 16½, 16½, 16½, 16½)"
37 (37.5, 38, 38.5, 39.5, 40, 40.5, 40.5, 42, 42, 42, 42) cm

6 14¾ (15½, 17¼, 18, 18¾, 19½, 21¼, 22, 22¾, 23½, 25¼, 26¾)"
hip and bust
37.5 (39.5, 44, 45.5, 47.5, 49.5, 54, 56, 58, 59.5, 64, 68) cm

7 13¼ (14, 15½, 16½, 17¼, 18, 19½, 20½, 21¼, 22, 23½, 25¼)" waist
33.5 (35.5, 39.5, 42, 44, 45.5, 49.5, 52, 54, 56, 59.5, 64) cm

8 8"/20.5 cm

9 21½ (22¼, 22¾, 23¼, 24, 24½, 25, 25½, 26¼, 26¾, 27, 27½)"
54.5 (56.5, 58, 59, 61, 62, 63.5, 65, 66.5, 68, 68.5, 70) cm

10 1½"/4 cm

FRONT

11 5¼ (5¼, 5½, 5½, 6, 6¼, 6¾, 6¾, 6¾, 7¼, 7¼, 7½)"
13.5 (13.5, 14, 14, 15, 16, 17, 17, 17, 18.5, 18.5, 19) cm

12 14¾ (15½, 17¼, 18, 18¾, 19½, 21¼, 22, 22¾, 23½, 25¼, 26¾)"
37.5 (39.5, 44, 45.5, 47.5, 49.5, 54, 56, 58, 59.5, 64, 68) cm

13 6½ (7, 7¼, 7½, 8, 8¼, 8½, 9, 9¼, 9¾, 10, 10½)"
16.5 (18, 18.5, 19, 20.5, 21, 21.5, 23, 23.5, 25, 25.5, 26.5) cm

SLEEVE

14 10¾ (11½, 12, 12½, 12¾, 13¼, 14, 15¼, 16, 17¼, 18, 18¾)"
27.5 (29.5, 30.5, 32, 32.5, 33.5, 35.5, 38.5, 40.5, 44, 45.5, 47.5) cm

15 4¼ (4¼, 5¼, 5½, 6, 6¼, 6½, 6¾, 6½, 7, 7½, 8¼)"
11 (11, 13.5, 14, 15, 16, 16.5, 17, 16.5, 18, 19, 21) cm

16 8 (8, 8, 8½, 8½, 8½, 9, 9, 9, 9, 9½, 9½)"
20.5 (20.5, 20.5, 21.5, 21.5, 21.5, 23, 23, 23, 23, 24, 24) cm

17 10 (10¾, 11¼, 11½, 11½, 12, 12, 12¾, 13½, 14¾, 15¼, 16)"
25.5 (27.5, 28.5, 29, 29, 30.5, 30.5, 32.5, 34.5, 37.5, 38.5, 40.5) cm

2, 2, 2, 2, 0, 2, 2) sts evenly on first row—50 (54, 56, 58, 58, 60, 60, 64, 68, 74, 76, 80) sts.

SHAPE SLEEVE

INCREASE ROW (RS): Increase 1 st each side this row, then every 28 (28, 28, 32, 16, 16, 8, 6, 6, 6, 6, 6) rows 1 (1, 1, 1, 2, 2, 2, 2, 2, 2, 4, 4) time(s), then every 0 (0, 0, 0, 0, 0, 10, 8, 8, 8, 8, 8) rows 0 (0, 0, 0, 0, 0, 2, 3, 3, 3, 2, 2) times, as follows: K1, M1R, knit to last st, M1L, k1—54 (58, 60, 62, 64, 66, 70, 76, 80, 86, 90, 94) sts. Work even until piece measures 8 (8, 8, 8½, 8½, 8½, 9, 9, 9, 9, 9½, 9½)" [20.5 (20.5, 20.5, 21.5, 21.5, 21.5, 23, 23, 23, 23, 24, 24) cm] from the beginning, ending with a WS row.

SHAPE CAP

BO 6 (6, 6, 6, 6, 6, 6, 6, 8, 8, 10, 10) sts at beginning of next 2 rows, then 0 (0, 2, 2, 2, 2, 2, 4, 4, 4, 6, 8) sts at beginning of next 2 rows—42 (46, 44, 46, 48, 50, 54, 56, 56, 62, 58, 58) sts remain. Work even for 4 (2, 4, 4, 4, 4, 4, 4, 4, 4, 4, 4) rows.

DECREASE ROW (RS): Decrease 1 st each side this row, then every 6 rows 1 (0, 2, 2, 2, 2, 2, 2, 3, 3, 5, 6) time(s), then every 4 rows 0 (1, 0, 0, 1, 1, 0, 0, 1, 0, 0, 1) time(s), then every RS row

8 (10, 8, 9, 9, 10, 13, 14, 8, 12, 8, 6) times, then BO 2 (2, 2, 2, 2, 2, 2, 2, 3, 3, 3, 3) sts at beginning of next 4 rows. BO remaining 14 (14, 14, 14, 14, 14, 14, 14, 18, 18, 18, 18) sts.

FINISHING

Block pieces as desired. Sew shoulder seams. Set in Sleeves; sew side and Sleeve seams.

NECKBAND

With RS facing, using circular needle and beginning at right Back shoulder, pick up and knit 8 sts along right Back neck edge, 22 (22, 24, 24, 26, 28, 30, 30, 30, 32, 32, 34) sts from BO Back neck sts, 8 sts along left Back neck edge, 31 (33, 36, 36, 38, 41, 41, 43, 45, 48, 48, 52) sts along left Front neck edge, 20 (20, 20, 20, 22, 22, 24, 24, 24, 24, 24, 26) sts from BO Front neck sts, and 31 (33, 36, 36, 38, 41, 41, 43, 45, 48, 48, 52) sts along right Front neck edge—120 (124, 132, 132, 140, 148, 152, 156, 160, 168, 168, 180) sts. Join for working in the rnd; pm for beginning of rnd. Begin 2x2 Rib in the Rnd; work even for 1" (2.5 cm). BO all sts in pattern.

HORSESHOE CABLE PANEL
(see Chart)
(panel of 40 sts; 8-row repeat)

ROW 1 (RS): K1-tbl, p2, C4F, C4B, p2, k1-tbl, p2, C4B, C4F, p2, k1-tbl, p2, C4F, C4B, p2, k1-tbl.

ROW 2 AND ALL WS ROWS: P1-tbl, *k2, p8, k2, p1-tbl; repeat from * to end.

ROWS 3, 5, AND 7: K1-tbl, *p2, k8, p2, k1-tbl; repeat from * to end.

ROW 8: Repeat Row 2.
Repeat Rows 1–8 for Horseshoe Cable Panel.

HORSESHOE CABLE PANEL

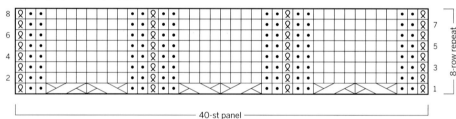

40-st panel

8-row repeat

☐ Knit on RS, purl on WS.

• Purl on RS, knit on WS.

Ⓧ K1-tbl on RS, p1-tbl on WS.

C4B: Cable 4 Back. Slip 2 sts to cable needle, hold to back, k2, k2 from cable needle.

C4F: Cable 4 Front. Slip 2 sts to cable needle, hold to front, k2, k2 from cable needle.

Collegiate Cardi

This preppy cardigan features thin stripes on the hem and sleeves, and a cable-like texture pattern on the front. The deep V neckline is flattering to many figure types, and the waist shaping (once more, worked on the back only) keeps the cardigan from being too boxy. Patch pockets are a fun addition, but can be eliminated if you don't like them.

FINISHED MEASUREMENTS

30¾ (33, 34¾, 37, 37¾, 40¾, 43, 43¾, 46¾, 49, 49¾, 55)" [78 (84, 88.5, 94, 96, 103.5, 109, 111, 118.5, 124.5, 126.5, 139.5) cm] bust, buttoned

NOTE: Cardigan is intended to be worn with 2" (5 cm) ease in the bust.

YARN

Louet Gems Worsted [100% merino wool; 175 yards (160 meters)/100 grams]: 6 (6, 7, 7, 7, 8, 8, 9, 9, 10, 10, 11) skeins #80.2564 Navy **(MC)**; 1 skein #80.2704 Pure White **(CC)**

NEEDLES

One pair straight needles size US 7 (4.5 mm)

One 24" (60 cm) long circular needle size US 7 (4.5 mm), for Front Bands/Neckband

Change needle size if necessary to obtain correct gauge.

NOTIONS

Stitch markers; removable markers; cable needle; eight ¾" (19 mm) buttons

GAUGES

21 sts and 32 rows = 4" (10cm) in St st

21 sts and 32 rows = 4" (10cm) in Gull Twist Texture

STITCH PATTERN

2X2 RIB

(multiple of 4 sts + 2; 2-row repeat)

ROW 1 (RS): *K2, p2; repeat from * to last 2 sts, k2.

ROW 2: *P2, k2; rep from * to last 2 sts, p2.

Repeat Rows 1 and 2 for 2x2 Rib.

SPECIAL ABBREVIATIONS

LT (LEFT TWIST): Slip 1 st to cable needle, hold to front, k1, k1 from cable needle. To work without a cable needle, insert needle from back to front between first and second sts on left needle and knit the second st through the front loop; knit first st, slip both sts from left needle together.

RT (RIGHT TWIST): Slip 1 st to cable needle, hold to back, k1, k1 from cable needle. To work without a cable needle, k2tog but do not drop sts from left needle, insert right needle between 2 sts just worked and knit first st again, slip both sts from left needle together.

NOTES

Armhole, neck, and Sleeve cap decreases should be worked to match the slant of the edge being shaped, as follows:

FOR LEFT-SLANTING EDGES:
K1, ssk, work to end.

FOR RIGHT-SLANTING EDGES:
Work to last 3 sts, k2tog, k1.

You may work Gull Twist Texture from text or Chart.

BACK

Using MC, CO 78 (82, 90, 94, 98, 106, 110, 114, 122, 126, 130, 142) sts. Begin 2x2 Rib; work even for 1½" (4 cm), ending with a WS row.

Continuing in rib pattern, work 1 row in CC, 2 rows in MC, then 1 row in CC. Cut CC.

Continuing in MC and rib pattern, work even until piece measures 2½" (6.5 cm) from the beginning, ending with a WS row.

Change to St st; work even until piece measures 3½" (9 cm) from the beginning, ending with a RS row.

NEXT ROW (WS): P26 (27, 30, 31, 33, 35, 37, 38, 41, 42, 43, 47), pm, p26 (28, 30, 32, 32, 36, 36, 38, 40, 42, 44, 48) sts, pm, purl to end.

SHAPE WAIST

DECREASE ROW (RS): Decrease 2 sts this row, then every 12 rows 3 times, as follows: Knit to 2 sts before first marker, ssk, sm, knit to next marker, sm, k2tog, knit to end—70 (74, 82, 86, 90, 98, 102, 106, 114, 118, 122, 134) sts remain. Work even until piece measures 9" (23 cm) from the beginning, ending with a WS row.

Twisted
stitch pattern
on cardigan
fronts only

DIFFICULTY LEVEL:

SET-IN
SLEEVES

COLLEGIATE CARDI

Pockets and
easy-care yarn
make this a
daily favorite

SHAPE BUST

INCREASE ROW (RS): Increase 2 sts this row, then every 12 rows 3 times, as follows: Knit to first marker, M1R, sm, knit to next marker, sm, M1L, knit to end—78 (82, 90, 94, 98, 106, 110, 114, 122, 126, 130, 142) sts. Work even, removing markers on first row, until piece measures 15½ (15¾, 16, 16¼, 16½, 16¾, 17, 17, 17½, 17½, 17½, 17½)" [39.5 (40, 40.5, 41.5, 42, 42.5, 43, 43, 44.5, 44.5, 44.5, 44.5) cm] from the beginning, ending with a WS row.

SHAPE ARMHOLES

BO 6 (6, 6, 6, 6, 6, 6, 8, 8, 10, 12) sts at beginning of next 2 rows, then 0 (0, 2, 2, 2, 2, 2, 4, 6, 6, 6, 8) sts at beginning of next 2 rows, then decrease 1 st each side every RS row 2 (3, 4, 4, 4, 6, 7, 6, 6, 7, 7, 6) times—62 (64, 66, 70, 74, 78, 80, 82, 82, 84, 84, 90) sts remain. Work even until armhole measures 5½ (6, 6¼, 6½, 7, 7¼, 7½, 8, 8¼, 8¾, 9, 9½)" [14 (15, 16, 16.5, 18, 18.5, 19, 20.5, 21, 22, 23, 24) cm], ending with a WS row.

SHAPE NECK

NEXT ROW (RS): K20 (20, 21, 22, 23, 24, 24, 25, 25, 26, 26, 27), join a second ball of yarn, BO center 22 (24, 24, 26, 28, 30, 32, 32, 32, 32, 32, 36) sts, knit to end. Working both sides at the same time, decrease 1 st at each neck edge every RS row twice—18 (18, 19, 20, 21, 22, 22, 23, 23, 24, 24, 25) sts remain each shoulder. Work even until armhole measures 6½ (7, 7¼, 7½, 8, 8¼, 8½, 9, 9¼, 9¾, 10, 10½)" [16.5 (18, 18.5, 19, 20.5, 21, 21.5, 23, 23.5, 25, 25.5, 26.5) cm], ending with a WS row.

SHAPE SHOULDERS

BO 9 (9, 10, 10, 11, 11, 11, 12, 12, 12, 12, 13) sts at each armhole edge once, then 9 (9, 9, 10, 10, 11, 11, 11, 11, 12, 12, 12) sts once.

RIGHT FRONT

Using MC, CO 38 (42, 42, 46, 46, 50, 54, 54, 58, 62, 62, 70) sts. Begin 2x2 Rib; work even for 1½" (4 cm), ending with a WS row.

Continuing in rib pattern, work 1 row in CC, 2 rows in MC, then 1 row in CC. Cut CC.

Continuing in MC and rib pattern, work even until piece measures 2½" (6.5 cm) from the beginning, ending with a WS row.

NEXT ROW (RS): K0 (0, 0, 1, 1, 0, 0, 0, 1, 0, 0, 1), work in Gull Twist Texture (see page 169) to last 2 (0, 0, 3, 3, 2, 0, 0, 3, 2, 2, 3) sts, knit to end.

NEXT ROW: P2 (0, 0, 3, 3, 2, 0, 0, 3, 2, 2, 3), work in Gull Twist Texture to last 0 (0, 0, 1, 1, 0, 0, 0, 1, 0, 0, 1) st(s), purl to end. Work even until piece measures 14 (14¼, 14½, 14¾, 15, 15¼, 15½, 15½, 16, 16, 16, 16)" [35.5 (36, 37, 37.5, 38, 38.5, 39.5, 39.5, 40.5, 40.5, 40.5, 40.5) cm] from CO edge, ending with a WS row.

SHAPE NECK

Note: Neck and armhole shaping are worked at the same time; please read entire section through before beginning.

DECREASE ROW (RS): Continuing in pattern, decrease 1 st at neck edge this row, then every 4 rows 4 (11, 0, 6, 1, 3, 11, 3, 2, 6, 0, 9) time(s), then every 6 rows 7 (3, 10, 7, 11, 10, 5, 11, 12, 10, 14, 9) times, as follows: K2tog, work to end. AT THE SAME TIME, when piece measures 15½ (15¾, 16, 16¼, 16½, 16¾, 17, 17, 17½, 17½, 17½, 17½)" [39.5 (40, 40.5, 41.5, 42, 42.5, 43, 43, 44.5, 44.5, 44.5, 44.5) cm] from the beginning, ending with a RS row, work armhole shaping as follows:

NEXT ROW (WS): BO 6 (6, 6, 6, 6, 6, 6, 8, 8, 10, 12) sts at armhole edge once, then 0 (0, 2, 2, 2, 2, 2, 4, 6, 6, 6, 8) sts once, then decrease 1 st at armhole edge every RS row 2 (3, 4, 4, 4, 6, 7, 6, 6, 7, 7, 6) times—18 (18, 19, 20, 21, 22, 22, 23, 23, 24, 24, 25) sts remain when all shaping is complete. Work even until armhole measures 6½ (7, 7¼, 7½, 8, 8¼, 8½, 9, 9¼, 9¾, 10, 10½)" [16.5 (18, 18.5, 19, 20.5, 21, 21.5, 23, 23.5, 25, 25.5, 26.5) cm], ending with a RS row.

SHAPE SHOULDER

BO 9 (9, 10, 10, 11, 11, 11, 12, 12, 12, 12, 13) sts at armhole edge once, then 9 (9, 9, 10, 10, 11, 11, 11, 11, 12, 12, 12) sts once.

LEFT FRONT

Using MC, CO 38 (42, 42, 46, 46, 50, 54, 54, 58, 62, 62, 70) sts. Begin 2x2 Rib; work even for 1½" (4 cm), ending with a WS row.

Continuing in rib pattern, work 1 row in CC, 2 rows in MC, then 1 row in CC. Cut CC.

Continuing in MC and rib pattern, work even until piece measures 2½" (6.5 cm) from the beginning, ending with a WS row.

NEXT ROW (RS): K2 (0, 0, 3, 3, 2, 0, 0, 3, 2, 2, 3), work in Gull Twist Texture to last 0 (0, 0, 1, 1, 0, 0, 0, 1, 0, 0, 1) st(s), knit to end.

NEXT ROW: P0 (0, 0, 1, 1, 0, 0, 0, 1, 0, 0, 1), work in Gull Twist Texture to last 2 (0, 0, 3, 3, 2, 0, 0, 3, 2, 2, 3) sts, purl to end. Work even until piece measures 14 (14¼, 14½, 14¾, 15, 15¼, 15½, 15½, 16, 16, 16, 16)" [35.5 (36, 37, 37.5, 38, 38.5, 39.5, 39.5, 40.5, 40.5, 40.5, 40.5) cm] from the beginning, ending with a WS row.

SHAPE NECK

Note: Neck and armhole shaping are worked at the same time; please read entire section through before beginning.

DECREASE ROW (RS): Continuing in pattern, decrease 1 st at neck edge this row, then every 4 rows 4 (11, 0, 6, 1, 3, 11, 3, 2, 6, 0, 9) times, then every 6 rows 7 (3, 10, 7, 11, 10, 5, 11, 12, 10, 14, 9) times, as follows: Work to last 2 sts, ssk. AT THE SAME TIME, when piece measures 15½ (15¾, 16, 16¼, 16½, 16¾, 17, 17, 17½, 17½, 17½, 17½)" [39.5 (40, 40.5, 41.5, 42, 42.5, 43, 43, 44.5, 44.5, 44.5, 44.5) cm] from the beginning, ending with a WS row, work armhole shaping as follows:

NEXT ROW (RS): BO 6 (6, 6, 6, 6, 6, 6, 6, 8, 8, 10, 12) sts at armhole edge once, then 0 (0, 2, 2, 2, 2, 2, 4, 6, 6, 6, 8) sts once, then decrease 1 st at armhole edge every RS row 2 (3, 4, 4, 4, 6, 7, 6, 6, 7, 7, 6) times—18 (18, 19, 20, 21, 22, 22, 23, 23, 24, 24, 25) sts remain when all shaping is complete. Work even until armhole measures 6½ (7, 7¼, 7½, 8, 8¼, 8½, 9, 9¼, 9¾, 10, 10½)" [16.5 (18, 18.5, 19, 20.5, 21, 21.5, 23, 23.5, 25, 25.5, 26.5) cm], ending with a WS row.

SHAPE SHOULDER

BO 9 (9, 10, 10, 11, 11, 11, 12, 12, 12, 12, 13) sts at armhole edge once, then 9 (9, 9, 10, 10, 11, 11, 11, 11, 12, 12, 12) sts once.

SLEEVES

Using MC, CO 42 (46, 46, 46, 46, 46, 46, 46, 50, 50, 54, 54) sts. Begin 2x2 Rib; work even for 2½" (6.5 cm), ending with a WS row.

Continuing in rib pattern, work 1 row in CC, 2 rows in MC, then 1 row in CC. Cut CC.

Continuing in MC and rib pattern, work even until piece measures 4" (10 cm) from the beginning, ending with a WS row.

Change to St st; work even for 2 rows, increasing 0 (0, 0, 0, 2, 2, 2, 2, 0, 0, 0, 2) sts evenly on first row—42 (46, 46, 46, 48, 48, 48, 48, 50, 50, 54, 56) sts.

SHAPE SLEEVE

INCREASE ROW (RS): Increase 1 st each side this row, then every 14 (14, 10, 10, 10, 8, 8, 6, 6, 4, 4, 4) rows 1 (1, 1, 5, 5, 1, 9, 5, 13, 3, 7, 10) time(s), then every 16 (16, 12, 12, 12, 10, 10, 8, 8, 6, 6, 6) rows 5 (5, 7, 4, 4, 9, 3, 9, 3, 15, 13, 11) times, as follows: K1, M1R, knit to last st, M1L, knit 1—56 (60, 64, 66, 68, 70, 74, 78, 84, 88, 96, 100) sts. Work even until piece measures 18 (18, 18, 18½, 18½, 18½, 19, 19, 19, 19, 19½, 19½)" [45.5 (45.5, 45.5, 47, 47, 47, 48.5, 48.5, 48.5, 48.5, 49.5, 49.5) cm] from the beginning, ending with a WS row.

SHAPE CAP

BO 6 (6, 6, 6, 6, 6, 6, 8, 8, 10, 12) sts at beginning of next 2 rows, then 0 (0, 2, 2, 2, 2, 2, 4, 6, 6, 6, 7) sts at beginning of next 2 rows—44 (48, 48, 50, 52, 54, 58, 58, 56, 60, 64, 62) sts remain. Work even for 2 (2, 4, 4, 4, 4, 4, 4, 4, 4, 4) rows.

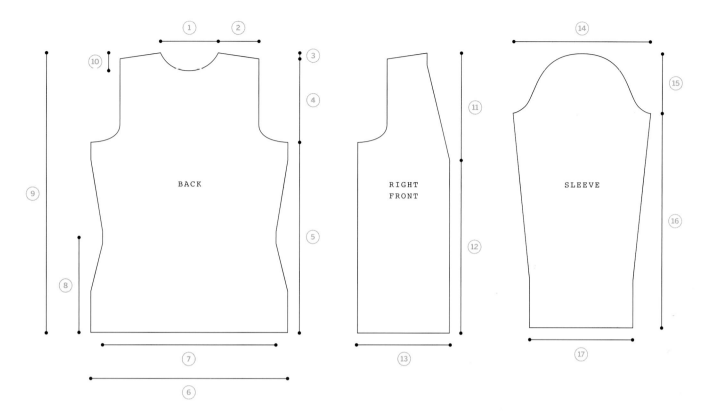

BACK

1 5 (5¼, 5¼, 5¾, 6, 6½, 6¾, 6¾, 6¾, 6¾, 6¾, 7½)"
   12.5 (13.5, 13.5, 14.5, 15, 16.5, 17, 17, 17, 17, 17, 19) cm

2 3½ (3½, 3½, 3¾, 4, 4¼, 4¼, 4½, 4½, 4½, 4½, 4¾)"
   9 (9, 9, 9.5, 10, 11, 11, 11.5, 11.5, 11.5, 11.5, 12) cm

3 ½"/1.5 cm

4 6½ (7, 7¼, 7½, 8, 8¼, 8½, 9, 9¼, 9¾, 10, 10½)"
   16.5 (18, 18.5, 19, 20.5, 21, 21.5, 23, 23.5, 25, 25.5, 26.5) cm

5 15½ (15¾, 16, 16¼, 16½, 16¾, 17, 17, 17½, 17½, 17½, 17½)"
   39.5 (40, 40.5, 41.5, 42, 42.5, 43, 43, 44.5, 44.5, 44.5, 44.5) cm

6 14¾ (15½, 17¼, 18, 18¾, 20¼, 21, 21¾, 23¼, 24, 24¾, 27)" hip and bust
   37.5 (39.5, 44, 45.5, 47.5, 51.5, 53.5, 55, 59, 61, 63, 68.5) cm

7 13¼ (14, 15½, 16½, 17¼, 18¾, 19½, 20¼, 21¾, 22½, 23¼, 25½)" waist
   33.5 (35.5, 39.5, 42, 44, 47.5, 49.5, 51.5, 55, 57, 59, 65) cm

8 8½"/21 cm

9 22½ (23¼, 23¾, 24¼, 25, 25½, 26, 26½, 27¼, 27¾, 28, 28½)"
   57 (59, 60.5, 61.5, 63.5, 65, 66, 67.5, 69, 70.5, 71, 72.5) cm

10 1½"/4 cm

RIGHT FRONT

11 8½ (9, 9¼, 9½, 10, 10¼, 10½, 11, 11¼, 11¾, 12, 12½)"
    21.5 (23, 23.5, 24, 25.5, 26, 26.5, 28, 28.5, 30, 30.5, 32) cm

12 14 (14¼, 14½, 14¾, 15, 15¼, 15½, 15½, 16, 16, 16, 16)"
    35.5 (36, 37, 37.5, 38, 38.5, 39.5, 39.5, 40.5, 40.5, 40.5, 40.5) cm

13 7¼ (8, 8, 8¾, 8¾, 9½, 10¼, 10¼, 11, 11¾, 11¾, 13¼)"
    18.5 (20.5, 20.5, 22.5, 22.5, 24, 26, 26, 28, 30, 30, 34) cm

SLEEVE

14 10¾ (11½, 12¼, 12½, 13, 13¼, 14, 14¾, 16, 16¾, 18¼, 19)"
    27.5 (29, 31, 32, 33.5, 34, 35.5, 37.5, 40.5, 42.5, 46.5, 48.5) cm

15 4 (4½, 5¼, 5½, 6, 6¼, 6¼, 7, 6¾, 7, 7¼, 8)"
    10 (11.5, 13.5, 14, 15, 16, 16, 18, 17, 18, 18.5, 20.5) cm

16 18 (18, 18, 18½, 18½, 18½, 19, 19, 19, 19, 19½, 19½)"
    45.5 (45.5, 45.5, 47, 47, 47, 48.5, 48.5, 48.5, 48.5, 49.5, 49.5) cm

17 8 (8¾, 8¾, 8¾, 9¼, 9¼, 9¼, 9¼, 9½, 9½, 10¼, 10¾)"
    20.5 (22, 22, 22, 22, 22, 22, 24, 24, 26, 26) cm

DECREASE ROW (RS): Decrease 1 st each side this row, then every 6 rows 0 (0, 1, 1, 1, 1, 0, 2, 4, 4, 3, 5) time(s), then every 4 rows 1 (1, 0, 0, 1, 1, 1, 0, 1, 0, 1, 1) time(s), then every RS row 9 (11, 11, 11, 12, 12, 13, 16, 15, 6, 9, 11, 8) times, then BO 2 (2, 2, 2, 2, 2, 2, 2, 3, 3, 3, 3) sts at beginning of next 4 rows. BO remaining 14 (14, 14, 14, 14, 14, 14, 14, 20, 20, 20, 20) sts.

FINISHING

Block pieces as desired. Sew shoulder seams. Set in Sleeves; sew side and Sleeve seams.

FRONT BANDS/NECKBAND

With RS facing, using MC and circular needle and beginning at right Back shoulder, pick up and knit sts around neck shaping, picking up 1 st for every BO st, 3 sts for every 4 rows along vertical edges, and 4 sts for every 5 rows along diagonal edges, making sure to end with a multiple of 4 sts + 2. Place markers for 7 buttonholes along Right Front edge, the first 1" (2.5 cm) up from bottom edge, the last at beginning of neck shaping, and the remaining 5 evenly spaced between. Begin 2x2 Rib; work even for ¾" (2 cm), ending with a WS row.

BUTTONHOLE ROW (RS): [Work to marker, BO 2 sts] 7 times, work to end.

Work even, casting on 2 sts over BO sts on first row, until piece measures 1½" (4 cm) from pick-up row. BO all sts in pattern.

Sew buttons opposite buttonholes.

POCKETS

Using MC, CO 30 sts. Begin St st; work even until piece measures 4" (10 cm), ending with a WS row.

Change to 2x2 Rib; work even for 1" (2.5 cm), ending with a WS row.

Continuing in rib pattern, work 1 row in CC, 2 rows in MC, then 1 row in CC. Cut CC.

Continuing in MC and rib pattern, work even until piece measures 6" (15 cm) from the beginning, ending with a WS row. BO all sts in pattern.

Sew pockets to Fronts, 2 rows up from top of bottom ribbing and approx 1" (2.5 cm) in from Front bands.

GULL TWIST TEXTURE
(see Chart)
(multiple of 6 sts;
8-row repeat)

ROW 1 (RS): *K2, RT, LT; repeat from * to end.
ROW 2: Purl.
ROW 3: Knit.
ROW 4: Purl.
ROW 5: *RT, k2, LT; repeat from * to end.
ROW 6: Purl.
ROW 7: Knit.
ROW 8: Purl.
Repeat Rows 1–8 for Gull Twist Texture.

GULL TWIST TEXTURE

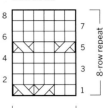

8-row repeat

6-st repeat

☐ Knit on RS, purl on WS.

◩ RT

◪ LT

A Super-Quick Guide to Super-Wearable Sweaters

It is my sincere hope that as you've flipped through this book, you've seen sweaters that excite you—sweaters you want to knit, sweaters you want to wear, sweaters you can't wait to show off.

And since I know sweater knitting can sometimes be intimidating (one of the questions I get asked in class most often is "Where would you recommend I even *start*?!"), I wanted to end our time together with a few concise pointers on how to choose a project, and then ensure it's as successful as it can be.

CHOOSING A PROJECT can be a pretty delicate dance—we've all gotten caught up in the glory of a well-taken pattern photo now and again! (I'm particularly guilty of wanting to knit anything that's photographed on an Icelandic hillside, despite repeated evidence that I won't wear the garment once it's finished.)

Once you've fallen in love with the thought of a particular sweater, it's sometimes hard to truly evaluate how much wear you'll get out of the garment. But it's so important to do so! Before you take the plunge and cast on, think about the following:

- *Do you wear anything like this?* Is there a store-bought item with a similar shape or feel in your closet's "heavy rotation" section? If not, what changes would you have to make to the sweater you're considering to bring it into your wardrobe comfort zone?

- *What will you wear with the sweater?* Take a good look at your swatch, and envision the sweater out of that fabric. Can you come up with a few outfits to wear with it?

- *Are you up for the challenge (or lack thereof)?* The last thing to consider is whether you'll be happy actually doing the work of fitting and knitting this sweater. Remember, knitting is your hobby—it should be fun! So if you've chosen something that seems super-daunting, fit-wise, or so boring you'll never want to work on it, stop now before you break your own heart.

ONCE YOU'RE SETTLED ON A PROJECT, I've got a few more tips to ensure your sweater immediately becomes your new BFF.

- *Keep your swatch helpful.* I can't emphasize this enough. Your swatch isn't a pop quiz on how to achieve a particular gauge, or an impediment to the "real" knitting. It's your chance to figure out and account for the size of your stitches and the fabric you create. So follow my tips on pages 9–11 to get a swatch that helps you make the sweater you want to wear.

- *Make sure your fabric matches your design.* By this point, you've got a silhouette you really want to wear and a fabric you like. Make sure they'll make great partners! If the sweater will be hard-working, make sure your fabric can stand up to the use. And if the silhouette is more formal, make sure your fabric is poised and polished, too!

- *Choose a size thoughtfully.* Before you settle on a particular size to knit, think about whether using your full bust measurement might lead you astray. If you're not an average size, as I discuss on pages 23–24, select a size based on your upper torso instead. (Want a refresher? My books *Knit to Flatter* and *Knit Wear Love* have even more information on fitting.)

STILL LOOKING FOR SUGGESTIONS to help lead you to the right garment?

- *If you're a first-time sweater knitter who really doesn't want to fuss with a lot of fit math,* my best suggestion is an easy, all-in-one silhouette made with a knockout, drapey fabric. My favorite sweater from this book, hands-down, is the Blaze Cardigan on page 73—and I think it makes a fantastic first (or 50th) sweater!

- *If you've done a couple of boxier sweaters and want to try something with a bit of shaping,* but still keep the finishing simple, try the Revive Cardigan on page 93. The drop shoulder seams are easy-peasy, and the waist shaping on the back of the sweater is super flattering.

- *If you'd like something a little sportier, with the option to keep the fit trim,* you might enjoy the Speedster Raglan on page 113. Bonus: The texture pattern looks *great* in subtly shaded yarns!

- *If you've done the rest, and now want something more fitted and tailored,* try taking the plunge with the Horseshoe Pullover on page 160. It's classic, trim, and gorgeous.

Whatever you choose, I hope your knitting is speedy and thoroughly enjoyable, and that you wear that sweater *All. The. Time.* Because you can knit that, and it's going to be amazing.

xoxo—

Amy

SOURCES

BERROCO YARNS
www.berroco.com

BLUE SKY ALPACAS
www.blueskyalpacas.com

CLASSIC ELITE YARNS
www.classiceliteyarns.com

ELSEBETH LAVOLD
www.knittingfever.com/brand/elsebeth-lavold

THE FIBRE COMPANY
www.thefibreco.com
kelbournewoolens.com

GREEN MOUNTAIN SPINNERY
www.spinnery.com

HARRISVILLE DESIGNS
www.harrisville.com

LOUET NORTH AMERICA
www.louet.com

MANOS DEL URUGUAY
www.manosyarns.com

MRS. CROSBY LOVES TO PLAY
www.mrscrosbyplays.com

ROWAN YARNS
www.knitrowan.com

SHIBUI KNITS
www.shibuiknits.com

SWANS ISLAND COMPANY
www.swansislandcompany.com

VALLEY YARNS
www.yarn.com/webs-knitting-crochet-yarns-valley-yarns

JUL CLOSURES
juldesigns.com/attach/screw-in-closures

RECOMMENDED READING LIST & RESOURCES

I hope this book has left you thirsty for more sweater exploration! To help in your journey, here's a list of my very favorite, most-essential books on sweater knitting:

A TREASURY OF KNITTING PATTERNS
A SECOND TREASURY OF KNITTING PATTERNS
CHARTED KNITTING DESIGNS: A THIRD TREASURY OF KNITTING PATTERNS
A FOURTH TREASURY OF KNITTING PATTERNS
by Barbara G. Walker

VOGUE KNITTING: THE ULTIMATE KNITTING BOOK
by Vogue Knitting Magazine Editors

FINISHING SCHOOL
by Deborah Newton

THE KNITTER'S BOOK OF FINISHING TECHNIQUES
by Nancie M. Wiseman

THE KNOWLEDGEABLE KNITTER
by Margaret Radcliffe

THE KNITTER'S BOOK OF YARN
THE KNITTER'S BOOK OF WOOL
by Clara Parkes

KNITTING ON THE EDGE
KNITTING OVER THE EDGE
by Nicky Epstein

And of course, I hope that if you haven't already, you'll explore style, fit, and flattering your figure through sweater knitting in my first two books, *Knit to Flatter* and *Knit Wear Love*.

ABBREVIATIONS

BO: Bind off

CC: Contrasting color

CN: Cable needle

CO: Cast on

DPN(S): Double-pointed needle(s)

K1-TBL: Knit 1 stitch through the back loop

K2TOG: Knit 2 stitches together

K3TOG: Knit 3 stitches together

K: Knit

MC: Main color

M1 or **M1L (MAKE 1—LEFT SLANTING):** With the tip of the left-hand needle inserted from front to back, lift the strand between the 2 needles onto the left-hand needle; knit the strand through the back loop to increase 1 stitch.

M1P or **M1PR (MAKE 1 PURLWISE—RIGHT SLANTING):** With the tip of the left-hand needle inserted from back to front, lift the strand between the 2 needles onto the left-hand needle; purl the strand through the front loop to increase 1 stitch.

M1R (MAKE 1—RIGHT SLANTING): With the tip of the left-hand needle inserted from back to front, lift the strand between the 2 needles onto the left-hand needle; knit the strand through the front loop to increase 1 stitch.

MC: Main color

P1-TBL: Purl 1 stitch through the back loop

P2TOG: Purl 2 stitches together

PM: Place marker

P: Purl

RND(S): Round(s)

RS: Right side

S2KP2: Slip the next 2 stitches together to the right-hand needle as if to knit 2 together, k1, pass the 2 slipped stitches over.

SKP (SLIP, KNIT, PASS): Slip the next stitch knitwise to the right-hand needle, k1, pass the slipped stitch over the knit stitch.

SM: Slip marker

SSK (SLIP, SLIP, KNIT): Slip the next 2 stitches to the right-hand needle one at a time as if to knit; return them to the left-hand needle one at a time in their new orientation; knit them together through the back loops.

SSSK: Same as ssk, but worked on the next 3 stitches.

SSP (SLIP, SLIP, PURL): Slip the next 2 stitches to the right-hand needle one at a time as if to knit; return them to the left-hand needle one at a time in their new orientation; purl them together through the back loops.

ST(S): Stitch(es)

ST ST: Stockinette stitch

TBL: Through the back loop

TOG: Together

WS: Wrong side

W&T: Wrap and turn (see Special Techniques)

YO: Yarnover

SPECIAL TECHNIQUE

SHORT ROW SHAPING: Work the number of sts specified in the instructions, wrap and turn (w&t) as follows:

To wrap a knit st, bring yarn to the front (purl position), slip the next st purlwise to the right-hand needle, bring yarn to the back of work, return the slipped st on the right-hand needle to the left-hand needle purlwise; turn, ready to work the next row, leaving the remaining sts unworked. To wrap a purl st, work as for wrapping a knit st, but bring yarn to the back (knit position) before slipping the st, and to the front after slipping the st.

When short rows are completed, or when working progressively longer short rows, work the wrap together with the wrapped st as you come to it as follows:

If st is to be worked as a knit st, insert the right-hand needle into the wrap, from below, then into the wrapped st; k2tog; if st to be worked is a purl st, insert needle into the wrapped st, then down into the wrap; p2tog. (Wrap may be lifted onto the left-hand needle, then worked together with the wrapped st if this is easier.)

ACKNOWLEDGMENTS

THIS BOOK IS DEDICATED TO BETH, who took up knitting with the perfection and enthusiasm with which she does everything—and who gently but persistently told me it needed to be written.

Although I'm sure this has been written in the acknowledgments of every book ever created: Books are intense, intricate, massive things that take a village of effort to reach their potential. I've been consistently and incredibly lucky with the support I've received for mine.

A single paragraph isn't nearly large enough to contain my gratitude to my family for being with me through this process. Jonathan, you've been amazing: From many (delicious) dinners and picking up my dropped household tasks, to what must have seemed like endless musing about design choices, to never blinking an eye when the knitting came with me everywhere, you've been my partner with humor and grace. There are not enough words for my thanks. Daniel and Jacob: A mother could never wish for better sons. You fill me with warmth and courage; you fill my days with laughter and joy; you make me a better person. Thank you.

My team at STC Craft continues to amaze: Thanks to my editors, Melanie Falick and Cristina Garces, for their tireless and patient work; my technical editors, Sue McCain and Therese Chynoweth, for their attention to detail and the occasional "what were you thinking?" reality-check; Astrid Scannell-Long for her creative and beautiful styling. Thanks to Karen Pearson, for continuing to put everyone at ease and capture incredible photographs, and Mary Jane Callister for translating who I am directly into the design of the book—it's a privilege to continue to work with you both. Thanks to our models, Jay, Sarah, and Liris, for their infectious smiles and beautiful selves; thanks to Stacy Beneke for helping make their loveliness shine.

The materials donated to this book to make the sweaters represent not only the very best choice for each garment, but some of the best hand-knitting yarns made in this world: Thanks to Louet North America, Harrisville Designs, Classic Elite Yarns, Blue Sky Alpacas, Knitting Fever International/Elsebeth Lavold, Rowan, Shibui Knits, Manos del Uruguay, Berroco, The Fibre Company, Green Mountain Spinnery, Swans Island, Mrs. Crosby Loves to Play, and Webs/Valley Yarns for their support. Further thanks are due to Deb, Lauren, Jennifer, Julie, Rae, Wendy, Kelly, Erin, and Audrey for lending their perfect stitches to me when the samples got overwhelming.

Thanks to Linda Roghaar, who continues to ensure my work is the best that it can possibly be, and to my amazing colleagues Andromeda, Jonathan, Lauren, and Jackie: You've made this wild ride more fun than I would have thought possible.

Finally, thanks *must* go to the thousands of knitters who make it possible for me to do what I do. I am humbled by you, I am grateful for you, and I cannot wait to see where we go from here.

Editor: Cristina Garces
Designer: Mary Jane Callister
Production Manager: Katie Gaffney

Library of Congress Control Number: 2015958243

ISBN: 978-1-4197-2247-9

Printed and bound in China
10 9 8 7 6 5 4 3 2 1

Abrams books are available at special discounts when purchased
in quantity for premiums and promotions as well as fundraising
or educational use. Special editions can also be created to specifi-
cation. For details, contact specialsales@abramsbooks.com or
the address below.

ABRAMS
The Art of Books
115 West 18th Street
New York, NY 10011
www.abramsbooks.com